The Jewel of Knightsbridge

ROBIN HARROD

THE JEWEL OF KNIGHTSBRIDGE

THE ORIGINS OF THE HARRODS EMPIRE

The History Press

Cover illustrations: *Front*: Harrods store (Gibson Blanc/Alamy); *Rear*: Harrods frontage about 1901 (Harrods).

First published 2017

The History Press
The Mill, Brimscombe Port
Stroud, Gloucestershire, GL5 2QG
www.thehistorypress.co.uk

© Robin Harrod, 2017

The right of Robin Harrod to be identified as the Author of this work has been asserted in accordance with the Copyright, Designs and Patents Act 1988.

All rights reserved. No part of this book may be reprinted or reproduced or utilised in any form or by any electronic, mechanical or other means, now known or hereafter invented, including photocopying and recording, or in any information storage or retrieval system, without the permission in writing from the Publishers.

British Library Cataloguing in Publication Data.
A catalogue record for this book is available from the British Library.

ISBN 978 0 7509 6813 3

Typesetting and origination by The History Press
Printed in Great Britain by TJ International Ltd, Padstow, Cornwall

CONTENTS

	Introduction	7
1	In the Beginning, there was a Draper	13
2	Out of Essex – The Origin of the Harrod Family	25
3	The First Grocery	51
4	The Move to Kensington	87
5	Charles Digby Takes Over	117
6	Out of the Ashes	135
7	Harrods Goes Public	167
8	Retirement	185
9	Charles Digby's Family	215
	Epilogue	245
	Acknowledgements	249
	Index	250

INTRODUCTION

'Harrods of London', 'Harrods of Knightsbridge' or just plain 'Harrods' are all names that are used for the famous London store and are recognised instantly worldwide. The shop is an institution. Although it's always described as being on Knightsbridge, the splendid seven-storey building with its Edwardian terracotta facade is actually situated on the Brompton Road. Even in the early part of the twentieth century, any post addressed to 'Harrods, England' would be safely delivered. The store was by then so confident of its place in the world that it used the telegraphic address, 'Everything, London', and adopted the motto, *Omnia, Omnibus, Ubique*, meaning 'Everything for Everybody, Everywhere'.

Some facts about the store will illustrate the enormity of the place:

> The main building has about 1 million sq.ft of sales floor, with more again being allocated to offices, staff areas and stockrooms. In addition, Harrods also uses other buildings in the immediate area. As a comparison, Selfridges is just over half that size.
>
> At night the facade of Harrods is lit up with 12,000 light bulbs, several hundred of which need replacing each day.
>
> The baroque dome at the highest point contains a water storage tank, filled from its own source. Harrods, in common with several other well-known London institutions, has its own water supply, derived from artesian wells that were sunk under the building many years ago. There are three wells, and one is nearly 500ft deep.

> The store makes more money per square foot than any other store in the world and attracts 15 million customers a year.
>
> Until 2014, there was a model of the store on display in the shop in the form of a silver cigar box, which dated back to 1927. This was the result of a wager 100 years ago regarding the turnover of the shop. In 1917 Harry Selfridge made a bet with Richard Burbidge, the managing director of Harrods at the time, that Selfridges would overtake Harrods in annual returns within six years of the declaration of peace at the end of the First World War. The prize was to be a model of the loser's shop. By 1927 Harry Selfridge admitted defeat and agreed to change the model to one of Harrods. The model was crafted in Harrods' own workshops in Trevor Square, representing the store in that year, and the £400 bill was sent to Selfridge. Despite the loss, good relations between the two individuals and their shops were maintained. For many years, the model graced first Sir Richard's and then his son's desk. This cigar box was sold recently at auction by Christie's for £85,000.

The research that has formed the basis for this history of the early days of Harrods revealed that the founding Mr Harrod, Charles Henry Harrod, actually started trading in 1824, a decade earlier than previously thought, at premises on the south side of the Thames. The first shop was not, however, a grocery business; the grocery store was started in the 1830s and moved to the present site twenty years later. The first version of a Harrod's grocery shop, in the East End of London, was a truly humble affair, and the next shop, now sited on the Brompton Road, started life as a simple one-storey shop with the living accommodation attached behind.

The success and growth of Harrod's grocery business was kick-started by tea. Events in China during the 1830s, and later in Assam, were the driving force behind the growth in the tea trade in Britain. Until 1833, the East India Company had held a monopoly over the trade in China tea and had ignored the native tea produced in the

INTRODUCTION

northern part of India. When the monopoly was removed in that year, there was an explosion of wholesale tea dealers, and then retailers, in London. Tea plants were imported from China to India and production of the Assam black tea continued to grow. Harrod and many others took advantage of the new prospects the trade offered.

Once the shop had moved to Brompton Road, it grew organically on the same site, gradually acquiring the historic features which have epitomised its image over the last 100 years. Members of the Harrod family remained in charge of the business until 1891, when it was sold and a limited company was formed. The rate of expansion continued at a pace after the change of ownership.

The last part of the present rectangular site was finally acquired in 1911, and the splendid building has occupied the same footprint since that year. Almost all the improvements and innovations to the store that followed were either in a vertical direction or were internal changes. The Brompton Road aspect was faced with Doulton terracotta tiles, and the lavish interiors, also decorated with Doulton tiles, were the work of the designer Frederick Sage.

The year 1911 was a momentous one for the store, and for the country, for it was the year that saw the coronation of King George V. *Harrods: The Store and the Legend*, a book written by Tim Dale in 1981, states that in 1911:

> A souvenir brochure printed by the store at that time starts, 'His Most Gracious Majesty's memorable words, "Wake up England" have not been forgotten by his people, and Harrods today presents a striking example of what can be done by British Capital and British Labour combined with British Enterprise.' Stirring words indeed.

Perhaps today we would have said, 'Let's make britain great again.'

How did a small local grocery shop that started 185 years ago grow into the successful department store that now dominates the Brompton Road in London? The chapters that follow will answer the question.

Harrods has certainly been very successful, but it has never claimed to be the oldest department store in Britain. Which store can claim that accolade depends on how one defines a department store – and there are several candidates. The list is not confined to London, and some provincial stores that started trading in the eighteenth century can probably be included in the genre, and were certainly in existence before Harrods. One of them, Bennett's, on Irongate in Derby, which was founded in 1734, exists to this day, 282 years later. Although it was threatened by the nearby Westfield Centre a few years ago, the store modernised and seems to be thriving again.

Several other London stores claim their origins in the 1830s, but Fortnum & Mason probably lays claim to be the oldest; they have been on the same site since 1707. However, they have never diversified into the full complement of departments which many would consider needed to be included as a 'department store'. Selfridges, the second largest store in the UK, did not open until 1909.

Harrods have often led the trade in innovative retailing. It was the first store to take out a full-page advertisement in the *Times*, and the first store to boast a 'moving stair', a primitive form of escalator which was presented to an interested but mistrustful public in 1898.

The present store still boasts the green and gold liveried doormen and the green-and-gold-painted delivery vans that were introduced decades ago. The original vans were of course horse-drawn, and the mechanised vans which followed were well in advance of what we now think of as part of our modern eco-sensitive era. The first electric Harrods van, running on solid tyres, was in use in 1919, and between 1936 and 1939 Harrods built a fleet of sixty such vans.

The ownership of Harrods has often been a subject of speculation during the last sixty years or so. After decades of ownership by the Harrod family, my great-grandfather sold the store in 1889, and it was floated as a limited liability company.

The Burbidge family, father Richard, then son, Woodman, and finally grandson, Richard, ran the store for many years and introduced some dramatic and groundbreaking innovations during their tenure. They continued the tradition of my ancestors by putting the customer first, and concentrating on the quality of the goods and service. In the 1920s Woodman Burbidge began to build a Harrods empire, acquiring other London shops, including Dickens & Jones and Swan & Edgar. Further stores were added after the Second World War.

A takeover battle took place in 1959 involving Debenhams, House of Fraser and United Drapery Stores, and eventually Harrods became part of the House of Fraser Group.

In the late 1970s Lonrho acquired a substantial holding and then in 1985 the Investment and Trust Company owned by Mohamed Al-Fayed took over the store. Although thought by many to be 'over the top', and too 'show business' and eccentric to be a successful businessman, Al Fayed was a natural shopkeeper. He was more like Charles Henry Harrod than most would credit. He reputedly started life as a stallholder in his home town of Alexandria and he had the same attention to detail which characterised the Harrods ethos. During his years in charge the shop grew into a tourist attraction as much as a luxury store.

Al Fayed was in control until May 2010 when Harrods was sold to Qatar Holdings, the sovereign wealth fund of the State of Qatar. Harrods remains in their hands to date. After many years of involvement with other stores as part of a group, Harrods now stands alone, but boasts Air Harrod, Harrods Aviation, Harrods Estates and Harrods Bank as parts of the business.

Although to the local inhabitants of the area, now mostly very well-heeled, Harrods is still their local grocery store, the shop has become progressively more upmarket in the last few decades. For the multitude of visitors to London, and especially to those from the United States, the Far East, Russia and the Arabian Peninsula, it is an iconic showcase for luxury goods.

My interest in the store and the Harrod family began in 1986 when my 11-year-old daughter came home from school, asking if my wife and I could help to fill in a family history tree that she had been studying in class. I was in trouble with the family tree. My mother had died earlier that year and my father had died some years before. I knew a limited amount about my mother's family but nothing about my father's. He had been an orphan and had 'changed hands' several times during his early life. He had always had strong views regarding his birth family, saying, 'If they didn't want me, I don't want them.'

So, although my brothers and I had speculated whether we might be related to the Harrods family, we did not know anything, and in any case had respected his wishes and not pursued any investigation during his lifetime. Our speculations were fuelled by one of the few facts known by my father – that he had been born in a nursing home in Kensington, not very far from the Brompton Road.

Until I started my research, my family in East Yorkshire and I had been blissfully unaware that we actually had anything to do with Harrods apart from sharing the name. My story of discovery is documented elsewhere, but to cut a very long story short, I subsequently found that I was the great-great-grandson of the founder, Charles Henry Harrod. By a quirk of fate, my brothers and I were the only direct descendants of both the founder and his son to have retained the surname 'Harrod'.

What followed for me was thirty years of research into the Harrod family and its ramifications, and this has inevitably led me into the story of the early history of the store. I have been well supported in my research by other living members of my newly found family and by successive archivists at Harrods, although Harrods have not in any other way been involved in the writing or production of this book. The family have given me photographs and stories of my ancestors, and the archivists have been very helpful in granting access to their records and images. I could not have completed this book without their help and I acknowledge their contribution here, rather than repeatedly with each individual piece of information or document used.

So, how did this magnificent institution begin and develop into what it is today? I hope to answer here most of the why, when and how questions you might ask about its origins.

I

IN THE BEGINNING, THERE WAS A DRAPER

In 1824 Charles Henry Harrod, later to become a giant of the grocery business, was a single man of 25 and of no great consequence. He was living in Southwark. Though referred to here as Charles Henry, to differentiate him from his son, Charles Digby, certainly at times he was known as Henry or Henry Charles.

Contrary to what has previously been documented in various descriptions of Harrods, his first shop was not a grocery shop. In his books about Harrods, Tim Dale points out that there are many articles about Harrods which state that it was the only large London store not to have started life as a draper's, but as a grocer's shop. British History Online, for instance, states, 'Harrods is untypical of the great London department stores in having risen not from a drapery or general goods business but from a grocer's shop.' These statements have proved to be incorrect and Harrods was not especially thrilled to hear the news when this was discovered.

Charles Henry started renting premises at 228 Borough High Street, Southwark, in the April of 1824. The rate records and the Surrey land tax records for the parish of St George the Martyr, Southwark, list him there in every quarter until 1831 but give no indication of his occupation.

Southwark, the district south of London Bridge, has been populated since the Roman era. For most of that time the only crossing of the Thames had been London Bridge and its precursors. The area of London south of the Thames grew much more slowly than the rest of the city. The growth was limited by a lack of additional bridges across the river and the relatively marshy ground. Following the opening of Westminster Bridge in 1750 and then Blackfriars Bridge in 1769, the area blossomed. In 1800 the population of Southwark was about 66,000, only about 7 per cent of the city as a whole, and then between 1801 and 1851 the population nearly doubled.

Southwark and its high street, known as Borough High Street, were full of craftsmen and shopkeepers. There were a disproportionately large number of inns, partly due to the proximity of the riverside and its trade, but more particularly because of the presence of a thriving local brewing industry. Several prisons were also located here, including the King's Bench Prison and the Marshalsea Debtors' Prison. The Marshalsea, featured in Dickens' novels, had been founded in the 1300s and had been rebuilt in the early 1800s. Best known as a debtors' prison, it also housed those convicted of subversion, sailors who had mutinied and those accused of piracy. It closed in 1842.

The brewing connection with the district came about because until 1750 the High Street and London Bridge was the sole route for all the hop trade traffic from Kent, Surrey and Sussex. The proprietors of the coaching inns thrived on the trade and became very affluent. The medieval pilgrimage route to and from Canterbury and the route from the hop fields of Kent lay through Borough High Street. Warehouses for the hops, managed by brokers called hop factors, were built together with showrooms for the goods. Breweries followed in the same area. The two main breweries in Southwark were, rather oddly, both called the Anchor Brewery. One eventually became the Courage Brewery, and the other, much older, eventually merged with Courage in 1955.

Many of the warehouses and breweries were destroyed by bombing in the Second World War and the industry then moved to Paddocks Wood, near Tunbridge Wells in Kent. (Coincidentally, one of my uncles managed a hop farm in Paddock Wood for about ten years in the 1950s.)

Charles Harrod may have frequented the inns, though this is doubtful as he is known in later life to have been teetotal. He certainly did not get involved in the brewing industry. The first records listing Charles's occupation are in the London street directories held at Southwark Local Studies Library and now available partially online. In the Pigot & Co. Directory for 1826 and 1827, the entry for 228 High Street, Borough, lists 'Harrod & Wicking, Linen Drapers, retail'. The next listing is in the 1829 Post Office Directory, which shows Charles Harrod working on his own at the same address as 'Harrod C.H., Mercer & Haberdasher'.

The Wicking connection in 1826 and 1827 was obviously a transient one, as there is no mention of him at the same address again. In Pigot's 1839 Directory, there is a Matthew Wicking who was a 'Linen Draper and Silk Mercer' at 9 Ludgate Hill, just west of St Paul's Cathedral. To muddy the water further, the 1846 Post Office Directory lists a James Wicking at the Half Moon Public House, 132 Borough High Street – that would be real diversification!

Contact with a living descendant of the Wicking family who was doing his own family research confirmed the presence of his family in Southwark, but no further details were available and no obvious connection was known to the Harrod family. Further confirmation of the transient relationship between Harrod and Wicking was found when an online version of the *London Gazette* was searched. Issue 18210, published on 10 January 1826, page 57, contained the following announcement:

> Notice is hereby given, that the Partnership which subsisted between the undersigned, William Wicking and Charles Henry Harrod, in the business of Linen-Drapers, at No. 228, High Street, Southwark, was dissolved by mutual consent on 31 December last; and that the business will in future be carried on by the said Charles Henry Harrod only, by whom all debts due to and from the late firm are to be received and paid – Witness their hands this 3rd day of January 1826.
>
> Charles Henry Harrod
>
> William Wicking

What a relief; 'Harrod and Wicking's of Knightsbridge' just does not sound as good as 'Harrods'!

The records reveal that Charles Harrod continued as the ratepayer and tenant at 228 High Street from 1824 until 1831. He was listed in Robson's 1832 Directory at the same address, and in other directories prior to that variously as 'Harrod, Draper', 'Harrod. C.H., Mercer & Haberdasher', and 'C.H. Harrod, Haberdasher'.

My conclusion at the time of that research was that Charles Harrod had started in business in 1824 and then taken Wicking into partnership for a couple of years. When things did not work out, for whatever reason, he had continued once again on his own until 1831. Further research, however, revealed different information. Sometimes in retrospect, it is perhaps a bad idea to continue researching the same subject repeatedly.

William Wicking was almost certainly born in Surrey. The Wicking family were based in Crowhurst in Surrey which, although just south of the M25 near Oxted, was still in the diocese of Southwark. There are two likely 'William' candidates in the records, one baptised in 1801 and the other in 1802. The two may have been cousins.

Prior to the 1826 partnership with Charles Harrod, a different combination was listed in the 1822 Pigot's Street Directory at 228 High Street. 'Gainsford & Wicking, Linen Drapers, Retail' were the residents that year and also in 1825–26. They had another business at 119 King Street in 1821, and at Mermaid Court in 1831, both called 'Gainsford & Wicking, Linen Drapers'. King Street and Mermaid Court were almost opposite 228 High Street. An entry in British History Online mentions the partnership:

> The old Marshalsea site was sold to Samuel Davis, cooper, in 1802, but the prisoners were not removed until 1811. No. 119 [now 163] Borough High Street, and the building over the entrance to Mermaid Court were acquired about 1824 by a firm of wholesale drapers, Gainsford and Wicking, who erected a five-storey building with a double-fronted shop there.

So it looks as though the Harrod story in Southwark was a little more complicated than I had originally thought. William Wicking, or at least someone in his family, was already running a business at the same premises before Charles Harrod became the rate payer. Harrod took over the rent in 1824 despite not being involved in the partnership until 1826. 'Gainsford & Wicking' appear to have built their own premises across the road so were obviously not short of funds.

There is no obvious way to explain these confusing facts. Perhaps 'Gainsford & Wicking' involved one member of the Wicking family and a different member of the family set up with Harrod for those two years. That Harrod was responsible for the rent from 1824 onwards suggests that he must have had some money to invest in the existing business, which cannot be confirmed. It is possible the dates are blurred by the delay inevitable in reporting changes of ownership and then a new printing of a directory.

It is also possible that Harrod and Wicking just fell out. However, outside events may also have influenced the changes in partnerships. The competition between mercers could have forced closures of shops and realignments in their ownership. Checking the listed shops in Borough High Street for 1838 shows that there were no fewer than eleven silk or linen mercers in the same road, so competition was strong. Further evidence for this is another entry in Pigot's 1839 London Directory for 'Gainsford & Gaude' at 119 High Street – yet another combination.

Another factor which might be of some importance is that in 1825 there was a financial crash, something which may sound very familiar to present-day readers. After the austerity years of the Napoleonic Wars, which ended in 1815, a few months after the Battle of Waterloo Britain was ready to change direction but was left with large debts. The National Debt was 200 per cent, twice the country's GDP. Compared this with today's, which is just above 80 per cent.

The state of industrialisation and low cost of the workforce meant that the country was in a good position to reverse the problem, and in a wave of overenthusiasm there had been a huge investment by British individuals and banks in overseas ventures and trade. The almost inevitable result was called 'the Panic of 1825'.

The stock market crash started in the Bank of England following the collapse of speculative investments in Latin America. The crisis was felt most in England, where it resulted in the closing of six London banks and sixty country banks – about 10 per cent of the total. Inaction by the Bank of England led to delay and backlogs, and was followed by widespread bankruptcies, recession and unemployment. Documents about Charles Harrod written several years later report that he 'was ruined by the mercantile Panic of 1825', having been a 'respectable and responsible tradesman'.

Although the financial crash might have been a problem in his life, Harrod was obviously not completely ruined. He continued the business on his own at 228 High Street and, between 1827 and 1831 or 1832, both there and at another premises in the area at Maidstone Buildings, a cul-de-sac next door to No. 228.

Despite that report, Charles Henry must have turned things around or been rescued, as he was confident enough about his future to get married. On 18 February 1830, a year before he moved away from the Southwark area, Charles Henry Harrod married Elizabeth Digby in the parish church of Birch in Essex. A special licence was required from Lambeth Palace as Elizabeth was under 21 years old. There is some confusion about her birthdate but Elizabeth was born around 1810 and so she was probably 19 years old.

The licence was dated 15 February in the same year, and stated, 'Appeared Personally, Charles Henry Harrod of the Parish of St George Southwark in the County of Surrey a Bachelor aged twenty one years and upwards.' Charles Henry swore an oath that the consent of Elizabeth's father, James Digby, had been obtained. The witnesses at the wedding were William Digby and James Digby Junior, who were the eldest two of Elizabeth's brothers; Eliza Mason, probably a relation from Charles's mother's family; and Mary Bateman, who is not known.

Elizabeth Digby was the eldest daughter of James Digby Senior, a successful Essex pork butcher and miller. The Digby connection may have been the source of some financial support for Charles. The Digby family were for many generations butchers, millers, farmers or agricultural workers in and around Birch, a couple of miles south of Colchester, and certainly, for a while, were quite an affluent lot, owning mills and land locally. We shall hear more about the Digbys later.

Maidstone Buildings, Harrod's second property in the area, was also found in the rate records, but proved to be in the parish of St Saviour's, Southwark, whereas 228 High Street was in the parish of St George the Martyr. Tallis's brilliant drawings and maps of early nineteenth-century London (1838–40), and Horwood's map of Southwark, updated in 1813, show that although Maidstone

Buildings and 228 High Street are in different parishes, Maidstone Buildings is a mews street off the west side of Borough High Street, the entrance being under an archway on the building listed as No. 231, next door to No. 228. The boundary between St George and St Saviour's falls, remarkably, exactly between the two buildings.

The Tallis drawings are well worth a look for anyone interested in the London of the early nineteenth century. They show in some detail the facades of the buildings, their relationship with other buildings and the side streets, and list the ownership. The Tallis drawings also show the 'Gainsford & Wicking' premises at 119 High Street, almost opposite 228 and next to King Street and Mermaid Court.

The numbering of High Street, Southwark, has changed completely since the 1830s. The site of Harrod's premises can be found on the west side of the present High Street, just north of Union Street; 228 Borough High Street is now numbered 76 High Street and is a cafe, with a gated and locked archway leading to Maidstone Buildings between Nos 72 and 76 High Street. Though the High Street itself now has a variable standard of retail premises and is a bustling road with heavy traffic, Maidstone Buildings is, in contrast, a rather quiet and more fashionable mews area behind security gates, with a variety of offices and living accommodation.

The rate records show that after Harrod left the area in 1831, Maidstone Buildings was rented by James Pike, a hop factor. The buildings still boast the old winches on the outside of the upper floors for hoisting goods up and down. A 2006 planning application described Maidstone Buildings as follows:

> ... comprises former hop stores that have been converted into residential flats and they consist of two parallel, three and four-storey buildings that lie on either side of a central access road. The main entrance is via an archway between Nos 72 and 76 Borough High Street.

Other documents show that Charles Henry had interests in other premises south of the river. In his 1885 will, he leaves to one of his sons '4 leasehold messuages, Nos 11, 12, 13 and 14 New Church Street, Bermondsey'. New Church Street no longer exists but is in the same place that is now occupied by Llewellyn Street. This is about a mile as the crow flies from Borough High Street and backs onto the wharves of the river.

In an attempt to find out more about Charles Henry's presence in Southwark, contact was made with Duncan Field, the latest in a long line of Fields who own Field & Sons, an estate agency in the area, which was founded around 1804. He had already retired from the business, but was happy to meet and let me look at their archives. The Southwark branch of his firm is still run from their original building at what is now 54 Borough High Street and was previously No. 240. Quite probably a Field ancestor would have dealt with the letting of the property at No. 228 to Harrod.

My contact with Duncan Field came about by a rather devious route. His wife, Shirley Harrison, is a writer who had researched a book about Southwark. She had spent some time in 2008 in the Harrods archives looking for material for her book about Winnie the Pooh. Because of her interest in Southwark, the Harrods archivist Sebastian Wormell by chance mentioned my recent research there, and the connection was made. At Duncan's invitation, the cellar of their ancient premises was inspected to see if records of the properties at Nos 228 or 231 were still in existence. Sadly, no documents before 1850 had survived the many years of floods and fire, so the search was fruitless, but interesting.

My attempts to find more information about Charles Henry Harrod were confused by the discovery of several other Charles Henry Harrods in Southwark – three altogether, all in the same family. They proved to belong to a family who had originated in Lincolnshire and by chance are involved later in another part of the Harrod story.

So, Charles Henry Harrod had spent seven years in Southwark attempting to make a success of his drapery business. But, something made him change direction, both literally and metaphorically.

There were probably several different factors in his decision. The competition in the drapery trade, both locally and elsewhere in

London, may have overwhelmed Charles. In Pigot's 1839 London Directory, there are lists of wholesale and retail dealers and agents of most trades. Lumping them all together, there were just over 1,300 businesses involved in the linen, silk and haberdashery trade in London. In contrast, there were fewer than 300 involved in the tea business. As was discussed earlier in the introduction, there were enormous opportunities in tea following the loss of the East India Trading Company's monopoly in 1833. The tea trade alone had been worth £30 million a year to the company. Tea was one of the main consumer goods brought to Britain from the East and the trade expanded rapidly in the first half of the nineteenth century. Tea drinking was previously an expensive and fashionable pastime in Britain, but as tea became cheaper more people could afford it and perhaps Charles saw an opportunity.

The means to fulfil the promise of that opportunity was also being developed in London at this time. Until the early nineteenth century, all shipping had to unload their cargoes directly from the banks of the Thames in the Pool of London, just downstream of London Bridge. As trade increased, the riverside became more crowded and damage and delays became inevitable. In the early part of the century, large docks were opened on the north side of the Thames, firstly the West India Docks in the Isle of Dogs, for trade from that part of the world, then the East India Docks slightly further east. In 1820 the Regents Canal was opened, allowing travel by boat from Limehouse across London and into the canal network to the Midlands. Travel by canal was faster than road transport and steam-driven railways were as yet still in their infancy. This opened up a new faster distribution network. By 1835, three quarters of trade on this canal originated from the shipping on the Thames.

There were few warehouses in the larger docks, as goods were usually unloaded directly into transport and taken directly for delivery or for storage elsewhere in London. St Katharine Dock was completed and opened in 1828. This was the only project by Thomas Telford in London, built near the Tower of London on a site that required the demolition of the Hospital of St Katharine by the Tower and over 1,000 slum homes. It was almost unique in offering six-storey warehouses on the quayside to enable unloading directly into the storage area.

Before the existence of the new docks, eight days might be needed in the summer and fourteen in the winter to unload a ship of 350 tons. At St Katharine, however, the average time now occupied in discharging a ship of 250 tons was twelve hours, and one of 500 tons, two or three days. St Katherine Dock was, however, not a great success as it could not take the larger vessels, and eventually it was joined up with the Western Dock in Wapping. The result was that it had never been easier to dock and unload your cargo. It was a good time to be importing and selling goods from the rest of the world.

There was another factor which may have influenced Charles Henry's decision to change both his trade and his geographical location, and that was finance. It does not look as though he had been a very successful draper and haberdasher. He may have needed financial help to survive the 1825 crash. In 1834, just after the Harrods moved from Southwark, Charles's wife Elizabeth was left £300 following the death of her father. Depending upon which indices are used, this is something like £15,000 in today's buying power – just about enough to help him to set up the new business.

The last entry in the Southwark records for Charles Henry Harrod is in the 1832 Robson's Directory, where C.H. Harrod is listed once again as a haberdasher. A fresh start was in progress …

2

OUT OF ESSEX: THE ORIGIN OF THE HARROD FAMILY

How and why Charles Henry Harrod appeared in Southwark in 1824 is not clear, but any possible explanation requires a look back at his origins. Charles was the second son, and third child of William and Tamah Harrod. He was born in Lexden in Essex on 16 April 1799. Lexden was then a separate village entity but is now a suburb of Colchester.

Though the Harrod family at that time were almost certainly Nonconformists, Charles Henry was baptised on Christmas Day 1799 at the old medieval church of St Leonard in Lexden. St Leonard's was demolished in 1920 and replaced by a 'modern' church. Though unusual now, there is a certain historical and biblical logic to the choice of Christmas Day for baptism. It was a much more popular choice in times gone by. I have been told it might have been because the incumbents made no charge on Christmas Day.

The choice of a Church of England baptism was probably forced upon his parents by the lack of a local Nonconformist church at that time, although there were several not that far away. Charles later in his life seems to have been very relaxed about dipping into both the established Church of England and the Nonconformist religions as and when it suited him. In the eighteenth and nineteenth centuries, Nonconformists of all types sometimes had problems with the registration of births, marriages and deaths. 'Nonconformist' or 'Dissenter' was a term used in England and Wales after the Act of Uniformity of 1662, to apply to those who did not conform to, or dissented from, the teaching and practices of the 'accepted' Church. The term included Reformed Christians, Presbyterians, Congregationalists, Baptists and Methodists.

Lord Hardwicke's Act, passed in 1754, required that couples had to be married in the Church of England for their marriage to be legal, regardless of what religion they belonged to, although an exception was made for Jews and Quakers. This state of affairs lasted until 1837 when civil registration began and the law then just required Nonconformist groups to send their registers into the Public Record Office. Nonconformists were often buried in parish churchyards until a local chapel was established and obtained its own burial grounds, but this changed when civic cemeteries started opening in 1853.

William and Tamah Harrod, the parents of Charles Henry Harrod, are the earliest direct Harrod ancestors of the family who have been found to date. They were both born in the second half of the eighteenth century and their origins have proved resistant to research. During more than twenty-five years of research, I have discovered most of their descendants and have met most of the living ones, milking them of as much information as they held. I have not found any definite ancestors.

Many other Harrod families, both here and abroad, have made contact with me during this time. They have often been found to have family trees stretching back well beyond the time of our earliest ancestors in the mid 1700s, but so far I have not been able to find any connection between their families and mine. The connection must exist somewhere, as Harrod is not a particularly common name, and there will surely prove to be a common ancestor for most of us. The variations of the name, Herod, Harold, Hereward, Harwood and Harewood have led to confusion which will no doubt be sorted out in the not too distant future by wider DNA studies of families.

Contact with other researchers was mostly made through genealogical websites, where your family tree can be made available to others if you wish. I found some contacts via the archivist at Harrods Store, who gets letters from time to time from Harrod family 'wannabes'. Over the years I have developed a relationship with several of the Harrods archivists, and the letters are now often sent on to me to sort out and answer. Most of them hope that they, like us, were related to the 'Harrods of Knightsbridge'. Sadly, this is seldom the case, but each contact raises the possibility for me that further connections with our tree might be discovered.

William Harrod was my great-great-great-grandfather and was born in about 1767. His birth details have never been found and the birthdate is a calculation back from later dates in his life and from his given age at death. He was an exciseman (or tax collector and enforcer), and spent his working life initially in Suffolk and later in Essex. He may not have been the only family member working with the excise; as another, seemingly unlinked Harrod, George Gateland

Harrod, a resident of Southwark, also worked in the Excise Office in London. If they were related, the Southwark connection might also have decided Charles Henry's choice of district for his first shop.

William worked with the excise for twenty years, five years in Suffolk between 1792 and 1797, and fifteen years in Essex between 1797 and 1812. He died in 1812, perhaps during the course of his work. Despite hundreds of hours on the case, and visits to Suffolk and Essex, I have not been able to find his birthplace or parents. There were initially some reasons to believe that he may have his origins in London or close by, and only moved elsewhere with his work. Despite the research in Suffolk, Essex and Southwark, and more recently in Lincolnshire and Ireland, no definite record of his birth or baptism has been found, so no more distant ancestors have been discovered. A William Harrod of the right vintage in Lincolnshire looked promising for a while but lived out his life as a schoolmaster. The right William must be out there somewhere!

At the present moment, the villages in north-east Suffolk, just south of Lowestoft, seem the most likely bet for his birthplace. There are a clutch of Harrods around Thetford, Wangford and Blything in that part of Suffolk. There are also some at Henstead, and the surrounding villages of Barsham and Benacre. The National Gravestones Index records Harrods at the nearby villages of Kirkly, Rushmere and Worlingham – this part of England seems to be full of them. Situated in south-east Suffolk, Shotley is just north of the Stour Estuary, and the parish records there include a William Harrod as a taxpayer, but give no date.

So, what led William to start work for the excise at the age of 25 is a mystery. In the late eighteenth century, excise and customs were separate organisations with different tasks. Where they overlapped, such as with imported goods, there was often much rivalry and, not infrequently, skulduggery. An exciseman, sometimes called a 'gauger', was employed by the government in what today would be the joint HM Customs & Excise, to ensure that people paid their taxes. Gauger, pronounced 'gay-jer', comes from the old French *'jaugier'*, or someone who measures.

They were also known by the name 'collectors', and rode together on horseback in groups referred to as a 'ride', as part of a county, a 'collection'. It was not an occupation that was valued by ordinary people, and it would be fair to say that the excise men of this era were, to say the least, unpopular, and that attitudes towards them were ambivalent. Followers of *Poldark* will understand this! Many people, especially those living near the coast, were either involved in, dependent upon, or turned a blind eye to the proceeds of smuggling and contraband. As a consequence of this situation, excise men were often employed away from their home area so as to avoid any conflict of interest or retribution.

The Board of Excise is not as ancient as Customs. A Board of Excise was established by the Long Parliament, and excise duties first levied in 1643. The Board of Excise was merged with the existing Board of Taxes and Board of Stamps to create the new Board of Inland Revenue in 1849.

Excise duties are inland duties levied on articles at the time of their manufacture, such as alcoholic drinks and tobacco, but duties have also been levied in the past on salt, paper and windows. As the excise became increasingly well organised in the late eighteenth and early nineteenth century, the governments of the time started collecting excise duty on a wide range of goods. The numbers of officers also increased, partly helped by a small rise in their previously miserable pay. They took on 'supernumeraries', whose job it was to act as a clerk for the collector.

Famous excise officers include Robert Burns, the poet, and Thomas Paine, who later emigrated to America and became involved in the Independence movement. Though Robert Burns, who worked for the excise for eight years in Dumphries, found the work was relatively well paid, he was not totally comfortable in his profession. He was a diligent tax collector, and had to travel on horseback many hundreds of miles each week in pursuit of his duties, 'Five days in the week, or four at least I must be on horseback and very frequently thirty or forty miles ere I return; besides four different kinds of book-keeping to post every day.' He illustrates this part of his life in his poem, *The Devil's Awa wi' th' Exciseman* (The Devil has Taken the Exciseman):

The deil cam fiddlin' thro' the town,
And danc'd awa wi' th' Exciseman,
And ilka wife cries, 'Auld Mahoun,
I wish you luck o' the prize, man'.

[Chorus]
The deil's awa, the deil's awa,
The deil's awa wi' the Exciseman,
He's danc'd awa, he's danc'd awa,
He's danc'd awa wi' the Exciseman.

We'll mak our maut, and we'll brew our drink,
We'll laugh, sing, and rejoice, man,
And mony braw thanks to the meikle black deil,
That danc'd awa wi' th' Exciseman.
The deil's awa, &c.

There's threesome reels, there's foursome reels,
There's hornpipes and strathspeys, man,
But the ae best dance ere came to the land
Was-the deil's awa wi' the Exciseman.
The deil's awa, &c.

The job was not without its dangers, and at times the collectors carried large amounts of money, so were usually armed. On other occasions, they might meet resistance to pay or attempts at retribution when the trader felt aggrieved. Did this happen to William?

William Harrod married Tamah Mason on 18 September 1794, in Hartest, a village situated in the triangle between Clare, Long Melford and Bury St Edmunds in Suffolk. He was 27 years old and she was 18. Their banns of marriage were published on three consecutive Sundays – 10, 17 and 24 August. Both were listed in the Hartest parish records as 'of this Parish', though there is no evidence that William lived in Hartest for any length of time.

The witnesses were Edmund Coe and Hannah Pettit, both members of local families. There is a Hannah Pettit to be found in the parish records; she was baptised in Hartest in 1779, so would have been 15 years old at the time of Tamah's marriage. William's wife signed the register of marriage as 'Tamah'. She was recorded as 'Thamar' on the baptism entry for one of her children and 'Tamar' on the baptism entries for the rest of her children and in the register of her burial in Kelvedon, Essex. Her own signature as 'Tamah' seems likely to be the most accurate one.

The whole area around Hartest is on the edge of Constable country and much of the countryside looks like his paintings. It was one of the regions of the country where Nonconformist and Quaker activity increased during that time, and many Huguenots also came to live in the area. It does look, from their marriage and the children's baptisms, as though William and Tamah were Nonconformists, despite the parish entries.

No photographs of William or Tamah have ever been found – not surprising given their dates.

At the time of their marriage in Hartest, William had been working for eighteen months on the nearby Clare Ride in south-west Suffolk. Long enough, one presumes, to meet a local girl. Prior to this, as his first post with the excise, he was on the Saxmundham Ride, about 30 miles away to the north-east, as a 'supernumerary'. Saxmundham is about 20 miles south of Lowestoft and is not too far away from those Suffolk villages mentioned earlier. It would seem logical that his first job, though not actually in his home area, would be in the same county.

Hartest is a delightful Suffolk village, with a large triangular village green, a lovely simple church, and a pub which, prior to the 1830s, was a small manor house. The village is about 6 miles north of Clare, which is just on the Suffolk side of the Essex/Suffolk border. Clare is a small town with some seriously ancient houses and an enormous church. It had been a prosperous town since the Middle Ages and was heavily involved in the local wool and cloth trade, being especially renowned for its broad cloth until the 1600s, when different types of cloth began to be made and gradually took over.

I have assumed that William met Tamah during his time in the area and that she was local, despite the lack of any documentary evidence apart from the marriage banns. There are certainly a number of Mason families in the Hartest area, mostly poor families; the majority being agricultural labourers. No connection between Tamah and any of these families has yet been found. The village records of Hartest also show many Pettit families in the area, including a few Hannah Pettits, who might have been the witness, and in addition show the existence of an Edmund Coe who was probably the other witness. There was a family with three successive Edmund Coes living in the Hartest area; the most likely one would have been aged 51 at the time of the marriage, which would, however, seem to be a little old to be a friend of the young couple. There were still Pettits in the area a century later, as the war memorial on the green at Hartest reveals.

The Kelvedon records reveal that Tamah Harrod died on 16 June 1811; her age is given as 35. This confirms that she was about 17 or 18 at the time of her marriage and would suggest she was born in 1776. No other records have been found for her in the Hartest parish records, or any relevant baptism records in the surrounding parishes. There were plenty of other Masons in Clare, Hartest and nearby parishes, which suggests that she was probably from a local family, but none can be linked to Tamah and no burial records have been found for her possible parents.

William died in the year following Tamah's death, 1812. His age, given as 43 years, makes his year of birth around 1767. Although their burials are listed in the parish records, no sign of a gravestone for either William or Tamah was found during a visit to Kelvedon Church. A search of the local chapel records, just in case, was also fruitless.

There are several possible reasons. They may have been buried in a Nonconformist cemetery further afield, and listed only for legal reasons in the parish records. As William and Tamah died within a few months of each other, it is possible that they died in an epidemic, and so might have been buried in mass graves; although this is less likely. Perhaps they were too poor to afford stone gravestones. Death at the age of 43 was not that uncommon for a man at that time, most diseases being

OUT OF ESSEX: THE ORIGIN OF THE HARROD FAMILY

untreatable. The possibility that he died in the pursuit of his occupation is possible, but no local newspapers have listed any such event.

Many details of William's life as an excise man were supplied by Mary Rance, a fellow Harrod researcher. She is related to the other excise-employed Harrod in the records, George Gateland Harrod. She had written for information to the archivist at Harrods in 2000 and they had passed her letter on to me. She had researched the Harrod and related Digby families in order to see if her Harrod relatives were included in the Harrods family. We have corresponded frequently since then and eventually met when I visited the Essex Records Office in Chelmsford. (By coincidence, her husband David was, for twenty years, the personnel director at Freshfields, the City law firm where our eldest daughter worked for several years.)

Mary's research, based on the Minute Books of the Excise Board, London, held at the National Archives in Kew, supplied the details of his working life. The records show that excise officers changed posts every few years, presumably to reduce collusion with the locals and corruption:

Collection Book 383. 3/5/1792 – David Jones, Examiner being by minute of the 27th ultimo appointed Supervisor of Portsmouth District, ordered that William Harrod filled the Supernumerary vacancy on Mr Whiske's Motion of Suffolk. [Presumably David Jones had just been appointed as Portsmouth Supervisor, hence the rather odd geographical juxtaposition].

Collection Book 386. 27/2/1793 – that William Harrod, Officer of Saxmundham 2nd Ride exchange stations with John Colmer, Officer of Clare 3rd Ride, Suffolk. [William had progressed from supernumerary to Officer within ten months. Did he move to Clare in order to be nearer to Tamah, or did he meet her after the move? He eventually stayed there for four years.]

Collection Book 402. 19/5/1797 – that William Harrod, Officer of Clare 3rd Ride, Suffolk move to become Officer of Bury 2nd Ride, same Collection, exchanging with James King. [A stay of eleven weeks.]

Collection Book 403. 2/8/1797 – that William Harrod Officer of Bury Ride, succeed James Scutt as Officer, Grays Ride, Essex. [This was a move to the far end of the county of Essex, many miles away. He stayed for seven months.]

Collection Book 405. 23/2/1798 – that William Harrod succeed William Brown, as Officer of Colchester 3rd Ride, Essex. [This was three years.]

Collection Book 422. 19/5/1801 – that William Harrod Officer of Colchester 3rd Ride succeed Joseph Meredith as Officer of Manningtree 1st Ride, same Collection. [A stay, again, of three years.]

Collection Book 448. 15/8/1806 – that William Harrod succeed John Smith as Officer of Colchester 1st Ride when the latter was discharged after many transgressions. [Another five years in the area.]

Collection. Book 459. 20/6/1808 – that William Harrod exchange with Thomas Howard as Officer of Coggeshall Ride, Essex Collection. [Two years.]

Collection Book 480. 21/4/1812 – that William Harrod of Coggeshall Ride, being dead, as by letter of 12 Inst. from William Airy, Collector, order that George Clements Officer of Colchester 1st Ride succeed him. [He had worked with the excise for a month short of twenty years.]

Until a visit to the area in 2008 as a guest of Mary Rance and her husband David, it had looked to me from the records available online as though William and Tamah had had two children: Charles Henry Harrod was born in 1799 in Lexden, and Jane Harrod was born in 1809, at Kelvedon, where she was christened later that year.

It had seemed rather unusual to me that William and Tamah would have had only two children, as this would have constituted a very small family for the time. There were other factors which made me wary to accept this as fact. It was common practice to name the first-born son with the same name as that of his father, and also Charles and Jane were ten years apart in birthdates – quite a big gap.

A search of the parish records at the County Records Offices for Essex in Chelmsford and Suffolk in Bury St Edmunds, for the places where William had worked, proved very fruitful. Three additional children were found and researched, but there was more to be found out later.

All seems to have been well with the Harrod family of William and Tamah until 1811. William was working on the Coggeshall Ride, now an accomplished officer with nineteen years' experience in the job. Coggeshall was a village of about 3,000 inhabitants on the River Blackwater between Braintree and Colchester. William and Tamah may not, of course, have lived in Coggeshall itself.

Tamah died in 1811, followed by William himself ten months later. As discussed earlier, no details are known but the result was that five children aged between 20 months and 16 years old were left as orphans. Charles Henry was just short of his 13th birthday when his father died.

Putting this period of their lives into some sort of historical context, it was in 1811 that Jane Austen wrote *Sense and Sensibility*, and the Prince of Wales (the future George IV) was made regent when his father George III was deemed insane. In 1812, Charles Dickens was born; Napoleon retreated from Moscow and Wellington was fighting the French in the Peninsular War. Britain was fighting on another front in the 1812 war against the fledgling American state, which conflict included the burning of Washington in 1813. Spencer Perceval, the only British Prime Minister to be assassinated, was shot as he entered the House of Commons.

There is absolutely no evidence of what happened to the remaining young Harrods between 1812 and about 1821, when most of them start to appear in the records in various parts of London. The eldest child, Caroline, was then 17 years old and old enough to look after her siblings, although she would have needed support, both physical and financial. If William died in harness (pun intended), his family may have had a pension granted to help them.

The Colchester Union Workhouse was not opened until 1837 and much of the support of the homeless and destitute in 1812 would have fallen upon the local parish. There is likely to have been support from Tamah's family, who were 25 miles away in Hartest, although 25 miles across country in those days for five orphans might have been like an ocean to cross. I do not know the whereabouts of William's family, but they were likely to have been much farther away.

My best guess, considering that there was a future connection with a farming and milling family in nearby Birch, the Digbys, was that the Harrods may have been friends of theirs before William and Tamah's deaths, and that they might have helped them for a while. Birch was only 5 miles away from Coggeshall, and might have been even closer to where the family were living.

This scenario fits in with several known facts. The Harrods disappeared from the records for nine years or so until 1821 when the eldest two siblings can be found in London, then aged 26 and 24 and presumably fully independent. Charles Henry followed his siblings a couple of years later when he appears in Southwark. Charles Henry married Elizabeth Digby in Birch in 1830, having been living in Southwark since at least 1824. He must have had an opportunity to meet her previously. Birch was such a tiny place that a chance meeting would have been very unlikely.

In 1812, when his father died, Charles would have been 13 years old and Elizabeth Digby would have been only 2 or 3 years old. Even if they had been taken in by the Digbys immediately, no romance between the two would have blossomed until several years later. It would have had to start before Charles went to live in Southwark in 1824, when Elizabeth would have been 14 years old. This suggests a relationship with the Digby family and their daughter over some time.

According to some historians, Charles Henry Harrod was said to have started his working life as a miller in Clacton, the Essex seaside town about 20 miles to the east of Coggeshall. This might seem to corroborate the idea of a longer stay in Essex, and to fit in with the Digby milling activities, but has not been backed up by my research.

The idea was suggested in a history of Harrods by Tim Dale about twenty years ago. Dale was probably repeating the story as recounted by another historian, Frankau, who was commissioned to write a history of Harrods in about 1943. Frankau certainly had access to living direct relatives at that time, although Frankau's history was never published.

I have researched Clacton's mills with the help of the Clacton and District Local History Society. There were two windmills in Clacton between 1756 and 1918. The first, at Foot's Farm, Little Clacton, is thought to have been built around 1808 to cater for the large number of soldiers who were stationed in and around Clacton, prepared for a Napoleonic invasion. It came up for sale in 1813 but I do not know who bought it. It was eventually destroyed in a storm. The second was at Bull Hill Farm in Great Clacton. In 1810, this mill, at what is now Windmill Park in Clacton, was conveyed to Thomas Harding, who owned it until 1845. There were four millers who occupied it as tenants between 1808 and 1823, but there is no mention of Charles Harrod as a tenant or worker. In 1867, it was owned by Charles Beckwith, who built a steam mill. After 1886 the windmill was closed but remained in place, and not working, until 1918 when it was demolished.

Charles Henry's son, Charles Digby Harrod, was also involved with the area. He was for a while sent to school in a small village called Edwardstone, 12 miles north of Birch – a school with seven pupils. This would have been an unusual choice for his father, by then a successful grocer in East London. Later in life, Charles Digby purchased the lordship of the manor for Layer Breton, a village close to Birch. It was probably purchased from a close relative of the Digbys, whose family had previously owned the title.

There were many other ties between the Harrod and Digby family during the later nineteenth century. All in all, it is pretty certain that the Harrod and Digby families had made a close connection with each other at some time before the marriage in 1830.

A brief look at William's other children, Charles Henry's siblings, will help clarify the link between Essex and London.

Caroline Harrod, the eldest, was born in 1795, in Hartest, just over eight months after her parents were married. Probably par for the course, but she might have been premature. She was baptised privately two weeks later and 'received' into the Church two years later with her younger brother. Many religions believe that even newly born babies need to be baptised as soon as possible, especially when not likely to survive, so that they join the religious family and all that entails if they die. They can then be 'received' into the Church itself at a later date.

In 1795 William Harrod was working with the nearby Clare Ride, so Tamah had gone home to Hartest to give birth. That would have been very sensible, considering her husband was probably spending much of his time gallivanting around the county on horseback, chasing ne'er-do-wells.

Further information about Caroline has been very difficult to find. There are a few Caroline Harrods around in the records, and it was difficult to link any one of them more definitely. One was aged 42 (and if this were the same Caroline, this would be three years out from her birth details, a level of disparity that is common) and married in 1840, at St Peter's Church, Sible Hedingham, a village 10 miles south of Hartest, in Essex. Another Caroline died, aged 61, in July 1856, in Mile End, in the East End of London. This age would have fitted with her birth, as would the location, but the death certificate, when received, showed she was the wife of another unrelated William Harrod, so was not a Harrod at birth. The most likely candidate was a Caroline Harrod found in the Nonconformist burial records held at the National Archives (now available more widely online). She died at the young age of 26 years, and was buried in 1821 at Bunhill Fields Burial Grounds on City Road, near Old Street in London. The age was correct for her birthdate, as was her religion. She had lived prior to her death in Whitfield Street, just west of Tottenham Court Road.

The proximity of this address to her younger sister, described below, and her Nonconformist religion make her the most likely candidate. If so, it confirms the family move to London in the early 1820s. Her unmarried status at the age of 26 might fit with her previous status as a 'little mother' for the family.

Bunhill, the name of the cemetery, is derived from 'bone hill'. It was a small, wooded Dissenters' burial ground in the city. Bunhill Fields was soon known as 'the cemetery of Puritan England'. William Blake, John Bunyan and Daniel Defoe are amongst over 120,000 Nonconformists whose bodies are squeezed tightly together within only 4 acres. Bunhill's graves are crammed one on top of the other, as was the custom before the 1830s and the introduction of bigger out-of-town cemeteries. It was closed as a site for burials in the 1850s. Following extensive bombing during the Second World War and a subsequent redesign of the damaged area, nearly half of the site is free of tombstones and has been transformed into a garden area for recreational purposes.

William Harrod, the second child and first son, was born in 1797, also in Hartest. He was baptised privately in 1797, and received into the church sixteen days later with his older sister. As was the fashion, he was given his father's name. William, his father, was still working in Clare on the date of his son's birth, but moved to nearby Bury a month later. For the immediate period following the discovery of these baptisms in the Hartest parish records, nothing else was found out about him until the record of a very young William Harrod was found in the same Nonconformist burial records as his sister Caroline, but in a different cemetery. He was buried, aged 1 year and 4 months, in the Countess of Huntington's Chapel, Spa Fields, in Clerkenwell, not far from Bunhill Fields. Some details about this latter William make him look like the one baptised in Hartest. His age at burial is only one month out from his birthdate and he was Nonconformist.

Research into the Countess of Huntington produced a torrent of interesting information. Selina Hastings was born into an aristocratic Leicestershire family in 1707. Her marriage to the Earl of Huntingdon in 1728 was a love match that produced seven children before his death after seven years. Selina underwent an evangelical conversion in 1739, and came into contact with many Dissenters including the Wesleys. She gradually assumed a position of influence and used her position to further her religion within fashionable society. The Countess of Huntingdon's Connexion, as it became known, was one of the most significant of the non-Wesleyan groups within the Revival. It had its own training college and formed a network of chapels across the country, including the Spa Chapel at Spa Fields. Selina died in 1804 and was buried at Bunhill Fields.

The Spa Fields Burial Ground was one of the most appalling cemeteries in London. Shortage of space led to a rapid recycling of grave space and a lot of suspicious fires, suspected to be the disposal of bodies! Contemporaries described the burning of coffins and body parts, and the sale of bodies for dissection; recycling the space allowed 1,500 bodies a year to go into an area of 2 acres for fifty years. By the time it was closed in 1849, it is estimated that 80,000 bodies had been 'buried' there. Lady Huntingdon would have turned in her own grave! Since 1885 the ground has been used as an open space and tennis courts which is now maintained by the council.

The discovery, some years later, of a brother for Charles Henry named William Frederick, who lived into the mid 1850s, called into question the connection of the William born in 1797 with the poor young child buried in Spa Fields. Although the birthdate calculated from William Frederick's death details was a few years different to the actual date (1793–94, rather than 1797), no other William Harrod's birth or baptism has been found and so perhaps the William buried in Spa Fields was not related.

Once discovered, the life of William Frederick was traced from the records. He reappears ten years after his parents' death in London, when he married Nancy Bryant at St Andrew's, Holborn, in 1822. There were three witnesses, but none of them were Harrods. The following year, William and Nancy were living in Clerkenwell, and he was working as a 'seal maker' (probably exactly what it says on the tin). Soon afterwards he became a goldsmith and then a jeweller, living initially in Regent Street and later Southwark. They had four children; tragically, three died in infancy and the other in their 20s. Nancy died in 1829 two months after the birth, and one week after the death, of their last child.

Now a bachelor with just one child of 3 years of age to look after, he decided, like his brother Charles, to go into partnership. Together with George Fielding he ran a goldsmith and watchmaker's business in Nelson Street, Greenwich. Again, like his brother, the partnership did not survive for long. The *London Gazette* reported the dissolution of their partnership in 1833.

William Frederick died in 1840 in Gravesend. It was apparent he was just visiting the area when he died, as he was buried a few days later back in Clerkenwell. There is more to tell about William Frederick Harrod's connection to Charles in the next chapter.

Charles Henry Harrod, the third child, was born in 1799 in Lexden. The birth coincides with William's posting to nearby Colchester.

Mary Ann Harrod, the fourth child, was born in Manningtree in Essex during William's stay there. She was christened at St Michael & All Angels Church, Manningtree, at the end of 1803. Manningtree is a small town on the southern bank at the head of the Stour River estuary, inland from Harwich. Although Mary Ann is listed in the parish records as the daughter of a Thomas & Tamar Harrod, it seems most likely that this was a clerical error. There is no trace of another Tamah Harrod anywhere, let alone in Manningtree at a time when William was working there.

Further information about Mary Ann was obtained by the chance finding of a family tree online, which also included Jane Harrod, her younger sister. Mary Ann married William Augustus Press in 1831 at St James, Clerkenwell, in London. It was beginning to look as though all the children had gravitated to London. Both of them were listed as 'of this Parish', and their banns had been published there in March that year. William Press was born in about 1810 in Fleet Street, and worked as a mechanical draughtsman, then later in life as a chimney sweep. They lived in St Pancras, and later Finsbury. They definitely had three children, possibly a fourth, all born in St Pancras. Mary Ann is listed in 1861 as a 'shoe binder'.

It looks as though Mary Ann died sometime before the mid 1860s, as there is no sign of her after the 1861 census and her husband was alone by 1867. In that year, he was admitted to the Marylebone Workhouse. The early Victorian workhouses were pretty grim places, but they fulfilled a very necessary function in a world without social services and government benefits. As it happened, Marylebone Workhouse, which housed about 1,500 inmates at the time, had a facelift and a new ward built in 1867. The records show that altogether he had three separate admissions to the workhouse.

His admission in February 1867 shows that he arrived in a cab, ill with pneumonia, destitute and homeless. He gave an address in south-east Bloomsbury. Who sent him in the cab is not known. He stayed for sixteen days and was discharged 'cured'. He was readmitted from a different address fifteen months later, in 1868, and stayed for seven days, requesting his own discharge. Following the last admission a year later in 1869, he stayed for the rest of his life, dying a remarkable ten years later in 1879.

Although I have assumed, from the fact that all the Harrod children ended up in London, that they may have remained friends and supported each other, this now seems unlikely. Some were in contact, as you will see later, but Charles Henry's brother-in-law, William Press, died a pauper whilst Charles was by then a relatively rich man. We all know that families drift apart and fall out, so it is possible there had been no contact between them.

A little more is known about William and Mary Ann's second son, John Harrod Press, which raised my hopes of a connection. John started off his working life, according to the 1861 census, as a 'shopman' for George Poulter, a grocer in Putney. By 1871, he was a grocer himself in St Pancras, but by 1881 he had become an insurance agent and was living in Wandsworth. He was married with three daughters. Again, one wonders if had fallen out with his father.

A final footnote to the Press family: A William Press was tried at the Old Bailey on two occasions for theft, in 1826 and 1829. He was found guilty on both occasions and given mercy, with sentences of two months and six months in jail respectively. There are not enough details apart from his age to link him definitely to our William Press.

Jane Harrod, the fifth child, was born in 1809 in Kelvedon whilst her father was working locally at Coggeshall. She also disappears from the records for a number of years. She reappears, aged 20, in 1829, when she marries Samuel Thomas Vernell at All Souls, Marylebone, in London.

Samuel, a builder, had been born in Bristol in 1806. They lived all of their lives in the St Pancras and Regents Park areas of London, living at 6 Albany Street, Regent's Park, for a large part of their lives, then later at No. 28. Rather oddly, frequent newspaper adverts for Horniman's Tea, a famous brand of the day, list Jane Vernell at 7 Albany Street as one of their stockists. They were comfortably off, some censuses show the odd servant in their house. Albany Street is now a very smart thoroughfare to the east of Regent's Park, with expensive flats, apartments and small hotels. Regent's Park barracks are on the northern end of the street.

They had ten children between 1830 and 1846, five boys and five girls. As often happened, four died in infancy or early childhood. They were a close family, all their children and grandchildren continued living in the same area, and followed various occupations – a plumber, a house painter and a solicitor's managing clerk. None became involved with their Uncle Charles or the Harrods shop.

Apart from Charles Henry, none of the children of William and Tamah maintained any obvious connection with their Suffolk or Essex roots. Perhaps Charles had deeper roots there. If he had indeed worked for a while as a miller with the Digby family his marriage to the eldest daughter of James Digby Senior, a pork butcher and miller, and his wife Martha, would have cemented the relationship. Like Charles and his family, the Digby family were Nonconformists. Perhaps they met at the chapel.

I embark with some trepidation on a description of the Digby family. They were a family of farmers and millers in north-east Essex. The many branches each had large families, often with eight or more children; they were all born and lived in close proximity to each other, and all the siblings called their own children by the same names as the previous generation. What this means to a family history researcher is that you are faced by a bewildering array of ancestors with the same name and similar dates of birth. Confusion is inevitable. It frustrated me for some years. Even in the direct line of the Digbys with which the Harrods were involved, there were eight generations in a row with James as the name of the firstborn son.

When I was investigating the Digbys, I was in contact with several other branches of the family who were conducting their own research, some still living locally and others as far afield as New Zealand and Scandinavia. We had constructed slightly different family trees as we tried to fit names to families, and I must have set about modifying what I thought was my final family tree at least a dozen times. After I had just finished the final, final version, I came across a small book about the Digby family written by a John G. Digby, another New Zealand descendant. This was quite comprehensive. Most of his detail matched my own, and reassuringly he had found the same gaps. What his book provided was some flesh to put upon the previously rather bare bones.

In the 1881 England census, a total of 1,500 Digbys were listed, almost all in Suffolk and Essex. To put this in perspective, there were about 1,000 Harrods in the same census. The Digby family were involved with the Harrods over three generations. Charles Henry married one and gave his children the name Digby as a middle name. Some Digbys were witnesses at his marriage.

The Digby family probably hailed from Norfolk between 1600 and 1700, although there are traces of them further south in 1550. The Digbys in our story worked and held land in Birch and the nearby villages of Peldon, Lexden, Layer Breton and Layer de la Haye, all in that part of Essex, just south of Colchester and quite near to Kelvedon. They were a very affluent family in the 1700s and 1800s.

In 1831 the population of Birch was 764 persons. In contrast, nearby Colchester was a town of several thousand people. Birch existed long before the reign of Edward the Confessor, and consisted of two parishes, Great and Little Birch. Today Birch is a rather straggling village spread over an area that merges with Layer Breton and Layer Marney. It is set on gently undulating arable land, rising to the heath at Layer Breton then falling towards Abberton Reservoir and falling further towards the coast in the direction of Peldon.

For many years the Digbys leased several mills south-east of Colchester and this was their principal occupation, although they also worked as tenant farmers in the area. The mill in Birch was a 'post' mill, meaning the whole mill turned on a central post allowing the sails to move into the wind. Birch Mill (which was also known as Digby's Mill) was built in 1724 and boasted a windmill and a watermill. The Digby family held the lease on the property and ran the mill from 1794 until 1855. The Digbys faced competition from another mill in Birch run by Mr Royce.

There is a hymn-like ditty once current in the village:

All people that on earth do dwell,
Shall grind their corn at Digby's Mill;
If not they'll have to buy their bread
And flour off old John Royce instead.

The family features quite prominently in the history of milling in Essex in the eighteenth century. Three of James Digby's sons followed him in the trade. Almost all the mills and the land were owned by the Round family, who were the lords of the manor in Birch. The Digby family flame burned bright in the area for over sixty years. They increased in wealth and stature in the first half of the nineteenth century, and then in 1855 everything changed.

In that year they ceased working at both Birch Mill and Bourne Mill. Some branches of the family then slipped from relative wealth to poverty. James Digby Junior, Elizabeth Digby's brother, was declared bankrupt that year, having apparently lived in poverty for some time before that. His total debt was £850 (probably something like £100,000 today). This change of circumstances may have been due to poor individual management, but in the years preceding 1855 there were several years of poor harvests and a general economic depression. Problems for farmers and millers increased from the mid 1800s and large parts of the local community were caught by the downturn of events when corn production declined after the Repeal of the Corn Laws.

The Corn Laws were enacted between 1815 and 1846 and kept corn and other grain prices at an artificially high level. This was intended to protect English farmers from cheap foreign imports of grain following the end of the Napoleonic Wars in 1815. During the conflict the British blockaded Europe, with the result that goods within Britain were protected against competition from outside.

Farming became extremely lucrative and farming land profitable. Voting Members of Parliament had no interest in repealing the Corn Laws, as the voting franchise depended on land ownership.

The high corn price meant that the urban working class had to spend much of their income on corn just to survive. With little left over, they could not afford manufactured goods and so manufacturers suffered and had to lay off workers. These workers had difficulty finding employment, so the economic spiral worsened for everyone involved.

The reform of the Corn Laws started in 1828 and the right to vote was extended by the Reform Act to many middle-class merchants in 1832. The movement to continue reform of the Corn Laws included the Chartists and the final repeal took place under Sir Robert Peel in 1846. In the following decades, the farmers and millers of corn went through some very bad times, and this would have hit the Digby family badly.

Some of the Digby family had intermarried with a local family of butchers, the Tiffens (sometimes spelt Tiffin), and as the nineteenth century progressed, perhaps prompted by the difficulties surrounding corn production, more of the Digbys became involved in the butchery trade, cattle dealing and more varied farming. Others left England to seek their future abroad.

Our Digby family have been traced back ten generations to Richard Digby, who was born in Essex in 1560. The move to Birch took place in the late seventeenth century. Our James Digby, Elizabeth's father, was the sixth in a line of seven James's. James Digby Senior (1775–1834) was the last direct male ancestor of this branch of the family to remain in England all of his life. His sons and grandsons spread into North America or Australasia. He was at times a farmer, a pork butcher, a miller and a corn merchant. Whilst James prospered, one of his brothers spent most of his life in poverty. It was James's will which left money to his children, including daughter Elizabeth. In that will, he spread his mills and properties out between his sons, three of whom stayed in the milling business. His eldest son, James Junior, a witness at Elizabeth's marriage to Charles Harrod, continued to work the Birch Mill.

William Digby, Elizabeth Digby's brother, and his family left for Pittsburgh, Pennsylvania, in 1834 around the time of his father's death. William became a very successful tailor and clothier in Pittsburgh. William's great-great-grandson, Joseph H. Digby, of Pittsburgh, had some personal correspondence with John G. Digby, the writer of the Digby story. He said that James Digby Senior, in Essex, had 'advanced them the money for their transportation to the United States,' and 'they left England to avoid religious persecution.' According to anecdotal recollections of his family, 'William's brother James left to go to Australia at about the same time.'

A chance finding of a 'funeral card' during the research highlighted one of the perils of life at this time. Black-edged, ornately decorated funeral cards were often sent out in Victorian times to inform others of deaths. Clara Selina Mason, born in 1850, was the granddaughter of James Junior by his third marriage. Her parents and siblings lived all their lives in either Dover or London, and she was working as a domestic servant for the family of Joseph Digby, the younger brother of James Digby Junior, in Peldon, when she met her untimely death. She died one month short of her 16th birthday. Her cause of death was given by the coroner at Maldon, Mr Codd: 'From eating greens which had been put by her by mistake into a sauce pan containing a solution of arsenic, 21 hours.'

Despite her being such a distant relative, it was too intriguing not to investigate. The story was carried in the *Essex Standard* and *Chelmsford Chronicle*, and parts of the story follow:

A FAMILY POISONED AT PELDON.
A fatal and painful case has occurred at the village of Peldon, the family of Mr J. Digby, miller of that place, having been poisoned through a saucepan in which arsenic had been boiled having been incautiously left on the fire place, from which it was taken for the purpose of cooking. Clara Mason, the niece of Mr Digby [in fact, Joseph was the brother of her maternal grandfather, Joseph Digby Junior] died on Thursday, and the details of the case were given at the inquest, which was held before W. Codd Esq. on Friday.

Mr Joseph Digby, miller, of Peldon, said – 'The deceased Clara Mason was my great-niece, and was 15 years and 11 months old; she acted as servant in my house. On the morning of the Tuesday, 7th inst., I left home, and on my return about three in the afternoon, I found the deceased and three members of my family suffering from the effects of some poison, which was no doubt arsenic. Between seven and eight that morning I had put two ounces of stone arsenic into two quarts of water in a saucepan, to be used for destroying vermin, and left it standing on the kitchen fender. The deceased and my wife and daughter were present at the time. I held up a little piece of arsenic, saying at the time, "That little piece would kill any of us"; my wife was to boil the arsenic as soon as the kettle which was on the fire was taken off; on my arrival at home that afternoon I found that Mr Green, the surgeon, had been there; and he came again to see deceased in the evening, when he expressed his opinion that she would die; she died yesterday morning about eleven o'clock; my wife, wife's mother, and my little girl were all affected.' [That would have been his wife, Ann, his mother in law, Jemima Birkin, and his granddaughter.]

Emily Digby, daughter of the last witness, deposed – 'On the afternoon of Tuesday last, between one and two o'clock, my mother, grandmother, the deceased and my little niece sat down together for dinner; one dish consisted of boiled greens; I did not like the look of them, as they were brown, and didn't eat any; all the rest did; immediately after dinner the deceased was taken with sickness, and complained of pain in her inside and head ache; she went upstairs and laid down, and soon after the rest were taken with sickness; not having myself been affected, I began to suspect there was something wrong in the greens, and I told deceased what I thought, when she said she thought she had put the greens into the wrong saucepan; the deceased was attended by Mr Green, the surgeon, soon after the occurrence, but she died yesterday morning about a quarter before 11; she complained greatly of thirst and of feeling very hot about her throat; I saw the saucepan containing the arsenic on the fire, and afterwards on the side of the stove.'

Mr Green gave his evidence. There was little he could do apart from giving a mustard emetic and drinks. He saw her three times in all. He tasted the liquid in the saucepan and was in no doubt this was arsenic. The coroner admonished the Digby family for the lack of caution, and the Jury returned a verdict of 'Accidental Death'.

James Digby Junior was initially successful after his father's death, but at around the age of 50 in the early 1850s he fell upon hard times. In 1855 he became bankrupt and his creditors reluctantly auctioned his goods, the mill and its contents at the Ship Inn.

The *Essex County Standard* advertised the auction in the edition of 19 January 1855:

Birch Mill, Essex. Near Colchester. To be sold by auction by Messrs. Smith & Ward on Wednesday, January 24th, 1855. All the excellent household furniture, outdoor effects, utensils of trade, useful brown mare, grey ditto, miller's van and miller's cart, light chaise-cart, brewing utensils, etc. etc. by order of the assignee of Mr James Digby, a bankrupt. Sale to commence at half past ten o'clock.

The mill itself appeared in the same paper three weeks later:

To Millers and others. To be sold by auction by Messrs. Smith & Ward. At the Ship Inn, Headgate, Colchester on Wednesday February 14th 1855 at 5 o'clock in the afternoon, in one lot and to be removed by the purchaser.

All that excellent POST WINDMILL, known by the name of 'Birch Mill' lately held by Mr James Digby, now standing near the Church at Birch, in the County of Essex, together with all machinery, 2 pairs of French stones, and all going gears to same belonging; and the materials of the Round-house.

James had been in trouble for a while and at one time was accused of fraud.

But enough of the Digbys and Essex for the moment. Both will keep popping up throughout the story.

3

THE FIRST GROCERY

Charles Henry gave up his drapery and haberdashery business in Southwark in 1831 or 1832 and started up a grocery business north of the Thames. The possible reasons have been discussed earlier. It looks as though the drapery business had not been successful and there was a lot of competition.

His wife Elizabeth was left some money in her father James's will after he died in 1834, which might have aided the move retrospectively. However, a closer examination of the will shows that the money was to be paid by Elizabeth's brother Joseph from his share of the estate, after the death or remarriage of their mother, Martha. She died ten years later in 1844 so the money would not have been paid until that year at the earliest.

With my knowledge of Charles Henry's tactics in later life, I could easily be persuaded that he moved because he thought he could make more money somewhere else trading in tea. His situation had changed in 1830, he was then a married man, so he might in addition have been influenced by his wife.

Charles Henry is said to have established his 'Wholesale Grocery and Tea Dealer' business in Cable Street, east London, in 1834, but his first premises north of the Thames were actually in Upper Whitecross Street, just north of the Barbican. Depending which source you consult, he had premises there from somewhere between 1831 and 1833. Robson's Directory, which had him still in Southwark as a haberdasher in 1832, lists him in 1833 as 'Harrod & Co., Grocers', 163 Upper Whitecross Street, London EC1. By 1834, he was definitely trading at or near 4 Cable Street, where he stayed for a number of years. This hesitation about his first address in that area is explained below.

Robson's lists him there as 'Harrod Chas. Grocer & Co.' in 1834, and Kelly's Post Office Directory confirms his business was there until 1855. At an early stage of my research, when street directories were one of my main sources of information, I was confused by an entry in Pigot's 1839 Commercial Directory, which gave a Frederick William Harrod as a grocer at 4 Cable Street. At that time, I had not yet 'discovered' Charles's brother, so assumed this entry was a clerical error. Later work clarified the reason for the entry.

THE FIRST GROCERY

Errors in records are quite common. They can sometimes be recording errors, but probably more often than not they are transcription errors, occurring particularly when records are digitised. In the 1980s, one of the best record databases available was that of the Mormon Church, or the Church of Jesus Christ of Latter-day Saints, as it is now better known. The Church is based in Salt Lake City in the USA, and because of their rules about intermarriage between closely related family members, they have accumulated thousands of birth and baptism records to allow members to check their origins.

When very little else was available to study apart from paper records at the Public Record Office based in Portugal Street in London (a precursor of the National Archives), the births marriages and deaths in large bound books at Somerset House and later St Catherine's House, and the Family Records Centre at Myddleton Street, all in London, the Mormon records could be studied on microfilm at many centres, including my home town of Cheltenham.

This resource was invaluable, but not always completely accurate. I was told that the UK records had been transcribed by American students on holiday in Britain who had used local parish records and other sources. It was inevitable that, apart from simple transcription errors, their unfamiliarity with British names and places led to other errors. These records were eventually digitised as the International Genealogical Index (IGI), but many of the errors remain, so beware.

Once in Cable Street, which seems to have been a retail business selling groceries and tea, Charles Henry seemed to have vacated the premises in Upper Whitecross Street. Cable Street, which runs from the direction of the Tower of London in the west to Ratcliff in the east, probably dates back to the sixteenth century when it was just a pathway. The original length of Cable Street was the standard length of hemp rope, twisted into a cable, which was required for sailing ships (in the British Navy this length was about 100 fathoms/608ft/185m, one tenth of a nautical mile or one cable).

A modern visitor to east London would find 4 Cable Street on the south side of the street, recently the site of the Cirilo Noodle Bar and Grill. Whether this is the site of the original No. 4 in the nineteenth century is difficult to prove, but from the census descriptions, it looks likely. The area is very close to Tower Hill, and is still run down despite much of the redevelopment in the surrounding areas. Cable Street runs west from Dock Street, and the north side has been completely demolished and taken over by parking and the Docklands Light Railway (DLR). There has been a railway line there since the mid 1800s but it was taken over latterly by the DLR. With the opening up of the Isle of Dogs and Canary Wharf, and particularly since the Olympics in 2012, the area has improved.

The whole district was once called Well Close. It is suggested that Well Street (now called Ensign Street) and Well Close were so called because of the well in nearby Goodman's Fields to the west. A tributary of the Thames originally ran parallel to Well Street into the river. Well Close Square is on the south side of Cable Street a few doors east of No. 4. Only buildings on the northern side of the square remain.

From the eighteenth century until early in the nineteenth century it was a rather fashionable suburb, attracting well-to-do merchants, sea officers and doctors. The area deteriorated in the 1800s and has only improved in recent years. At the north-west corner of the square, on Grace's Alley, stands the famous Wilton's Music Hall. Billed as the world's oldest functioning grand music hall, it was built in 1858 behind the Prince of Denmark Tavern, which is now called the Mahogany Bar and is attached to the music hall.

The tavern opened in 1839, and was reputedly the first in London to have mahogany counters and fittings. The tavern was often frequented by people of 'ill repute' and had a poor reputation. Sailors were induced to enter, to drink and to dance. These men were plied with drink, knocked senseless, and after being robbed were thrown out into Grace's Alley. An alternative method of distribution was to drop the victim through a trapdoor (which is still to be seen there) and leave them to get out when sober. The original entertainment was pretty basic, and many fights and the occasional murder occurred. I visited the area about seven years ago when a restoration was underway, but it was still in a very sad state. It has since been fully restored to its magnificent glory and is in regular use.

THE FIRST GROCERY

As stated above, there is some confusion in the records regarding the shop at 4 Cable Street, and where Charles and his family actually lived and worked. In the 1841 census, the address of the Harrod family is given as Rosemary Lane, Cable Street, in Registration District 9 of the parish of St Mary Whitechapel. Rosemary Lane and Cable Street are often bracketed together in the directories as though they were parts of the same street, and they were originally just that. Rosemary Lane, now named Royal Mint Street, runs from Tower Hill in the west and becomes Cable Street at the junction with Dock Street. However, even though the heading on the pertinent page of the 1841 census starts confusingly with the address, 'Cable Street/Rosemary Lane', the south side of Rosemary Lane is in Registration District 9, whilst the south side of Cable Street is in Registration District 10. To make matters more confusing, according to the 1841 census 4 Cable Street was occupied by John Relzbach and his family, a 'pork butcher', who is listed as 'born in foreign parts'.

Further information in this chapter will suggest that in 1836 the shop was in Rosemary Lane, not Cable Street. In 1839 the business was in Cable Street, but by 1841 John Relzbach was at that address. Either Charles held both properties, and used Cable Street on occasions and rented it out at other times whilst living in Rosemary Lane, or they were repeatedly confused with each other.

The area surrounding Well Close was, and still is, referred to as the Minories. This name remains as the road running south from Aldgate to Tower Hill, and is derived from the abbey of the 'minoresses', or nuns, of St Mary of the Order of St Clare, founded in 1294, which stood on the site. In 1686 the area became part of the Liberties of the Tower of London, granted by King James II. It was the location of Minories Railway Station, built in 1840 as a part of the London & Blackwall Railway – a 3½ mile (5.6km) cable railway. The site is now occupied by a Docklands Light Railway station, opened in 1989 as the western terminus of the system.

The area was quite cosmopolitan and has accommodated waves of immigrants over many generations. It was renowned as an area for Dissenters and Nonconformists. It was home to several German owned sugar refineries and warehouses, and part of the surrounding area was also known as Rag Fair, as it was the district for the sale of second-hand clothes. George Godwin, in *London Shadows* (1854), described the wares available:

> A missionary, who recently explored Rag-fair, reported that a man and his wife might be clothed from head to foot for from 10 to 15 shillings. Another missionary stated that 8 shillings would buy every article of clothing required by either a man or a woman, singly ... A third missionary reported: There is as great a variety of articles in pattern, and shape, and size, as I think could be found in any draper's shop in London. The mother may go to 'Rag-fair' with the whole of her family, both boys and girls, – yes, and her husband, too, and for a very few shillings deck them out from top to toe. I have no doubt that for a man and his wife, and five or six children, £1 at their disposal, judiciously laid out, would purchase them all an entire change. This may appear to some an exaggeration: but I actually overheard a conversation in which two women were trying to bargain for a child's frock; the sum asked for it was 1½d and the sum offered was a penny, and they parted on the difference.

During the first half of the nineteenth century, it was one of several no-go areas for the authorities in East London, so-called safe havens for the criminal elements of the day. The illustrations of London by Gustave Doré, especially those of the East End, published in 1872 in his *London, A Pilgrimage*, show the industry in the docks, the riverside, and the pitiful state of the streets in the area. This was the area where many Dickens novels were set, north and south of docklands. As a young man Dickens lived in the worst parts of London, and although his novels were not published until after the mid 1800s they drew on his earlier experiences. His father and the whole family, apart from Charles, were sent to Marshalsea Debtors' Prison in 1824, whilst Charles continued at work.

So, Charles Henry and Elizabeth had settled and started to bring up their family in an area that was far from gentrified and salubrious.

Later evidence suggests that by the time of their move from Southwark to east London, they already had one child. Elizabeth, their second child, was born in 1835 after their move. By 1836, they had two young children and as far as I can ascertain, a functioning grocery business.

At one stage in my research, when I knew nothing about the first child, and thought Elizabeth was the first, and I knew that their next child had been born in 1841, I was puzzled by the pattern of pregnancies. Charles Henry and Elizabeth had married in 1830, and had no children until 1835, which was unusual in those days of limited or no contraception. It was possible that they had lost children in earlier pregnancies or in early childhood during this period in Southwark, but there was no evidence to support this idea. Then there was a five or six year gap between Elizabeth and their next child, following which children had followed with the regularity normally expected. Had something happened in those intervening years or was this just serendipity?

In the early years of this century the Ancestry.com website added a search facility for the England and Wales Criminal Registers, including details of Proceedings of the Old Bailey between 1674 and 1913. A search for 'Harrod' threw up several results. There were reports of thefts from Harrods Stores, but two reports where a Charles Harrod or Charles Henry Harrod was the defendant – this rapidly got my attention.

A 'Charles Henry Harrod' was accused in 1888 of breaking the peace and libel, and appeared at the Old Bailey on 30 July of that year. He pleaded guilty to 'unlawfully publishing certain libels of and concerning Sir Reginald Hanson'. Sir Reginald Hanson Bt Kt JP DL FSA and his family had a large wholesale grocery business. This led me to assume that this was *our* Charles Henry, but I was proved wrong.

Sir Reginald was born in 1840 and after education at Tonbridge, Rugby and Trinity College joined the Commercial Union Assurance Company which had been founded by his father, Samuel. He was made a director a year later, and then joined the family business, Samuel Hanson & Son Limited. After a number of City appointments, he became Lord Mayor of London in 1886, during which time Queen Victoria celebrated her jubilee year, and was entertained by Sir Reginald at the Mansion House, where his creation as a baronet superseded his previous knighthood. He was the Conservative Member of Parliament for the City of London from 1891 to 1900, and an honorary colonel in the 6th Battalion, Royal Fusiliers, City of London Regiment. Not a man to libel or take on lightly!

Wisely, Harrod apologised for his conduct, and pledged his word not to repeat the offence. He was sentenced 'to enter into his own recognisance in £40 to appear for judgement if called upon, and to keep the peace for Twelve Months'. Despite the initial excitement, I realised it was obviously not our Charles Henry, who I then realised had died three years earlier in 1885.

My research then unearthed several other Charles Henry Harrods in Southwark – three, in fact – all in the same family, whose origins were in Lincolnshire. To date, no connection to our family has been found, but the proximity of this family in Southwark to our Charles Henry and their origin in Lincolnshire might suggest we were connected by previous generations. This Harrod family originated in the Billinghay/Kyme area of Lincolnshire, midway between Lincoln and Boston, and were mostly agricultural labourers.

John Harrod (1826–63) made the move to Southwark somewhere between 1853 and 1861 and was the only branch of that family to have moved away from Lincolnshire. John became a 'fellowship porter', and lived with his family in Great Maze Street, in the parish of St Olave's, Southwark. This street no longer exists; it was swallowed up by the development of Guys and St Thomas's Hospital and London Bridge Station in the area east of Borough High Street and south of Tooley Street. His second son, Charles Henry Harrod (1851–1904), after a spell as a seaman on the river in Bermondsey, also became a fellowship porter – this was the man in the libel case.

The Index of Old Occupations states that a fellowship porter was a kind of uniformed, bonded messenger, vetted for honesty etc., before admission to the Guild of Fellowship Porters, to whom they were accountable. You could trust your valuables to them for transport

THE FIRST GROCERY

from your London office to another warehouse, shop or office – the equivalent of today's couriers.

The second and the more interesting case proved to be that of *my* Charles Harrod, held at the Old Bailey on 8 May 1836 before the Recorder, T. Clarkson Esq:

> RICHARD MORAN was indicted for stealing, on 2 April, 112lbs weight of currants, value £3 5s; and 1 bag, value 6d; the goods of John Healey Booth and others, his masters; and CHARLES HARROD for feloniously receiving the same, well knowing them to be the same, well knowing them to be stolen; against the statute.

I asked myself if this could be the previously squeaky-clean Charles Harrod, founder of the prestigious shop – and indeed it was.

Richard Moran, a year older than Charles Henry, was a porter at Messrs Booth, Ingledew & Co., who were wholesale grocers at 68 Upper Thames Street. From the evidence presented, it was likely that Harrod had been accepting stolen goods for some time and that the police had been watching him, and persuaded the carman involved (the cart driver named John Warner) to turn Queen's Evidence.

The quite complex and co-ordinated police operation was undertaken by the Thames River Police, or Mariners, as they were then called. They had been formed at the beginning of the nineteenth century to cut down the huge amount of theft taking place from ships and wharves on the river. They used auxiliaries called surveyors, or watchers, to collect evidence. This force was one of the first organised full-time forces and joined up with the land-based 'Peelers' in 1839 to form the Metropolitan Police.

The case was widely reported and followed blow by blow in the press, including the *Public Ledger & Daily Advertiser*, the *Evening Chronicle*, *Bell's New Weekly*, *Bell's Life in London & the Sporting Chronicle*, *Bell's Weekly Messenger*, the *Evening Standard*, the *Morning Post*, and last but not least, the *London Times*. What follows is a short version taken from many reports. The reports contained some errors, at times mixing up dates and the sequence of events.

Those involved were initially brought before the Recorder for a preliminary examination, but it became evident from the evidence that Moran and Warner, the employees at the wholesale grocer, had been apprehended and examined previously:

4 May 1836, *Public Ledger & Daily Advertiser*
Police Intelligence – Thames office. Extensive System of Robbery
Yesterday, John Warner, a carman, and Richard Moran, a porter, late in the employ of Messrs. Booth, Ingledew and Knott, wholesale grocers, in Upper Thames Street, and Charles Henry Harrod, a grocer and tea-dealer, who had for many years carried on business in Rosemary Lane, were brought before Mr Clarkson yesterday, charged, the two former with stealing property to a large amount, the property of their employers, and Harrod with receiving the same knowing it to be stolen.

Mr Hobler, jun., appeared for the prosecution, and Mr Wooler for the prisoners. The examination lasted several hours.

Mr John Preston said he was clerk and assistant to Messrs. Booth and Co., the prisoners Warner and Moran were in their employ as carman and porter. On Monday, 4th April, the firm received a letter stating that a system of robbery had been carried on for some time to a great extent. On the Saturday previous stock had been taken, and considerable deficiencies were discovered. On the receipt of the letter –

Mr Wooler – Which you have no business to mention, unless you have the person here who wrote it to give evidence.

Mr Clarkson said the witness must relate what he saw, not what he heard.

The witness then proceeded to state, that understanding the prisoners Moran and Warner had been delivering goods to Harrod, stock was taken on the Saturday previous to the receipt of the letter, and on the following Monday, a bag containing 100lbs of currants was missing. The currants had not been sold, nor were any goods consigned to Harrod nor any other person in Rosemary Lane.

Warner was taken into custody, and his wife afterwards brought me a paper produced by Mr Hobler, which stated –

Mr Wooler – The paper can't be made evidence unless the party is here who wrote it.

Mr Hobler said it was a confession of the prisoner Warner, and written at his dictation, by a man who was now in confinement in the Giltspur Street Compter. He had not brought him here. [The Giltspur Street Compter was a small prison, mainly used to hold debtors. It was situated in Smithfield, close to Newgate, in the City of London.]

Mr Clarkson – Then you can't make it evidence.

In cross-examination by Mr Wooler, Mr Preston said the porter and Warner had been taken before the Lord Mayor, remanded twice, and finally discharged. They could make nothing of the case before the Lord Mayor. [Before 1856, cases could be brought before the Lord Mayor of London at his Sessions.]

Mr Wooler – Then what charge have you against them?

Mr Hobler – Stop; we have other evidence.

Mr J.C. Evans jun., a surveyor of Thames police [or watcher], stated that on the evening of Saturday, 2 April, about half-past nine o'clock, he saw a woman drive a cart belonging to the prosecutors to Harrod's door. The after-part of the tilt [usually a fabric weather cover above the cart] was hanging down and the forward part was over some bales. He saw the carman, and saw him take a bag out of the cart and leave it in Harrod's shop. He received no bill of parcels. He kept his eye on the shop a short time, but was compelled to leave for a short time, and on his return the bag was gone. He had seen bags in Messrs. Booth and Ingram's warehouse exactly similar.

Luton, a river constable, said that by direction of his surveyor, the last witness, he went into Harrod's shop to purchase some tea for the purpose of hearing the conversation between Warner and Harrod. The carman left a bag of currants with the grocer, and said that is all I have got tonight. Harrod said, 'Very well,' and that was all that passed. No bill of parcels was delivered.

James Fogg, a surveyor of the Thames police, said that in consequence of information that Harrod was in the habit of receiving large quantities of grocery from the other prisoners, he watched his shop, and saw Warner and Moran repeatedly there towards the end of March. One night he saw Warner drive up to the door. He left the horse and cart in the street, and went into the shop; while he was there witness lifted up the tilt of the cart, and saw beneath it several bags of currants and sugar. Warner had some conversation with Harrod. The shop at the time was full of customers. Warner left nothing at Harrod's shop that night, and drove to Scott's stables, in Princes Street, Drury Lane, and left the cart and horse. [Despite extensive searches of old London maps and gazettes, I have not found a Princes Street, Drury Lane, anywhere near Cable Street or Rosemary Lane. There is, of course, the famous theatre-land Drury Lane some distance away, but no Princes Street near it; and there was a Princes Street in Spitalfields.]

On Tuesday week last he searched Harrod's house. He was not then at home, nor did he return until last Friday, two days after Moran and Warner had been discharged by the Lord Mayor. On seeing him, the prisoner Harrod said, 'Step into the parlour, Mr Fogg, what is the charge against me.' Witness said, 'I suppose you are aware we searched your house the other day.' The prisoner said he was; and witness informed him that Booth, Ingledew and Knott had been robbed by their carman and porter of currants, pepper, sugar and many other things, to a very great extent.

Harrod said, 'What am I to do? I am a guilty man: but look at my wife and children. She is in bed; come and look at her.' Witness told him he could do nothing for him, but take him into custody. Harrod said, 'Yes, you can if you like; let me run away, and I'll never come in the neighbourhood any more; nobody shall see me here; and I'll give you £20, or anything you require; or £50, if you like.' Witness then took him into custody.

Mr Wooler said that upon this evidence there was nothing to warrant the detention of the prisoners. The case had been given up before the Lord Mayor, and was now dragged before a county magistrate.

Mr Hobler said the fact was, the prisoners Warner and Moran were under certain advice, prematurely apprehended in the city, and Harrod, the receiver, kept out of the way. They suffered the case to drop, and directly after the carman and porter were discharged Harrod returned to his shop and was taken into custody. The ruse, as he expected, had so far succeeded.

Mr Wooler said it was not fair to drag the prisoners a second time before a magistrate. There was not a tittle of evidence to inculpate Moran.

Mr Austin said Moran assisted to load the cart on the night the bag of currants was left in Harrod's shop.

Mr Wooler – There was evidence a bag of something was left in the shop, but what was it or who it belonged to no one can tell.

Mr Hobler said Warner had dictated a confession to a prisoner in Guiltspur Street Compter, in which he acknowledged selling his employers' bag of currants to Harrod on the Saturday night, for £2 5*s*, and disposing of other property belonging to his employers.

Warner – No, I have nothing to do with it.

Mr Hobler – Here is the document – a complete confession of the whole case. The horse and cart were kept close to Harrod's house all night.

Mr Wooler – that singularity is explained away at once. The horse and cart is kept in Scott's stables, near Harrod's house. That has been done for some time – This was admitted.

Mr Clarkson said robberies to a great extent had been committed, and the case was one of great importance.

He should remand the prisoners for a week. Bail was offered, but declined.

They were all brought back for a final examination before Mr Clarkson six days later. Much of the evidence presented was as before, though there was some new evidence, as Warner had decided to tell all to save his own skin:

10 May 1836, *Public Ledger & Daily Advertiser*
Police Intelligence – Thames office. Extensive System of Robbery
Mr Hobler, jun., said he appeared as solicitor for the prosecutors.

THE JEWEL OF KNIGHTSBRIDGE

Since the last examination, the prisoner Warner had offered to disclose all he knew of the transactions in which he and the other prisoners had been engaged, and with the permission of the magistrate he should now put him in the box as a witness for the Crown.

Mr Clarkson consented to take Warner's evidence.

Others gave evidence that 'The cart and horse were then driven to Scott's stables at the back of Harrod's premises (the place where they were always kept) and left there.'

Fogg proceeded to the place early next morning, when he found the cart gone. On the night of Saturday, 2nd April, Evans was watching Harrod's shop with one of his men named Luton, and the prosecutor's cart again stopped opposite the house. Warner took out a bag and carried it into the shop. Luton was sent in to buy some tea; and he saw Warner leave the bag at the back of the shop. He brought no bill of parcels with it, and said that was all he had got. Luton returned to Evans, and related to him what he had seen. He was sent in a second time, and the bag was gone. Information was immediately forwarded to Messrs. Booth and Ingledew, and the porter and carmen were prematurely apprehended under their directions by a City officer, and Harrod absconded.

After the two men had been in custody for a fortnight, and undergone three examinations by the Lord Mayor, they were discharged for want of sufficient evidence, though Warner made a confidant of a person in Giltspur Street Compter for a breach of the peace, and related to him a series of depredations on the property of his employers which could not be used in evidence. Two days after the carman and porter were liberated, Harrod returned to his house, and Fogg went there to apprehend him.

That evidence having been taken, Warner, the carman, was removed from the bar and sworn.

He said he had been in the employ of Messrs. Booth, Ingledew and Knott for five years. Moran had lived with them eight or nine months. Moran had not been there long before they began robbing their employers. Moran first said, 'Take this,' and gave him a bag of sugar, but he refused to do so. He was afterwards induced to take away property, which was sold to Mr Harrod. He had been in Harrod's shop several times. Moran generally dealt with him. He remembered the Saturday before Easter Monday. They stole a bag containing 112lbs of currants [50kg]. Moran took it out of the cellar, and he, the approver, put it into the cart. They took it to Harrod's shop. Harrod was there, and he told him that was all he had. After he had put up his cart, he went home; and next day Moran called upon him, and said he had been to Harrod and got the money for the currants. Moran paid him his share of the money; he could not tell the exact amount he received, because there were some other matters settles at the same time. The price paid for the currants was 45s. The same price had been paid for currants before that. He believed George, who was dead, had done the same as he and Moran had done.

Mr Preston, in an answer to a question from Mr Clarkson, said the wholesale price of currants was 65s.

The prisoners were then called upon for their defence, and, by advice of Mr Wooler, declined making any: but Harrod said the conversation related by Fogg was correct, but what he said was in the irritation of the moment.

Mr Wooler – I have advised you to reserve your defence.

Mr Clarkson then committed Moran for trial for stealing the property; Harrod as the receiver; and ordered Warner to be detained to give evidence.

The inquiry excited great interest.

Justice proceeded rapidly in those days. The offence with which they had been charged had been committed on 2 April, Warner and Moran were taken into custody and examined by the lord mayor, remanded twice and then discharged. Charles Harrod had 'done a runner' when they were arrested, and reappeared upon their discharge. They were all taken before the Recorder on 3 May, then again on 8 May before being committed for trial at the Central Criminal Court, or Old Bailey, on 17 May. That is just over six weeks from offence to final trial and sentencing:

THE JEWEL OF KNIGHTSBRIDGE

17th May 1836, Central Criminal Court, before the Recorder Messrs. Bodkin and Ballantine conducted the case for the prosecution, and Mr Phillips appeared for the defence.

Moran denied all knowledge of the robbery. Harrod denied saying anything in his defence.

Selwood, a confectioner, and a brother of Harrod, deposed hearing Fogg say to Mrs Warner that if she would not induce her husband to make a confession, he [Fogg] would convict him; this was previous to the final examination at the Thames Police office.

Fogg was recalled and said there was not a word of truth in the statement made by Selwood and Harrod. There were two females talking to Warner's wife, and he said to them, go away, or else you will get your husband transported.

A great number of witnesses gave Harrod an excellent character for honesty.

The Recorder summed up the evidence, observing, that if the jury were satisfied that the evidence of the accomplice was confirmed by other witnesses for the prosecution, there could be little doubt of the guilt of both prisoners.

The Jury returned a verdict of Guilty against both prisoners.

The Recorder ordered them to be called up for judgement, observing that if the Court should allow itself to be influenced by feelings of compassion, the wretchedness and misery which the conduct of the prisoner Harrod had entailed upon his wife and children might have some weight in mitigating the sentence about to be passed upon him. But, as the object of all punishment was example, private feeling could not be allowed to interfere with the duty which a Judge owed to the public welfare. With regard to the prisoner Moran, the fact could not be lost sight of that he was a servant in the confidence of the prosecutors, and, taking advantage of that confidence, he had been guilty of robbing his employers from time to time to a considerable extent. The sentence of the Court was that they should be severally transported for seven years.

This looked like the end of Harrod's career as a grocer – and strange to think that Harrods may never have existed.

There is a long list of those people who gave 'the prisoner Harrod' a good character. They were:

James Baker, a surgeon, of Dorchester Place, New North Road, in the Shoreditch area.
William Mason, a draper, of Fore Street, in the Barbican/Moorgate area.
Richard Burton, a silk manufacturer, of Wood Street, Cheapside.
Charles Edward Walker, of London Road, Southwark, a tea dealer.
James Bateman, a carpenter and builder, of Dorchester Place, New North Road.
William Carter, a wholesale coffee dealer, of the Barbican.
James Bower, a linen draper.
John P. Searle, a tailor, of Tabernacle Row, City Road, north of Liverpool Street.
John Hewett, a druggist, of Well Street, Well Close Square. He lived three doors away from Harrod in Rosemary Lane.
Henry Cowley, a tea dealer, of New Road in the Whitechapel area.
Mr Bacon and Alice Bacon.

He seemed to have a lot of loyal friends, none of whom had previously featured in the research. They all lived at addresses in a small local area, on just a single page of the present-day London A–Z.

The mention of Harrod's brother was, at that time, the first I had heard of him – it became apparent that Charles Henry had a brother called William Frederick Harrod. In the full transcription of the trial, one of the witnesses stated, 'Harrod's brother was with me at the time', and 'I know Harrod's brother, but not the prisoner', and later, William Frederick Harrod spoke on his brother's behalf:

I am the prisoner's brother, and am a working jeweller, living at No. 129, Tooley Street. Mr Selwood and I have been intimate some time – I was with him at the Thames police-office, on Saturday, 7th of May, when my brother was there, under charge – I heard Fogg say …

James Fogg, the police officer, was later re-examined and gave evidence that, 'the witness Harrod asked me to be as lenient with his brother as I could and asked me to take something to drink ...'

So, where did this William Frederick Harrod come from? The reader will remember he was found earlier in the research and at that stage his existence had been discounted as an error. His discovery was a surprise, and it was initially difficult to get any information about him. I already knew that Charles Henry had a brother William, born and christened in Hartest in Suffolk in 1797. The baptism records of this William make no mention of the other Christian name, Frederick. It would have been common at the time that his parents would name their firstborn son William.

A burial record had been found for an infant William Harrod, of the right age, in Clerkenwell in 1798, in a Nonconformist cemetery, and the assumption was that this was the same William. But he probably wasn't, and he lived on to be William Frederick, the jeweller. The only other explanation is that the original son, William, had died and that the parents later had another son they also called William. However, there has been no further birth or baptism found.

Frederick William was found listed in the 1839 Pigot's Directory at Cable Street as a grocer, and an assumption had been made that this was a clerical error, as I had already found a William Frederick Harrod, working as a jeweller in Tooley Street, Southwark.

Quite a lot has since been found out about William Frederick. From the information on his marriage and death certificates and in censuses, it looks as though he was born in about 1797 or 1798, which tended to confirm the idea that he might have been the William born in Suffolk in 1797. However, calculating age from these sources is notoriously inaccurate. William Frederick worked as a jeweller from about 1826 onwards, and was by 1839 working in Southwark, quite close to the area where Charles Henry had his draper's shop in the previous decade. He was, intriguingly, working in the same street, Tooley Street, where the Lincolnshire family of Harrods had lived a couple of decades later.

William Frederick and his wife, Nancy, who had married in 1822, had four children and a lot of misfortune. Their first child, William Thomas, was born in 1823, but died in 1824, aged 19 months. Charles Thomas was born in 1825, and died after three days. William Frederick was born in 1826 whilst the family were living in Regent Street, London. He also died early, in 1853 aged 27, of a fistula (a fistula is an abnormal track from the inside to the outside of the body, often in those days the result of untreated abdominal infections, such as appendicitis). Emma was born in 1829 in Clerkenwell, and died aged 8 weeks. His wife Nancy died seven days after Emma was born, aged 34.

So tragically, by 1836 when William was involved in Charles Henry's story, he was already a widower with a single remaining 9-year-old son. In 1836 Charles Henry and Elizabeth would have had two children, aged 4 and 1. They were about to suffer from their own share of misfortune.

Charles Henry had obviously been involved in receiving stolen goods for some while, and had been given the standard sentence for such crimes, transportation to Van Diemen's Land, or Tasmania as we know it. He would be leaving England for a stay of seven years, and most convicts did not return. Tasmania had been discovered by Abel Tasman, a Dutch explorer in 1642. He named the island after the governor general of the Dutch East Indies, Anthoonij van Diemenslandt.

In 1803, a small British force was sent to establish a military post and prevent the French, who had been sniffing around the island for some time, from making any claims. A colony was eventually proclaimed in 1825. Tasmania became the principal destination for transported criminals after the early 1800s; 75,000 were sent there altogether. Two more convicts were soon to join them.

Considering that Charles Henry appears in the 1841 census, and accepting that he was the father of Charles Digby Harrod, born in January 1841, it looks as though he was definitely 'in circulation' in the spring of 1840, four years after his sentence. So, what had happened? Though the exact details of what happened to him are unclear, some facts are known and Charles Henry certainly disappeared from the scene after his sentence in 1836. It appears that in his absence, his brother William Frederick ran both his own jewellery business in Southwark and the grocery business in Rosemary Lane/Cable Street, where he was listed in an 1839 directory. He would have had his son with him and probably joined Elizabeth and her two children.

The Prison Hulk Registers and Letter Books for 1836, now available online, show that Charles Henry Harrod was taken to the prison ship *Leviathan*, moored in Portsmouth, and arrived there on 30 May 1836, three weeks after his trial. This is confirmed by the Newgate Prison records held at Kew. Newgate is next door to the Old Bailey, and Charles was incarcerated there between 7 May (the day of his arrest and two days before his trial) until 30 May.

Several prison hulks served as holding stations for prisoners, often for several weeks prior to transfer to other boats for the long journey to Australia. Most of them were literally hulks, usually old warships that were no longer seaworthy. The *Leviathan* was a third-rate ship of the line and in her prime was armed with seventy-four guns. She was built in 1790, based on a French design, and was probably larger than most third-rate ships. She had served at the Battle of Trafalgar in 1805. In the Royal Navy, a third-rate ship of the line had between sixty-four and eighty guns, usually with two gun decks (a 'two-decker'). Whilst first rates and second rates were larger and more powerful, these third-rate ships were the best compromise between agility and speed, firepower and cost. After active service, the *Leviathan* was de-masted and laid up in Portsmouth as a prison hulk. She was later to be broken up in 1848.

Between 1788 and 1868, over 160,000 prisoners were transported to Australia and Tasmania. The conditions on board would have been horrendous. An account was given by John Frederick Mortlock in his *Experiences of a Convict*, where he describes his time in *Leviathan* in 1843:

> They conveyed me (chained hand and foot to a man now driving a cab in Tasmania) by railroad to the hulk *Leviathan* at Portsmouth [the first railway route from London to Portsmouth was via

Eastleigh, Fareham and Gosport. The station at Gosport was opened on 29 November 1841 and passengers had to use the ferry to get to Portsmouth. Charles Henry must therefore have travelled by road or boat. Though the dates suggest he arrived in Portsmouth on the same day that he left Newgate, this which would have been quite a feat in 1836] ... and quickly transmogrified me into a strange-looking object, whom no one could recognise ... At any rate I was no longer shut up in gaol, to me the most dreadful of punishments, now, I hoped, done with for ever. This, however, as will be seen, turned out to be a mistaken expectation. The hulk, an old [Trafalgar] ninety-gun ship, being very full, contained more than six hundred convicts (from starvation and discipline, tame as rabbits), housed on the three decks, which were divided into compartments, separated from each other by bulkheads, and from the gangway down the centre, by iron bars, giving the appearance of a menagerie. Owing to the height of the wharf, alongside of which she lay, the larboard row of cells, on the lower deck, was nearly in darkness, and insufficiently ventilated. 'New chums', therefore, in their location down below, breathed very foul air ... A pernicious habit also existed of sluicing out all the decks every morning, with salt water ... The chilly dampness arising from this, proved a fertile source of sickness.

... As a reward for three months of good behaviour, a light ring [called a basil] above the ankle, scarcely to be felt, succeeded the irons. Upon losing the weightier decorations, my foot in walking used to fly up in an odd manner for some time afterwards, till the muscles grew accustomed to their lighter load ... I found the carrying of timber and other hard work very irksome at first, although labour is not severe punishment to a strong man well fed; but we suffered from a lack of sufficient food ... Hence the mortality was great, it being whispered that the head doctor at the hospital ship, enjoyed a contract for supplying surgeons in town with bodies for dissection at six guineas a piece.

The records confirm that the vast majority of the convicts on board were actually transported, there being an annotation in the 'how disposed of' column in the records, with the initials of the transport ship and the date. A few prisoners died, and a very few were pardoned.

In the 'how disposed of' column opposite Charles Henry's name, there is the annotation 'Penit … y', with the date 1 July, 1836. This indicates that he was sent to the Millbank Penitentiary Infirmary, presumably in poor health. There was an annotation stating he was not to go abroad until the case was decided.

Richard Moran, his co-defendant, also held on *Leviathan*, was sent off in the transport ship *Sarah* on 29 November 1836, six months after his arrival on the hulk. He reached Van Diemen's Land on 29 March 1837, accompanied on the voyage by 253 other convicts. The Tasmanian Records Office contains the records of each convict arriving there, and Moran's behaviour on the hulk and during the transportation was good. He was listed as having gone absent without leave a year after arrival, in December 1837, but he later returned of his own will to the penal settlement. After six years he was pardoned and he was declared free in 1842. No further information about him is available, so the presumption must be that he remained in Tasmania.

It was not clear initially why Charles was reprieved from his transportation. Perhaps he was too ill to transport. It is known that some captains of the transport ships were very reluctant to take on board prisoners who were ill, as there was an enormous amount of paperwork involved if any prisoner died during the voyage. In most cases, the convict transport ships were privately owned merchant ships that were chartered by the British government for one or more voyages to the Australian colonies. Following serious outbreaks of disease, with the heavy loss of life on board some early convict ship voyages suffered, later voyages were strictly regulated in terms of provisions and medical support. As a result, deaths on board ship during these long passages were generally lower than on assisted immigrant ships on similar voyages, and many convicts actually arrived in a better state of health than they had enjoyed before leaving!

More light was thrown on the whole episode with a further discovery early in 2013 of documents online relating to a 'memorial', or appeal, for Charles Henry Harrod, instigated in 1836. This consisted of thirteen original documents placed online, together with the original folder and the list of contents. I still find it amazing that documents such as these, so important to my understanding of my great-great-grandfather's life, but relatively unimportant to the rest of the world, have not only survived intact, but were available for me to search online. Each document consisted of several pages of handwritten letters and reports. I have attempted to transcribe them and have unravelled the story of Charles Henry's partial reprieve.

I will paraphrase the documents in approximate date order. The outer folder was a summary of the events, headed 'Petition of Charles Henry Harrod'. It was presented by George Grote, Esquire, the Liberal MP for the City of London, of 62 Threadneedle Street, and was addressed to the Right Honourable Lord John Russell, Home Secretary since the previous year. It was dated 25 May 1836, five days before Charles Henry arrived on *Leviathan*. The petitioners had moved rapidly.

Grote was from a successful banking family, and was renowned as a reformist and forward thinker. He spent much of his later life researching Greek history. His mother was the daughter of the minister at the Countess of Huntingdon's Chapel in London, so perhaps there was some sympathy there for Harrod's Nonconformist background. His portrait is at the National Portrait Gallery in London.

The document listed the dates and sentence of his Charles Henry's conviction, with a summary of his social status. It states that the surgeon, Mr Capper, had been asked for a report and that he had said, 'His constitution is weakly and his health bad.' The recipient enquires if this was true, asking for enquiry to be made by the police as to his character. Inside the folded document Charles starts his petition with his own personal statement:

The Humble Petition of the aforesaid Charles Henry Harrod late of Cable Street in the county of Middlesex, Grocer but now a prisoner in his Majesty's Gaol of Newgate.
  Respectfully Sheweth

That your unhappy Petitioner was convicted at the late Sessions of the Central Criminal Court for having received a bag of currants, the property of John Booth and Ingledew, of Thames Street, Wholesale Grocers.

That your unhappy Petitioner does not presume to impugn the verdict which has been found against him, but he humbly hopes that upon the merciful consideration of his case which it may receive from His Most Gracious Majesty's clemency, some modification of the punishment awarded to him, which is that of Seven Years Transportation, may be extended to his supplication for mercy upon the following circumstances.

That your Petitioner by the mercantile panic of the year 1825, was reduced from the competence of a respectable and responsible Tradesman, to encounter with all the difficulties of the commercial embarrassments at which the wealthiest trembled for the sufficiency of their immediate resources, when it was almost impossible for those in his situation to struggle successfully against circumstances which involved so many thousands in total ruin.

That since that period, your unhappy Petitioner has been arduously endeavouring, by incessant application and unwearied industry to repair his shattered fortune, and up to the present period has maintained an irreproachable character, and that even with the disclosure of the approver, his evidence went only to prove that your Petitioner received the single article of property in question, and that only a few days before his apprehension, although his house and premises are deposed to have been carefully watched, both day and night, for some time previous to the transaction.

That your petitioner has a wife and two Children, the eldest only three years and a half, and the youngest little more than a year old; both, as well as his most unfortunate partner, in delicate health, and threatened with the most unfortunate consequences, should your unhappy Petitioner be removed from this country for the term of seven years.

This statement revealed to me for the first time the existence of an older child, born in about 1832 (making an eventual total of six). The name and sex of this child is still not known. I had previously found the details of four, or possibly five, children for Charles and Elizabeth, but had seen no trace of another. From other correspondence I now know this child died less than a year later, whilst Charles was in prison in early 1837. The younger of the two children was Elizabeth Digby Harrod, who died in 1839.

By a process of deduction, it is possible to surmise that this unidentified older child, who would have been the eldest in the family, would have been a boy. As the firstborn children were named after father and/or mother, and Charles and Elizabeth incorporated Digby in all their children's names, he would have been called Charles Digby Harrod. As he died, the next boy, my great-grandfather, was given this name. If the child had been a girl, she would have been called Elizabeth Digby Harrod, but the baby could not have been a girl as their second child, born whilst the first was still alive, used this name. I have searched the records for the birth of another Charles Digby with no success.

Charles Henry concludes his statement:

For with his naturally weak constitution, now still more enfeebled by his anxiety and misery, and his general health very materially affected, he bitterly feels that he could have no hope of any return to his family but that a transportation for that period would find its termination only in the grave.

Your unfortunate Petitioner therefore, in the deepest affliction, most humbly implores of His Most Gracious Majesty's clemency that he may not be removed from this country; but that the punishment may be moderated so as to give him some hope of being restored to his family, and enable him to show his grateful sense of the mercy extended to him, by the propriety of his conduct for the remainder of his life.

And Your Petitioner shall ever pray, &c
Chs Henry Harrod
Dated May 20th 1836.

The other parts to the documents are:

1. A 'memorial', the equivalent of a petition, signed by a list of sixty-three colleagues and friends asking the Home Secretary for commutation of his sentence so that he can stay in the London environs. The list consists of businessmen mostly from the City of London, but ranging from a Dissenting minister, to a surgeon, builders, a coal merchant and numerous shopkeepers.
2. Another memorial signed by thirty-seven individuals, mostly from North London.
3. A memorial signed by a further thirty-seven individuals, mostly from the City and Southwark.
4. Another memorial signed by fifty-three individuals, mostly neighbours in the Cable Street and Well Close Square area.

(That makes a total of 190 people who had signed the various petitions.)

5. An appeal for mitigation from William Mason, a glover of Fore Street in the City. He wrote:

Feeling strongly for him and his family, having known him during a period of Five and Twenty Years, and being convinced that up to the time of this most unfortunate transaction, he had maintained an unblemished and irreproachable Character, I respectfully beg to offer my humble Testimonial in his favour. Allow me earnestly to solicit your Lordship's attention to the fact that he was originally a Linen Draper, but unsuccessful in Business, and was unacquainted with the Trade which he has had for the last Two or Three Years pursued.

A friendship of twenty-five years would take the date back to 1811, just when Charles's mother had died. Could William Mason be related to his mother's Mason family? An attempt to find out more about William Mason has so far not produced any results, though there are several William Masons in the Hartest parish records:

6. An appeal for mitigation from John Pollard Searle, a tailor from Shoreditch, who stated he had known Charles for some years and said, 'he has always sustained the character of an honest and upright tradesman.'
7. An appeal for mitigation from James Baker, a surgeon who had known him for five years.
8. An appeal for mitigation from James Brown.
9. An appeal for mitigation from John Hewitt, chemist and druggist of Cable Street, who stated:

> I beg further to inform your Lordship that from his heretofore sober & industrious habits and from his assiduity & perseverance in business which I have had daily opportunities of witnessing on account of his occupying the house adjoining mine, I should have no objection to become security for his future good conduct.

10. The report from Mr Capper, surgeon, mentioned earlier. He saw Charles on the *Leviathan* and his report was very brief, '… is rather a weakly and debilitated subject, altho' not labouring under any specific Disease'.
11. The police report from a superintendent at Whitechapel 1st Division. A rather mixed report, though on balance probably supportive. He stated:

> I should say he was irreproachable; a Mr Hewit who is a respectable Chymist living near his [Harrod's] late residence, assured me he would readily become security for him, to the amount of One Thousand Pounds and several others seem to have equal confidence in his honesty.
>
> A person named Habgood an Oilman, and a Mrs Henshaw, grocer, insinuate they had heard he was a receiver of stolen goods, but can prove nothing, and I fear they speak interestedly being in the same trade and it is evidence to me that there is a jealousy.

The basic argument of the various appeals for clemency for Charles were that he had maintained an irreproachable character; he had a wife and two young children, all in delicate health, to support; his own health was poor; the evidence of the principal witness for the prosecution was questionable; the prisoner had conducted himself well in Millbank Penitentiary; and his elder child had died during his imprisonment.

The outer folder concluded, 'Not to go abr'd – until the case is decided.' It ends, 'Inform all. Was ord'd to Pen'y 29 June 1836.' So, as a result of this appeal by a Member of Parliament, backed by statements from Charles Henry himself, many of his friends and colleagues, and medical and police reports, Charles Henry was reprieved from transportation to Australia and instead sent to prison after just four weeks on the hulk.

Charles was sent to Millbank Prison, an enormous prison which stood on the site now occupied by Tate Britain, the Chelsea College of Art and Design and the Millbank Housing Estate. In the meantime, his eldest child had died and his own health was failing. His widowed brother, William Frederick, had been running the shop and living on the premises.

After a year in prison, Charles's wife, Elizabeth, sent in her own petition. It was dated 1 May 1837 and it contained an impassioned plea:

To the Right Honourable His Majesty's Secretary of State for the Home department.
   The Humble Petition of Elizabeth Harrod the Wife of the above named Charles Henry Harrod.
   Sheweth,
   That in consequence of the nature of the case and previous unblemished character of your Petitioner's husband several memorials signed by a great number of very respectable persons were presented to your Lordship by G. Grote Esquire one of the members of the Honourable House of Commons.

That during the long confinement of nearly twelve months in the Penitentiary Mill Bank your Petitioner's husband has as your Petitioner is assured conducted himself with great propriety.

That your Petitioner is of a weakly constitution and incapable of supporting himself and Infant child.

That recently the Elder child of your Petitioner has been removed by death which has added to your Petitioner's afflictions.

That your Petitioner's husband is subject to illness which confinement is calculated seriously to increase and to render fatal to him.

That should your Petitioner's husband remain in confinement much longer your Petitioner can have no hope of ever overcoming the consequences.

Your Petitioner therefore must earnestly pray your Lordship to save her and her husband and child from absolute and irreparable ruin and premature death, by mercifully remitting further confinement of your Petitioner's husband.

And your Petitioner shall ever pray, Elizabeth Harrod. Cable St, May 1st 1837

Her letter was countersigned by another twenty-five local people, amongst whom were no fewer than four Mr Masons. This page was headed with the annotation:

We the undersigned beg very respectfully to recommend the case of Charles Henry Harrod to your Lordship's merciful consideration in consequence of his previous good conduct and unblemished character, and we beg also to assure your Lordship that we have no doubt of his after well doing.

It must have been difficult to ignore this plea, and the authorities obviously agreed that Charles had been punished enough. Although there is no official document available to confirm this, I suspect he was freed soon afterwards. There is a scribbled and only partially decipherable note across the top of her letter, my best interpretation of which is, 'Rec'd from Mr Ald'n Wood, Can't hold incarcerated, pardon when seen G. C?ance.'

From all the documents available that I have read, it looks to me as though Charles Henry had probably been involved in receiving stolen goods before the episode that led to his arrest. Perhaps it was common practice in the trade. He was a lucky man to survive this episode. Charles would have been reunited with his wife and remaining child sometime during the spring or summer of 1837. London would have been a different place without him!

Charles Henry was not the only one who had been in trouble. His brother William was arrested and put on trial in early 1839. Like his brother, he was charged with receiving stolen goods. The initial case, held at Union Hall, was reported in the *Morning Advertiser* of 14 January:

> On Saturday, John Terry, an errand boy in the service of Mr Paul, a surgeon, of Lambeth, and Wm. Dine, were placed at the bar on a charge of stealing, and Wm. Harrod, a silversmith and tobacconist, in Tooley Street, with receiving, knowing them to be stolen, a quantity of large silver spoons.
>
> The prosecutor had a few friends to dinner on New Year's day when the prisoner Terry was employed to clean the plate for his master; soon afterwards three large and two dessert silver spoons were missed, and on the boy being charged with the theft, he acknowledged that he and his 'pal' Dine had stolen the spoons, broken the bowls from the handles and sold them to Harrod, who gave them 5*s* for the large and 3*s* for the small spoons.
>
> Harrod recollected Dine's selling him some spoons, and expressed his sorrow that he took them from him without inquiry, and hoped his character would render him above suspicion.
>
> The boys acknowledged selling the spoons to Harrod. And the Magistrate committed all three for trial.

The main trial was held at the New Court a month later, and was again covered by the *Morning Advertiser*. By a piece of good fortune, William was acquitted:

Discharge by Proclamation
At nine o'clock, the Grand Jury having been discharged, the nineteen following prisoners, whose bills they had ignored, were brought into Court and discharged by proclamation.

William was one of these nineteen. I assume this must have been because of some technical problem. Another amongst those reprieved included a youth called Charles Atkins. The report recounts his cheeky words of thanks, 'this youth put himself in a Court attitude, and said, "My Lord, I'm very much obliged to you."'

Frederick's trial was only four months before Charles and Elizabeth's second child, Elizabeth Digby, died. She was buried at St Mary's, Whitechapel. She would have been 4 years old. In late 1839, Charles and Elizabeth had no children left alive, Charles had a criminal record and Charles's brother had one remaining child.

Following these events, the trail of Charles's life and business goes quiet for some years. Hopefully, he had learnt his lesson and spent his time building up his shop as a reformed man. I suspect he never strayed again after his release, and as we shall see, he later gained a reputation for honest dealing.

It was providential that Charles returned home when he did, as his brother William Frederick died just a year later in 1840, aged 43, according to his death certificate. Rather oddly, this event happened in Milton, Gravesend, in Kent, He was recorded as being a 'working jeweller' and his cause of death was given as 'rheumatism'. This term could have applied to any form of joint disease, and might have signified some bone disease such as osteomyelitis or tuberculous joint disease. Although he died in Gravesend, I think he was just visiting the area as his burial entry is in the parish of St James's, Clerkenwell, and shows that he was still living in Tooley Street, Southwark. He was probably buried in a Nonconformist cemetery in Clerkenwell. According to the burial entry he was aged 47 at death, making his year of birth 1793, which led to some of my confusion about dates.

William's only remaining child, William Frederick, would have been just a month or two short of his fourteenth birthday when his father died and, as such in the Victorian era, nearly at an age when he could become independent. He may have lived with Charles and Elizabeth for a while, but by 1842 he was living in Southwark, apprenticed to a vintner called Edward Cuff. He remained in Southwark for the rest of his life, dying in 1853 at the age of 27. He was at the time working as a cook. The whole of that branch of the family had been wiped out in the thirty years following William Frederick Senior's marriage.

Charles Henry was not totally dormant as, on 25 January 1841, Elizabeth gave birth in Cable Street to their third child, Charles Digby Harrod, then their only child. The 1841 census, which was held soon after on 6 June 1841, gives us some insight into the family at the time. Present, apart from mother, father and baby, Charles Digby, there was a 15-year-old girl, Ann Digby. Little is known about her otherwise. Perhaps she was a relation of Elizabeth's, staying with them as a servant to help with the new baby.

Making up for lost time, Charles and Elizabeth had three further children, all boys, whilst they lived at 4 Cable Street. William Digby was born in December 1842, Henry Digby was born in July 1845, and Joseph Digby was born in May 1847.

By the end of the 1840s, all seemed to be going well for the family. The four children were growing up, healthy as far as we know at this stage. The business was obviously thriving as by 1849 Charles Henry had opened a wholesale business at 38 Eastcheap. The Post Office Directory lists him there as 'Harrod Charles Henry, Wholesale Grocer'. He traded there for some years but by 1855 he had moved and the 1857 directory now shows him at 12 Eastcheap, in shared premises as 'Harrod, Chas. Henry wholes. Grocer'. The premises at No. 38 were taken over by a wholesale grocer and sugar merchant's company, Bristow, Warren & Harrison, who remained until 1864.

The 1857 directory shows that Harrod also had premises at 41 St Mary at Hill, which is near the corner with Eastcheap. He is listed as 'Harrod Charles, Colonial Produce Dealer'.

Sometime before 1851, Charles moved his family accommodation away from the less healthy area of Cable Street and they are to be found living in Seabright Street, in leafy Bethnal Green. The electoral register shows him at No. 8, as well as later at No. 14, where he was living in 1851. The move away from the docks area would have been a benefit for the family; with the poverty, crime and filth close to the river it was a very unhealthy place to live.

The dangers were not only aesthetic; the cholera epidemics claimed many lives in England and Wales (some 50,000 in 1849, with 14,600 in London alone). There were major cholera outbreaks, originally brought in by foreign seamen, in 1832, 1849, 1854 and 1856. Alongside the erupting epidemics of 'King Cholera', there was the more regular annual death toll from tuberculosis (50,000) convulsions (25,000), diarrhoea (20,000), scarlatina (12,000) and whooping cough (10,000). The epidemic in 1854 is famously remembered for the discovery of the cause of cholera by Dr John Snow, when he removed the handle from the Broad Street pump.

In 1858 the Thames was 'black with the filth and excrement of two million people, ebbing and flowing in the tide. The stench was so great that Members of Parliament were driven from the chamber.' The *Times* called it 'The Great Stink', and Parliament was driven to act, resulting in Sir Joseph Bazalgette's monumental engineering programme to construct London's sewers.

The usual daily amount of London sewerage discharged in about 1860 into the River Thames on the north side has been estimated as 7 million cu.ft, and on the south side, 9 million cu.ft, or a quantity equivalent to a surface of more than 36 acres in extent and 6ft in depth. When the tide rose above the orifices of the sewers, the whole drainage of the district was stopped until the tide receded again.

Seabright Street, on the north side of Bethnal Green Road, was in the suburbs of the day. Most of the street was built in 1822 and consisted of two-storey terraced houses, with some three-storey tenements as well. When first built, many were occupied by the local silk weavers from Spitalfields. Just south of Bethnal Green Road was a large green space known as Weaver's Green. It is still intact today. With the downturn in the silk trade and the expansion of the population into the area, it degenerated into a slum area and Charles moved away from here in the mid 1850s. He was still listed there on the electoral register until 1860 so must have kept an interest in the property.

In the ensuing years, the west end of Bethnal Green Road was part of the haunt of Jack the Ripper.

The 1851 census shows Charles and Elizabeth living in Seabright Street with the youngest three of their children and a 20-year-old servant, Jan Harrison. The whereabouts of the eldest child, Charles Digby, in 1851 remained a mystery for me until some time later; I eventually found him in the 1851 census with his name misspelt as Charles 'Harrud'. This was a transcription error from the original written record that was spelt correctly, but written in such a way that it could be easily misspelt. He was a schoolboy, aged 10, boarding at Edwardstone School in Suffolk.

I wondered what on earth the 10-year-old son of an East End grocer was doing in a small school in rural Suffolk. The 1851 census shows there were only six other pupils in the school, five boys and one girl, aged between 7 and 12. Four of them came from the London area, and there were two brothers from Weymouth. The schoolmaster was Mr John Smith, with his wife and his eldest daughter, the latter aged 21, given as the other teachers. Mr Smith's own four children and a 14-year-old niece were also present.

The choice of school is very unlikely to have been random. It may have been chosen after a recommendation by a friend or relative, but a private boarding school suggests the Harrod family trajectory was upwards. It was intriguing to find that Edwardstone is just 10 miles from Hartest in Suffolk, the centre of the William Harrod and Tamah Mason world. Many of the Digby family originally came from this area of south Suffolk and north Essex, so perhaps local family was the reason. It is not known how long Charles Digby stayed there, and I am not certain whether any of his brothers were sent there, though it is likely they were for a spell. No brothers were found there in the 1861 census, but a spell of three years or so at the school could easily be accommodated between the census dates.

The school seems to have continued for some time in Edwardstone, and was most recently called Edwardstone House School, working as some sort of reformatory. There was also a local Edwardstone School, which caused some confusion. Following contact with a local historian, a poster for an exhibition of old photographs held at the parish hall featured a lovely 'Dickensian' photograph of Victorian children at 'Edwardstone School'. Every pupil looked like the 'artful dodger'. Sadly, this lovely photograph proved to be of the local village school.

Having built up his business over the course of twenty years at Cable Street and his other premises, a move was in the pipeline. The premises in Cable Street remained in Harrod's name until 1856 and may have been used for a short while after that, but a foothold had been gradually established in West London from about 1849 onwards, and this was to lead to a momentous change of direction and situation.

4

THE MOVE TO KENSINGTON

Though Charles Henry Harrod and his family were living in Bethnal Green in 1851, and the shop in Cable Street was going strong for a few years beyond that, Charles had already sown the seeds of his future in west London, in the Brompton Road.

One of the customers of his Eastcheap wholesale grocery was Philip Henry Burden, who since at least 1851 ran a grocery business in Kensington. They had probably become friends. Burden is thought to have found himself in some financial difficulty, and his shop at 8 Middle Queen Buildings, Brompton, was becoming a problem. Charles Henry began to help him by paying the rent, presumably in return for some of the profits. Sometime after Charles Henry started the relationship with Burden, and prior to 1853 or 1854 when he took over the premises, there was a gradual handover of the shop. The Harrod family meantime lived in Bethnal Green, and the shop in Cable Street continued until 1856.

The *Sussex Express* reported in a review feature in September 1905 that Charles Henry had needed capital of £500 to take over the premises in 1854 (something like £50,000 today). He could only have found this from the profits earned in Cable Street. Perhaps they had saved some of the £300 bequest left to Elizabeth by her father and received in 1844. The move was timely, with the Great Exhibition of 1851 opening up the area to a wider audience.

Burden was, until recently, a mysterious character. Apart from an entry in the 1851 Post Office and 1853 Watkins Directories, listing him as a grocer at the Brompton address, there was not a single trace of him in the conventional British records. There was a Philip Henry Burden, born in the first quarter of 1851 in Kensington, who may have been his son, and a Frederick Burden, who appears in the 1851 census listed as an assistant draper at the same premises as William Neale, a master bootmaker.

One family source, Charles Henry's third son, Henry Digby Harrod, wrote a letter some years later which stated that Burden left England and went abroad. The miracle of the Internet has now, with the help of a distant Australian relative called David Burden, revealed all. The story now goes as follows.

THE MOVE TO KENSINGTON

Frederick Burden and his brother, Philip Henry, were born in Ledbury, Herefordshire; the latter in August 1824. Their father, John, was a draper. Several of the family moved to London, including an uncle who became a grocer in North London. Philip Henry set up his grocer's shop in Brompton. On the night of the 1851 census, by chance he was not at home; he was a visitor with the Goode family in Islington. By then, he was married to Mary Jones, and had a 2-month-old son, also called Philip Henry. Back at Philip's house in Brompton was his brother Frederick, a visitor to his house next door to William Neale. All was now explained.

Philip Henry Burden continued working at 8 Middle Queens Buildings until at least 1854. His son had been born there in 1851, as was his second son, Frederick Britten, born in 1852 and his daughter, Annie, born in 1854.

Soon after Annie's birth Philip and his family emigrated to South Australia. Once there, Philip worked as secretary to the *Adelaide Advertiser and Chronicle* Company, but died soon after in 1864, aged only 39, with 'congestion of the lungs' (probably meaning pneumonia). His widow Mary, obviously not one to let the grass grow under her skirt, married a widower, John Barrow, in 1865. He was the editor and one of the owners of the same newspaper. Philip and Mary's son, Frederick, later became editor of the newspaper.

So, the story of the handover of the Brompton shop is substantially correct. Charles Henry Harrod obviously started the connection in 1849, but it was not until 1854 that he actually took over the premises, and it would have been in the first half of 1854 that his family moved into the rooms behind the shop. It is interesting to note that Harrods has celebrated its anniversaries dated from the year 1849, which they have designated as the start of Harrods – they were perhaps a tad premature. An 1854 street directory confirms Charles's listing in Brompton Road as 'Grocers & Tea dealers: Harrod, C.H.'.

The only sadness for Charles and Elizabeth at this exciting time would have been the death of their youngest son, Joseph Digby, at 8 Middle Queens Buildings on 10 June 1854, aged 7 years. According to his death certificate, Joseph died from 'scarlatina' and 'albuminuria', present for four weeks.

Scarlatina, or scarlet fever, was an extremely dangerous childhood infection in those days. The cause was not known at the time, though now we know it is produced by a reaction to a streptococcal bacterial infection, usually in the throat. It exists mostly in a much milder form these days, causing a rash and minor symptoms. It is normally treated with antibiotics. In 1854 it was a more serious disease and there were no antibiotics. Death was quite common. The cause of death was often kidney failure, caused by glomerulonephritis, an inflammation of the kidney, and this took its toll over some weeks or months. Albuminuria is the name for the presence of protein in the urine caused by the kidney failure. In Joseph's case, it had taken four weeks from the onset of the illness. Like his sister, who died young, and most children who died in the nineteenth century, Joseph died at home. He is buried with his father and mother in Brompton Cemetery.

At this time, and for some years afterwards, the Brompton Road was not conspicuously salubrious. Queen's Gardens, a narrow lane two doors away from the shop, contained a few little cottages and a large wood yard, and North Street behind was said to be 'a mass of filth from one end to the other'. The shops on the Brompton Road were single-storey extensions tacked on to the fronts of the original houses which were built between 1781 and 1783. A rather sanitised artists' impression of the shop frontage and interior in 1849, produced by Harrods in 1949 for publicity surrounding their centenary, paints a more refined picture with clean streets and handsome carriages.

The move west has been ascribed to several factors. Charles probably saw the likelihood of a better life for his family in this part of London, and he had the vision to see potential in the site, and so had offered to buy Burden out of his lease. The fashionable parts of London were beginning to spread westwards, and in 1851 the Great Exhibition, with its Crystal Palace, was built in Hyde Park and opened by Queen Victoria. It drew much attention and enormous crowds to the area. By 1854 the Exhibition had closed and the Crystal Palace was moved to Sydenham Hill in South London, and reconstructed in what was, in effect, a 200-acre Victorian theme park.

THE MOVE TO KENSINGTON

In the early days, Charles Henry's initial customers must have been the small and poor community of locals, somewhat removed from fashionable London. In the three decades prior to 1850, the road west from Hyde Park Corner lay through the unsavoury Knightsbridge village, possessing none of the fine buildings now present, and on to a thoroughly rural Kensington. Knightsbridge was named after a bridge which crossed the River Westbourne at a point where Albert Gate and the French Embassy now stand. There was danger in the maze of dirty back streets along the route, and highway robberies in the district were common.

The area was gradually changing from semi-rural hamlet to built-up suburb, initially mostly by ribbon development and then by backfilling of those properties. Alongside Burden's shop in the 1851 census there were two cobblers, an apothecary and a draper, as well as some professional men. As the neighbourhood changed, Harrod's new residential neighbours, with their new money, learnt of his store and his willingness to sell what was wanted. Harrod had acquired experience in tea imports, so this principal part of the shop was a natural extension of his existing talents. Over time the grocery line expanded into glassware, linens and *objets d'art*.

This part of my story has relied heavily on British History Online for much of the history and details of the area, and a lot of the description which follows comes from this source.

The property was a small house at 8 Middle Queen's Buildings; this was renamed 105 Brompton Road a decade later. Even the name 'Brompton Road' did not exist before 1863. Until 1835 it extended only as far as the junction with Thurloe Place (opposite the Brompton Oratory); after this, Fulham Road began. It now denotes the portion of the old highway from London to Fulham stretching south-westwards from Knightsbridge as far as Pelham Street, beyond which it becomes Fulham Road.

There was always a lot of traffic on the old turnpike road which linked London not only with Little Chelsea and Fulham, but also (via Putney Bridge) with parts of Surrey. Putney Bridge, then known as Fulham Bridge until it was rebuilt in 1886, had replaced a ferry in 1729 and was the only crossing of the Thames between London Bridge and Kingston.

The area beyond Knightsbridge was surrounded by gardens and open fields and 'Brompton', the term now used loosely for the general area, then applied most precisely to the village which lay westwards. During the seventeenth and eighteenth centuries the village of Brompton was renowned for its wholesome, clean air and flourishing markets and nursery gardens. Brompton Park Nursery (where the V&A now stands), was occupied by Henry Wise, Queen Anne's celebrated gardener and a well-known property owner. Brompton, like much of Kensington, was excellent nursery ground and it was intensively cultivated. Gradually over the ensuing decades, the occasional cottages became more frequent and, more particularly, numerous hostelries were added.

The early nineteenth century saw a huge change in London's landscape. An increase in building developments led to the transformation of Brompton from a prosperous rural parish to a busy metropolitan borough. The first property boom took place between 1760 and 1770. From about 1764 terraced houses with large front gardens were built along present-day Brompton Road in the area including and surrounding Harrods. This newly developed part of Brompton Road came to be known as 'New Brompton', to distinguish it from the original village further west, which became 'Old Brompton'. The original Brompton Lane became known as Old Brompton Road.

Road widening after 1862 opened up the area further but restricted the size of the front gardens on Brompton Road, making those properties less desirable as residential properties and so more commercial activity followed. After 1864 Tattersalls, the famous racehorse auctioneers, removed from Hyde Park Corner to a large site behind Nos 38–58 Brompton Road, which was behind the houses opposite Harrods. It was the start of a friendship between the Tattersall and Harrod families. These were the days of hansom cabs and delivery carts rattling noisily over narrow streets, the days of beaver hats (made of felted beaver fur, these were very fashionable and the soft, yet resilient material could be easily combed to make a variety of hat shapes, including the familiar top hat) and billycocks (a felt hat with a rounded crown, similar to a bowler), and skin-tight trousers and near-crinolines.

It was about this time that the Crimean War began; the Great Exhibition moved from Hyde Park to Sydenham; the Houses of Parliament were in the course of construction; Cheltenham Ladies College opened its doors to pupils and the first pillar boxes appeared on Britain's streets, courtesy of Rowland Hill. It must have also been about this time that Charles Henry decided to commission photographs of himself and his wife. They were in their prime at around 55 and 45 respectively, and look suitably serious.

The family moved into the house at the back of the shop in 1854, and as said earlier, soon after that they lost their fourth son, Joseph Digby. The remaining children, Charles, William and Henry, were aged 13, 11 and 9 years old respectively, and although I do not know if Charles was yet back from his school in Suffolk, it is likely that all three of them were living in the house in Brompton Road most of the time.

Part of a letter from the third son, Henry Digby, written fifty years later and mentioned earlier, throws some light on this time:

> I can recollect my father took over the business from a Mr Burden who went to some other country as near as I know 1853 or 1854 and carried it on in conjunction with his Wholesale Business which he had in Eastcheap at the time. We all moved into the house at the back of the shop – I went to school close bye and helped in the shop on and off till about 1858 when I went away in the country to live.

Although I cannot be sure of all his dates and facts, as some proved wrong later, his suggestion that he went into the country to live might indicate a spell at Edwardstone School, like his brother.

The shop in 1854 consisted of three rooms, and Charles Henry employed two assistants and a messenger boy. The frontage of the shop was between 30–40ft and the shop sold mainly groceries and hardware goods, with a turnover of £20 a week. Charles Henry spent his time consolidating his ownership of the shop and appears to have made very few changes apart from some extension of the range of goods on offer.

Viewed through the retrospectroscope, it seems as if he was slow to expand the shop's activities in response to the gradually changing nature of his clientele. Perhaps he had only limited ambitions, but the purchase of the business may have left him short of capital and playing safe was the order of the day. After all, he had had the initial vision to make the purchase and the move, and the speed of change only looks slow in comparison to what was yet to come.

Over the following years, his growing children started to spend some time working with him. Charles Digby, the eldest, probably left school in 1857 when he was about 16, and was sent off to work in a wholesale grocery business in the City, probably at the Eastcheap site that Charles Henry had been running. Tim Dale states, in *Harrods: A Palace in Knightsbridge*, that he worked with a company called Read, Warren & Harrison. I have found no trace of them, although 38 Eastcheap was taken over by a Bristow, Warren & Harrison after 1856.

Charles was certainly back and working in Brompton Road by 1861, when the census has him listed as a 'commercial clerk'. It is likely he came back at the end of 1860 when his mother Elizabeth died, in the November of that year, at just 50 years old. Her death certificate states she died of 'Capillary Bronchitis – three weeks'. That diagnosis is quite an old-fashioned term, not used today, although the description is accurate. Often called 'bronchiolitis' in children, it is usually caused by a virus and causes severe breathing difficulties when the smaller tubes in the lungs get clogged with mucous. In severe cases, pneumonia follows and is the cause of death. The fact that she was ill for three weeks suggests she had never recovered from the original acute illness and would have gradually faded. Elizabeth was buried alongside her young son, Joseph, in Brompton Cemetery.

Left on his own, Charles would have needed all hands on deck to help with the shop. William Digby, his second son, worked in the shop as a youngster, just like his brothers. He was not at home for the 1861 census, but was living and working with one of his 'Tiffin' butcher relatives from Birch, who ran a shop in Munster Street in the St Pancras area. William, then aged 19, was one of three butchers working there. It is possible his father wanted him to learn the trade and run a butchery department at the Harrod shop, but equally, perhaps he had chosen not to stay at home with his father and brother, Charles Digby. There is quite a lot of circumstantial evidence to suggest that the sons of Charles Henry and Elizabeth did not get on well together, and indeed, William made a decision two years later to leave England.

Alfred Tiffin (or Tiffen) would have been 30 years old in 1861. He was the youngest son of Charles Tiffin, one of a family of butchers and cattle dealers in Birch and nearby Layer Breton, who were related to the Digbys by marriage. As a youngster, aged 19 in 1850, Alfred got into a bit of trouble with the authorities and his appearance before a court at the Mansion House is reported in several newspapers of the day. He had apparently bought a cow on the cheap that was not fit for human consumption. Such cattle were called, rather gruesomely, 'wet cows', and Alfred was trying to pass it off for sale at Smithfield as a healthy animal. He denied this, of course, saying the cow was sound. Under interrogation he admitted buying this cow for £2 2s 6d (which prompted laughter from the public), knowing the average price for a sound cow was £14 or £15. He was fined heavily – £20 – and warned about his future conduct.

Although this is no excuse, the availability online of newspaper archives and access to court and criminal records does on occasion lead to the conclusion that everybody in Victorian England was 'on the make' in one way or another. Novels by Dickens, like *Oliver Twist*, seem to confirm that minor crime was very common.

Henry Digby, the youngest son, had gone away to 'the country' in 1858 and like his eldest brother probably returned when his mother died two years later. In the 1861 census, now at home, he is listed as a 'shopman'. That same census showed that the family had a Digby cousin living with them, a granddaughter of James Digby Senior called Elizabeth Nevill Digby. She was then aged 20. She was to join William Digby when he emigrated two years later. There was also a 23-year-old domestic servant in the house. Accommodating the six residents in the house, with the shop and the stock, would have been difficult.

The death of Elizabeth, wife and mother to the household, would have been a tragedy for the family; but it proved to be a watershed, prompting changes for Charles Henry. The following year, 1861, was also a year of change in British and world history. On 25 May, the American Civil War began; on 14 December, Prince Albert died, prompting the start of one of the longest bereavements in history; the first horse-drawn trams started in London; the Metropolitan Railway, later the Metropolitan Line, was in the throes of construction, linking the mainline railway stations of London with underground tunnels (it would be a few years later however, in 1868, before it would extend to South Kensington); and Mrs Beeton published her *Book of Household Management*. The penny post had been established in the previous year, 1860, and remarkably, each day there were at least ten deliveries of letters and eight collections. The iron boxes for letters, first erected in 1855 on the kerbstones of the leading thoroughfares, had collections at 7.45 a.m., 10 a.m., 12 noon, 2 p.m., 4 p.m., 6 p.m. and 8 p.m.

Aged 61, Charles should have been looking forward soon to retirement with Elizabeth. They had married when she was young and had been through many hard times together. His three sons, now young men, would have been raring to take on more responsibility and make their own way in life.

The differences between the boys must have come to the surface over the next year or two. Charles Digby, the eldest and probably the most forceful, was set to take over the shop from his father, whilst his brothers went off in very different directions.

THE MOVE TO KENSINGTON

WILLIAM DIGBY HARROD

William Digby Harrod was a very different character to his older brother, Charles. He was much more of a loner and was less ambitious. In 1863, he decided there was no future for him in England and he emigrated with his Uncle John Digby and John's family, which included Elizabeth Nevill Digby and his cousin Joseph Sampson Digby. The destination was Christchurch, South Island, New Zealand.

William travelled as a remittance man in the ship *David G. Fleming*. Remittance men have been described as 'those who were either useless or superfluous to the family – who were shipped off by their families to Australia [or New Zealand] and paid a remittance to stay there. They were the troublemakers, non-achievers, or perhaps just the youngest of the sons.' It is impossible to know to which group William belonged. A New Zealand Digby descendant added another possibility to the list, that of fleeing London after getting a young woman 'in the family way'. No evidence for this was offered or has been found.

Much of the information about William Digby has come from New Zealand researchers, who have investigated him thoroughly to try to find a link with their own Harrod lines; none of which have so far found to be connected. After his arrival, William farmed for a short time with his Uncle John in Ashburton, on the Canterbury Plain near Christchurch. The Maori Wars had, by this time, been grumbling on and off for some years in New Zealand. In 1863, the year of William's arrival, the colonial government brought the Military Settlers Scheme into being. Service with the military would be rewarded by land on which to work and live. This must have seemed like just the right opportunity for William to kick-start his own life in New Zealand.

In January 1864, only a few weeks after he landed, William enlisted in the forces in Canterbury. He was appointed a private and was transferred to Okato, to the Taranaki Military Settlers. This contingent was deployed to help stop the fighting between Maori and *Pakeha*, the Maori term for New Zealanders of European origin.

Okato is a small coastal township in rural Taranaki, North Island. Today it is still a small town, with a population of about 520 people.

William's military service records reveal that on enlistment he was aged 22, 5ft 4in tall and single. It gives his ship of arrival in New Zealand as the *Phoebe*, which might have explained a lack of Digby or Harrod names on the passenger lists of the *David G. Fleming*, the ship they were said to have used. My research on New Zealand websites shows that there were no suitably timed trips for the *Phoebe*, but I have confirmed a journey for her sister ship, the *Phoebe Dunbar*, in 1863 to Port Chalmers, at the southern end of the Canterbury Plains. Sadly, no passenger lists exist online for either vessel, so which ship was actually used remains unknown.

The New Zealand Wars, also known as the Land Wars or Maori Wars, were a series of conflicts that took place between 1845 and 1872. They were fought over a number of issues; most prominently Maori land being sold to the white settlers. This is a period of history about which the British government of the time and the local settlers should not be proud. The Treaty of Waitangi, signed in 1840, had guaranteed the rights of the Maori tribes to their land, though some land sales to colonials had taken place. The British colonial authorities decreed that the Maoris could sell land only to the Crown. However, many settlers did not appreciate that the Maori owned their land communally and that permission to settle on land did not always imply sale of that land. Under pressure from settlers, the colonial government gradually ignored the provisions of the treaty and permitted settlers in areas that had uncertain ownership. The Maori began resisting the occupation of their land by British settlers, and the whole process sowed the seeds of eventual war.

By 1859, the Europeans in New Zealand had reached numerical parity with the Maori, at about 60,000 each. Whilst the Maori population was declining so fast that some people saw their extinction as a distinct possibility, immigrant ships were arriving from Britain on an almost weekly basis. As early as 1841, one Maori had asked if the whole British tribe was moving to New Zealand.

THE MOVE TO KENSINGTON

During their attacks on rural settlements, however, the Maoris often had overwhelming numbers. In time, it inevitably proved an unequal struggle; the economic base of industrial Britain, against the Maori rural economy. Their warriors were their farmers and food gatherers, not soldiers. What became known as the Second Taranaki War was a reaction by the Maori to the wholesale confiscation of their land by the colonial government who had used imperial troops to enforce this. After 1863, most of the fighting was conducted by the local organised units of settler militia.

William's local militia built a blockhouse to use as a storage and defensive base, and during continuing Maori raids the white population would flee to the safety of the blockhouse. A local resident told a story in an article about William Harrod, which had occurred when he, the correspondent, was only 3 weeks old:

> To help my mother, who was in a weak state through my recent birth, Harrod, our neighbour, carried me most of the way up the steep hill to the blockhouse, and that on the way up, hearing some noise in the fern, he and my mother had to hide for some time before they attempted to go on.

Many Maori died defending their land; others changed sides to settle old scores. In all, there were an estimated 3,000 casualties, the majority of which were Maori. To make matters worse, land confiscation was the fate of many of the survivors. Inevitably, the might of the Empire prevailed.

For his service with the Military Settlers, William was awarded the New Zealand Medal, which was presented by Governor George Gray in 1867. Following the war, a lot of land changed hands, forming the basis for continued legal disputes over the ensuing years. So rightly, or more likely by today's standards, wrongly, William was granted land in 1867 for his contribution as a member of the Taranaki Military Settlers. The land was No. 42 Town Lot, an acre in the middle of the Okato settlement, and Lot 8, a 57-acre plot just outside the town. On this smaller town lot William built a two-roomed hut, laid a cobblestoned courtyard and planted arum lilies. The larger site has since been divided into two parts, the Okato Domain and Terry O'Sullivan's Farm, off Old South Road – local knowledge!

Once at peace and settled on his land. William took a full part in local life. An article in the *Taranaki Daily News* in 1935 describes how the local pioneers had to band together to build and repair the roads and bridges. William was on the Okato Road Board which supervised this work throughout the late 1870s and early 1880s, latterly as chairman. William featured in another article in the *New Plymouth Daily News* in 1986. After berating Harrods Stores, which they labelled 'the hallowed hand', for giving some New Zealand businesses a legal rap over the knuckles for taking its name in vain, the article then gives the life story of William as an example of one tie that can never be cut!

The article draws on information in the local archives together with the memories of descendants of his friends. It describes the rationale of the remittance man as 'Here's a few quid from the family coffers, old chap, now kindly push off.' The article states William did not farm but just 'gardened', although the archives list him as a 'farmer'. It states that he was at one time county clerk for Okato County and in his later years was appointed a Justice of the Peace.

William never married, and the evidence suggests he lived alone all his life. If he had been interested, single girls were in any case at a premium in the rural settlements. William's closest friends in the town were Fred Roebuck and William Corbett and their families. Fred Roebuck was Okato's first blacksmith and went on to run a carrier service to New Plymouth. Fred gave his youngest son, Stephen, the middle name of Digby, after William. Stephen Roebuck was interviewed in that 1986 article, then aged 87. He said that his parents enjoyed William's company and he was spoken of as a thoroughly sociable old gentleman. It was well known that William was part of the Harrod family of the store fame and came from a wealthy family. William was said to have had a picture of Harrods in his home, which he told locals was the biggest store in the world.

The Corbetts described him as a highly educated man, with a love of poetry and reading. They thought he survived on a private income; perhaps his inheritance formed the basis of this. William Corbett's grandson, Des, told a story about how his grandfather had saved William's life one winter's night, when he was found lying injured after being crushed by a farm animal. Mrs Corbett had heard his cries for help. 'They had to take him to town in a gig. I don't know how old he would have been, but he had to have a spell in hospital.' Mr Corbett's son, Ernest, later became an MP from 1943–57 and was, at one time, Minister of Maori Affairs and Lands and Forests.

William was not liked by everyone. The same article told a story about William's support for the Corbett children, who William felt were being victimised by their school teacher. Des said, 'They got whacked for being late, for not having a handkerchief. Harrod went down to the school and tried to sort it out.' However, perhaps Des's memory of the events was flawed. The response is recorded in the Okato School headmaster's diary for 3 June 1905, which read:

> Mr Harrod has been putting himself to considerable pains to interest himself in the Corbetts' case without coming to see me about my side of the question. As a JP it is evident he should keep out of party quarrels, or at any rate, find out the truth before taking action on one side, more especially as he is an old bachelor without any children or even relations at the school.

He is mentioned in several other newspaper cuttings of the day. The *Taranaki Herald* in 1890 states he was in hospital that year with a poisoned hand. The same paper gives a description of an injury in an article on 15 May 1897, probably the same story as told by Des Corbett:

> Mr W.D. Harrod, a settler at Okato and clerk to the Okato Road Board, sustained a broken leg on Friday evening. He was milking his cows between 4 and 5 o'clock when one of the animals slipped and fell on his leg breaking the limb. Mr Harrod, as no help was near, crawled about 2 chains to his house [for the younger reader, a chain is 4 rods or perches, and is about the length of a cricket pitch, or 20m. So 2 chains are about 40m] and opened both doors, and then, as he lived alone, he tried to attract attention. It was

not, however, until about 8 o'clock that he managed to attract the attention of 2 lads, named Clarke and Humphreys, who were out fishing in the river. The lads gave the alarm, and Mr Harrod was at once attended to by the neighbours, and was eventually brought to the hospital for treatment.

You had to be tough to survive in those days!

In 1901, William sold his land and moved into a cottage built for him in the town in Oxford Road. In his last years he was looked after by his friends, the Corbetts. William Digby Harrod died in the Private Hospital, New Plymouth, in 1907. He was 64 years old. The death was reported by William Corbett and his death certificate states he had died of 'Hernia, senile heart decay, Cardiac Failure – 3 days'. It is possible he had had a strangulated hernia, on which surgery would have been available in 1907, but risky, and that this precipitated the heart failure.

He had been in New Zealand for nearly forty-five years. The *Taranaki Herald* described him:

> A well-known and highly respected resident of Okato. Mr Harrod arrived in Lyttleton in 1861, then a lad of nineteen. He came up to Taranaki about '64 ... When hostilities with the Natives ceased, he settled on his Government grant ... He was, we understand, one of the very few who retained their Government grants.

He was buried in the Corbett family plot, beneath the shadow of Mount Egmont at Okato Cemetery, with an expensive looking grey marble headstone. The *Herald* report of the funeral stated, 'He was not much known to the outside world, being of a retiring disposition.'

The handwritten will appointed the Public Trustee as executor. The *Evening Post* reported his estate as £3,804 (between £1–2 million today, depending upon how you compare monetary worth). He left bequests to members of the Roebuck and Corbett families, and the balance of his estate to 'my brother Henry Digby Harrod, at present residing at High Street, Winchester, England'. This suggests that the two brothers had remained friends and were still in touch.

The Public Trustee took the land back into the public domain, although the rationale was not explained. The descendants of Henry Digby might otherwise have found themselves very rich indeed. He directed his executor 'to have a polished granite recumbent stone laid over my grave with only my name and date of birth upon it, the cost not to exceed £80'.

Mrs Roebuck used her bequest to build a new family home at 19 Carthew Street, which she named 'Harrodsville'. It later became the site for Okato's first bowling green which was on the front lawn.

A sale of his livestock took place after his death. It included '25 Yearling; 4 2-year-old Heifers; 1 Empty Cow; 1 Mare, with foal at foot; 1 Yearling Filly by Berlin Abba; 4 Pairs good Working Bullocks, Yokes, Bows and Chains; 1 Dray – 5 inch tyres.' The average 'gardener' would have found no use for bullocks and yokes.

HENRY DIGBY HARROD

Henry Digby Harrod was the youngest of the three brothers, and probably had the most problems getting on with his brother, Charles Digby. He worked for a while in the shop before he went off to the country when aged about 13. After his mother's death in 1860 when he was aged 15, he worked in the shop as a 'shopman' whilst his brother William was working elsewhere as a butcher.

This time working with his brother, Charles Digby, may well have made his mind up that they could not continue together. Charles was that bit older and full of ideas, and his star shone brighter. As Charles Digby gradually took over the Brompton Road shop in the early 1860s as his father handed over the reins, William emigrated and Henry decided he must make a move. He was helped by his father, who took over a shop in Soho, at 40 Old Compton Street. Charles Henry remained the ratepayer and is listed on the electoral register at this address until 1869, but he handed this shop over to Henry who was running the shop by 1866.

Henry decided to use his acquired skills and run his own grocery business, with the initial support from his father, although he did not try to rival the shop in Kensington. Over many years Henry ran a large number of retail establishments, and although some were sequential, many overlapped for some time. The dates and places have been gleaned using the census records, the electoral register, trade directory entries, the places and dates of birth of his children, and some family gossip.

Henry Digby obviously felt that the route to success was with multiple small branches rather than one large shop. He was successful in a modest fashion; in 1891, for instance, he was employing nine men and a boy. His first shop, 40 Old Compton Street, was, like its neighbours, a four-storey house. From the 1820s onwards it had been a drapery store, but by the time of the 1871 census, Henry Digby was running the business with two assistants and a domestic servant, and his occupation is given as 'grocer and tea dealer'. He was single, but married in October of the same year.

Henry married 22-year-old Caroline Wade in Colchester, Essex, in 1871, and they set up home in Old Compton Street. She was the fourth daughter of Thomas Wade, a Suffolk ironmonger, and she was born in Clare, in south Suffolk, where her father worked for many years. They were a local family and Caroline was one of their eight children.

At the time of their marriage, Caroline was working as a milliner in London, less than half a mile from Old Compton Street. They may have met in London, but her home town of Clare was the birthplace of Henry's grandmother, Tamah Mason, almost 100 years earlier, and Henry's grandfather William Harrod had lived there for a while. So Henry, like his father, may have gone back to his roots to find his bride and perhaps she had moved to London to be closer.

Henry and his family lived in Old Compton Street for about thirteen years, and the first five of their twelve children were born there. Remarkably for the time, eleven survived to adulthood. He ran a business there for much longer, probably thirty years in total. He was in the trade directories at that address until 1886, and in the electoral registers until 1893, although by these dates he was no longer living there.

The British Library holds a publicity leaflet from the shop in Old Compton Street dated 26 May 1885 which, apart from the header, gives a price list for teas and coffees. It reads:

> H.D. Harrod (Grocery Stores) Best Grocery Stores, 40 Old Compton Street.
> Notice. The well-known Christmas Club; which always gives satisfaction to its supporters has commenced, and we invite all to join at once to secure the benefits. We present to every subscriber of 8/- a bottle of Foreign Port or Sherry, and to every subscriber of 6/- 1/4lb. of Black or Green tea … Sugars, Fruit, Sago, Tapioca, Rice … at smallest profit on cost and the best value in London.

During this period of apparent stability for Henry, Brompton Road had been transformed by his brother Charles. Henry seemed to be quite happy running his business on a smaller scale and had no wish to expand or emulate his brother's model. Henry did, however, expand in terms of the number of his shops.

He started shops in Theobalds Road, north of Holborn, the Caledonian Road, King Street in Hammersmith and Newington Butts in Southwark. As one closed, others were opened in other parts of London, although there was some overlap. Henry had two grocery shops in Theobalds Road, No. 92 in 1880 and No. 104 in 1890. Grocery shops at 41 King Street and 341 Caledonian Road followed in the last decade of the nineteenth and first decade of the twentieth century.

A confectionery shop at 7 Newington Butts ran between 1909 and 1913. He may have had a shop at 42 Half Moon Street in Piccadilly for a year or two; he is listed on the electoral register at this address, but this was a 'dwelling house' so may have been a domestic property he rented out. He may have had some sort of storage facility at 112 High Street, Peckham, as it is mentioned in a land registry document years later regarding transfer of the property to his wife after his death.

Henry and the family had moved to Goldhawk Road, just west of Shepherd's Bush, by the time of the 1881 census. The house, 'The Hawthorns' at 264 Goldhawk Road, was large enough to accommodate their burgeoning family. They had moved there with four children, a daughter Florence having died at the age of 1 in 1878. By 1881 there were two more in the house. A further child was born there during their three-year stay, making a total of seven. The 1881 census describes Henry as a 'grocer, employing nine men and one boy'.

A photograph of Henry Digby, probably around this time when he would have been in his 30s or early 40s, shows a handsome man, looking very much like his brother, Charles. Other photographs held by the family show Henry's wife, Caroline, at the same sort of age and also a decade or so older. Charles Digby's wife was also called Caroline, and the similarity in the ages of the two Carolines and the prevailing fashion and hairstyle of the era has led to the situation where both Charles's descendants and Henry's descendants have told to me that the same photograph labelled, 'Caroline Harrod', is *their* Caroline. Despite one Charles Digby descendant owning an old locket with that photograph inside, comparing other photographs of the two Carolines makes me lean towards the likelihood that the photograph is of Caroline Harrod née Wade, Henry's wife; but I cannot be certain.

By 1883, Henry, Caroline and family were living at 21 Oxford Road, Chiswick, and they stayed there for at least eight years. Their last four children were born there. The 1891 census reveals that nine of his children were at home and two were staying with their cousins, Charles Digby's children. At least that suggests the two families were on talking terms.

The end of the nineteenth century marked a distinct change for Henry and his family. Henry's father, Charles Henry, had died in 1885 and Henry decided to move out of London. Over the next twenty years or so he closed all of his London premises – the reason for this is unknown.

Henry Digby opened a shop at 25 High Street, in Winchester, sometime in the 1890s – probably in 1892. The shop in Winchester had been previously occupied by J. Tracey, another grocer, until 1890. In the street directories, the Harrod name first appears in Winchester in 1893 and is there until 1906. It is listed in the 1895

Kelly's Directory as 'Harrod & Co., Grocers and Wine Merchants, agents for W&A Gilbey'. The family lived at the shop from 1893 to 1904, and whilst running this Winchester shop several of the shops in London continued to trade, so Henry may have travelled back and forth.

In the course of correspondence with the Harrods' archivist in 1987, I was sent a letter which suggested that Henry Digby opened the Winchester shop ten years earlier in 1880, and ran this until 1907 when he returned to Knightsbridge to work. No evidence has been found to substantiate this. There is no evidence he was in Winchester before 1892 or that he returned to Harrods after 1906.

A flyer for the Winchester shop and a branch opened at 1 Market Street, dated 1905, was shown to me by Harrods archives, and gives the prices of his wines, spirits and beers. Port was 1/- to 4/- (1/-, or one shilling, was the equivalent of 5p in decimal coinage), gin from 1*s* 6*d* and tea 1/- to 3/-. 'Lowest cash prices' were offered.

By 1904, Henry and his family had moved to a new home, Ivydene, East Hill, in Winchester, where they remained at least until Henry's death in 1915, aged 69. East Hill later became known as Quarry Road. After Henry's death, Caroline continued living in Winchester, latterly looked after by her eldest daughter, Edith. Caroline died in 1938, aged 88.

The family has many photographs of Henry in late middle age in his garden with Caroline and their family. They were often dressed in tennis gear and obviously made good use of their tennis court. They looked a happy lot. There were still some of Henry Harrod's family in Winchester in 1965. An article in *The Hampshire* by Joy Peach recounted that her next-door neighbours were two spinster sisters, the oldest and youngest of a large Victorian family. Miss Edith Harrod was in her nineties, and Miss Eveline almost twenty years younger. Edith was by this time doubled up with spinal arthritis, and had to walk about with her eyes looking down at her feet. This sounds as though she had severe spinal osteoporosis.

The sisters had lived there for sixty years altogether; Miss Edith, the eldest daughter, had remained single and stayed at home to look after her ageing parents, whilst Eveline, in her turn, gave up her job as a supervisor at Edmunds, the drapers in the High Street, to look after her sister when she needed help. Joy repeated the story that Henry was reputed to have worked at Harrods some years after his brother had left the store, starting in the year he had bought Ivydene. I think perhaps she was getting mixed up with his brother, as we will see later.

A remarkable insight into Henry Digby's view on the Harrod shop and his relationship with his father and brother is revealed by a letter shown to me by Sebastian Wormell, the Harrods archivist, in 2008. The letter is itself a copy, as handwritten at the top it states, 'Copy of letter, supplied by Mr [William] Kibble to Harrods Secretary in 1924'.

William Kibble was a relation by marriage of the Harrods, via Charles Digby's wife, and so a cousin to Charles and Henry. He worked for a long time in the store, having taken Henry's place in the Brompton Road store when he left. The letter is from Henry, presumably to William Kibble, and probably written during the last few years of Henry's life. It sounds as though William Kibble had asked Henry for his recollections of the early days in the store. After Henry Digby had died in 1915, the letter was passed on to the Harrods archive in 1924. Sebastian thinks the typed copy was probably made around 1943 for the novelist Gilbert Frankau, who was working on an official history of Harrods at the time. The letter reads:

Ivy Dene, East Hill, Winchester.   Jan'y 27
Dear Sir,

    Yours to hand. I am glad to see you are still in the land of the living like myself and hope you will continue in good health and long life yet to come.

    You ask me for facts which I can't give as I was a boy and therefore am not clear. But I will tell you all I know and as far as I can recollect my father took over the business from a Mr Burdin [*sic*] who went to some other country as near as I know 1853 or 1854 and carried it on in conjunction with his Wholesale Business which he had in Eastcheap at the time. We all moved into the house at the back of the shop – I went to school close bye and helped in the shop on and off till about 1858 when I went away in the country to live. [He would have been about 13 years old then]. My brother C.D. Harrod took it over in 1861and my father went to live opposite the Museum. I returned home about 1863 and went and lived with my brother until as you know I went to Compton Limited and you came into my place. You would know the year, I think it was 1866. During my last term with my brother we made the first move to improve the business by having a new front put in which you recollect, and it was that that drew the attention of the Public to our shop and I dare say the windows the first time. We steadily advanced especially in the Tea Trade and built up as very nice counter trade which you know was when I left it about 200 to 250 per week and very profitable. The rest you know as you were on the spot when he took up the store trading and succeeded.

I have given you all I know except mere trifles. But if anything comes of it I should like my Father's name to be much honoured before all other things as he was the person which was the principal factor in the making of success, for without his Father's help my brother could have done nothing.

My Father's name was Charles Digby Harrod so there can be no mistake.

With kind regards and well wishes,

I remain,

Yours faithfully, [signed] H.D. Harrod

A fascinating letter for many reasons. It must have been written between 1905 (when Charles Digby died) and 1915, when Henry Digby died. The date at the top is 27 January, though no year is given. There are a number of mistakes in the letter, so perhaps Henry was having memory problems, and a few points merit further discussion. To have called his father 'Charles Digby Harrod' not 'Chares Henry' was, in the context of the letter, a Freudian slip. The point was being strongly made and came from a deep-seated mutual antipathy and perhaps jealousy – no love lost there. The letter was almost certainly handwritten, and was copy-typed either by Kibble himself or a Harrods secretary, so this might just be a terrible transcription error. Odd to address a cousin as 'Dear Sir', but letters were much more formal in those days. 'Yours to hand', is the equivalent of today's 'in reply to your letter'.

It is not clear whether the 200 to 250 per week refers to cash turnover or number of items. If the former, no wonder it was so profitable! He asserts that his father took over the Brompton business in around 1861. Although Henry says he was away until 1863, he must have come back when his mother died at the end of 1860, and he was back working with his father and brother at the time of the 1861 census, unless this was just a holiday job. The letter confirms that brothers Charles and Henry worked together for a while in the shop. When Charles took over in 1861, Henry would have been only 15 or 16 years old. Henry was keen to stress his role in the early changes to the shop.

Many of my details about Henry and Caroline's children were supplied by Brian Heather, who lived in Truro but sadly died in 2010. He was the cousin of Winifred Mabel Heather, a granddaughter of Henry Digby Harrod by his second child and daughter, Kate Emily. Brian had written in 1995 to the Harrods archivist, then Nadine Hansen, stating that he knew that Winifred Mabel Heather had a family Bible with family details, and Nadine passed the letter to me. My brothers and I were shown that book during a visit in 2008. It had apparently been bought by Harrods at auction after Winifred's and Marjorie's deaths, together with some photographs.

Henry and Caroline, through their children and their marriages, became quite involved in the commercial life of the area. Some of their more notable offspring are described below:

Their eldest child, Edith, born in 1873, was mentioned earlier. In the 1891 census, she and her sister Kate were staying with cousins, Amy and Beatrice, two of Charles Digby's children, in Allerford House, North Somerset. After taking care of her parents in their old age, Edith died in 1969, aged 96.

THE MOVE TO KENSINGTON

The second child, Kate, was born in 1874. She married Arthur Heather, the son of a pawnbroker in Winchester, and they moved to Newbury where they ran Heather's Stores, which was listed as a 'pawnbroker and furniture dealer'. Kate had a leather-bound book in which she noted the birthdays of her family and friends. Brian Heather, her nephew, initially lent me this book and then later decided I had better keep it for the family. It confirms many Harrod dates already discovered, suggesting that she remained in contact with her cousins, despite the rift between her father, Henry, and his brother, Charles. One of their daughters, Marjorie, was an artist and exhibited at the Royal Academy. Kate died in 1940, aged 73 and Arthur in 1943.

The fifth child, Ethel, was born in 1878. She married William Butt, whose family were boot and shoe makers with a shop in the High Street in Winchester.

Frank was the eighth child, and second son, of Henry and Caroline. He was born in 1882 and started his working life as a teacher in Swindon. He joined the Royal Hampshire Regiment early on in the First World War, aged 33. He was awarded the Military Cross in the Battle of the Somme in 1916, during an attack on German trenches near Gueudecourt in which the 2nd Hampshires were heavily involved. He was put forward for more honours by General Haig in early 1918 and later that year he was awarded the French decoration, the *Croix de Guerre*, by which time he was the Adjutant of the Regiment. After the war, in 1921, he married Charlotte David in Leeds. Frank went into the administrative side of education, working in local government. By 1936 he was Director of Education in Coventry, a post he held during the Second World War, until 1945. He was awarded an OBE in 1952, and advanced to CBE later.

One of Frank's children, Lionel, born 1924, also had an illustrious career in the army, and built up quite a CV. During his career he was awarded the OBE. He served in the Grenadier Guards during the Second World War, and later saw service in Suez, Cyprus and Hong Kong, before being posted to the Welsh Regiment. He was on the British Defence Staff Washington between 1969 and 1970, and Military

Attaché in Baghdad in 1971. In 1976 he was promoted to major general. He worked as Assistant Chief of Staff (Intelligence) to the Supreme Allied Commander Europe (SHAPE) between 1976 and 1979.

He became colonel of the Royal Regiment of Wales from 1977 to 1982, and this appointment proved to be his proudest moment. Having retired from the army in 1979, he became inspector of recruiting from 1979 until final retirement in 1990. His motto was 'Soldiering must be fun' – I think he found life fun as well.

At a point in the 1980s when I was desperately searching for Harrod relatives, I got in touch with him after seeing his entry in *Who's Who*. In his usual generous spirit, he was delighted to find new relatives and was very welcoming. He helped by putting us in touch with my father's paternal family, and we met on several occasions. He died in 1995, aged 70.

Dorothy Eveline was the twelfth and last child of Henry and Caroline, born in 1891. She remained single, looking after her eldest sister Edith into her old age. There was just over eighteen years between them. She lived for most of her life with her sisters Edith and Blanche at Ivydene, caring for her parents with them until their deaths. Dorothy died eight months after her oldest sister in 1969, aged 78.

Henry Digby Harrod died in 1915 in Winchester. He was aged 69, and had outlived his older brother Charles by almost ten years. At the time of his death, he still owned businesses in London in Newington Butts, High Street, Peckham and Hammersmith. His estate was valued at £2,853 9s, a value today of about £200,000. His wife Caroline survived until 1938, dying at the age of 89.

CHARLES DIGBY HARROD

Back in 1861, Charles Henry had decided to hand over the running of the business to his son, Charles Digby. The death of his wife Elizabeth, tiredness after many years of work, and a vigorous son full of new ideas must have helped to make the decision.

As the *Daily Mail* of 1949 puts it, in newspaper speak in an article to mark the 100th anniversary of Harrods:

The clarion call of opportunity was sounding, and by 1861, when a migration of 'gentry' to Knightsbridge had already begun, Henry's son, Charles Digby, heard the call so plainly that he persuaded his father to sell him the business.

Young Charles Digby, then 20 years old, was enthusiastic, ambitious and hard-working, and that year began to run the store himself. A deal was made between Charles Digby and his father that he would take over the running of the store, and buy his father out in instalments over the following three years. His father would stay on to help and advise, and then retire gracefully.

An added stimulus to business appeared at about this time. An International Exhibition, known as the Great London Exposition, was a form of world's fair. It was built in 1862, beside the gardens of the Royal Horticultural Society, South Kensington, on a site that now houses the Natural History Museum and the Science Museum. Queen Victoria did not attend the opening as she was in mourning. The exhibition, much like the Great Exhibition of a decade before, was to display the industrial, scientific and artistic advances of the day. It was intended to be permanent, but after six months a purchase was not confirmed by Parliament and the construction was removed and reused to build the Crystal Palace.

The directories, rating records and electoral registers show that Charles Henry remained in charge of the Brompton Road premises, at least nominally, until 1864, and was then replaced by Charles Digby. Charles Digby had been running the shop for three years by then and had made enough money to clear the debt and pay off his father. Charles Henry moved out to live elsewhere. At about this time, what had been 8 Middle Queens Buildings was renamed as 105 Brompton Road.

On Thursday, 31 March 1864, Charles Digby married Caroline Godsmark at St Mary's Church, West Brompton. My knowledge of the character of Charles Digby might suggest he chose to marry on a

Thursday as this was the quietest trading day of the week! Charles is listed on the marriage certificate as a 'tea dealer' of 105 Brompton Road, whilst Caroline is listed as a spinster of 'full age'. Caroline was living nearby at 4 Percy Terrace, Gloucester Grove West, now called Clareville Grove, on the Old Brompton Road.

Charles Digby's father is listed as a 'gentleman', which means that he was not working and was living on his own means. Caroline's father, James Godsmark, had died in 1849, aged 33, of meningitis, and was listed on the certificate as having been a 'grocer'. His widow, Caroline, had remarried in 1855 a commercial traveller from Builth Wells, Breconshire, called Robert Edward Jones. He was one of the witnesses.

The Godsmark family has been thoroughly investigated by several descendants. One, Peter Godsmark, sent me a resume of the family and some of it is repeated here. The earliest known record of the surname Godsmark is in the Sussex Subsidy Roll for 1296. The Subsidy Rolls were the lists of people who had paid the 'subsidy'. This was the tax levied by the king. It was usually one-fifteenth of the value of all movable property. The Godsmark family moved from Ashurst in the late 1600s to Cuckfield and Slaugham.

In the eighteenth century, the family were farmers and yeomen in the Horsham area of Sussex. One descendant, James Godsmark, became a grocer, initially in Lambeth and later in Chelsea. He had married Caroline Kibble, the daughter of a baker, James Kibble from Lewisham. Some of the Godsmark children continued in the grocery and tea business after James's death, and some of the Kibble part of the family were later to be heavily involved at the Harrods shop itself. It is tempting to think that the common factor between the families, the grocery business, was what brought Charles Digby and Caroline together. It might be that James Godsmark and Charles Henry Harrod had traded with each other in the 1840s. James's grocer son might have been a customer and Caroline's new husband, Robert Jones, also worked for a while after their marriage as a grocer and tea dealer in Chelsea.

Tim Dale, who wrote some of the previous books about Harrods, told me in 1987 that Charles Digby Harrod and Caroline Godsmark met when they both attended Trinity Chapel, situated on the south side of Knightsbridge, close to Albert Gate. (Although Trinity Chapel sounds like a Nonconformist church, it was in fact Church of England.) Charles Digby was appointed Honorary Librarian of Trinity Chapel in 1861 and Caroline Godsmark taught in the Sunday school and sang in the choir. They became engaged in 1862, two years before their marriage.

Both the Kibble family and Caroline Godsmark and her second husband, Robert Jones, remained heavily involved with Charles Digby and his family. Caroline Godsmark's father, James Kibble, was a much beloved great-grandfather to Charles Digby's children. The family sent me a lovely letter from him, written in 1875 to two of the children a few months after the birth of another daughter.

Once Charles Digby had married, he and his bride Caroline took over the living accommodation on Brompton Road and his father, Charles Henry, by 1865 had moved out to 9 York Cottages in Kensington. This was a leasehold property which had been built a few decades earlier on the south side of the triangular site opposite the Brompton Oratory. He lived there with a housekeeper for the majority of the rest of his life.

Although Charles Henry retired from Brompton Road in 1864, in 1866 he was still listed as a grocer at 40 Old Compton Street, in the shop taken over by Henry Digby, so he may well have been 'keeping his hand in'. His 'York Cottages' property was renamed between 1866 and 1871 and became 9 Thurloe Place.

The Essex connection continued, as in the 1871 census his housekeeper was Julia Digby, a cousin of his wife's, who was 30 years old in that year. She must have left soon after as she married in that same year. In 1881, he had a more mature housekeeper, a 64-year-old widow from Birch called Eleanor Murton (or Munton). There is a Digby relative by marriage called 'Murton', but no other connection has been found. It would certainly be in character for his housekeeper to be a relative.

There is nothing in the records to throw light on how Charles Henry spent his time in retirement. Perhaps he was just a doting grandfather. Charles Henry lived on twenty years in retirement and died aged 85, in 1885, at 2 Oxford Terrace, Chiswick. Oxford Terrace was a terrace of large villas, part of Oxford Street in Chiswick. The road still exists, just under the southern end of the M4 flyover, east of Kew Bridge. It is not known why or when Charles Henry moved to this address, but it is probably related to the fact that Henry Digby was living at a house just down the road at 15 Oxford Road. Charles Henry had presumably gone to live near his son as he became less independent. He had retained his Thurloe Place residence as this property appears in his will.

His cause of death was given as 'General Decay of Nature', what would now be called 'old age'. His death had been 'reported' by his son Henry. He was buried in Brompton Cemetery with his wife and his youngest son, Joseph. His will, made in 1879 whilst he was resident at Thurloe Place, states:

> My sons Charles Digby Harrod and Henry Digby Harrod are already indebted to me in the sum of one thousand pounds each and the sum owing from my said son Charles will if still due at my death form a fund to meet the legacy hereinafter bequeathed to my son William.

All the household goods were to be sold and the proceeds divided equally between his three sons, as were the plate and plated articles. To Charles Digby he bequeathed his 'leasehold messuage and premises at 9 Thurloe Place, with the appurtenances thereto belonging [appurtenances – the rights associated with the property]', and his life assurance policy with the National Life Society. To William Digby he bequeathed £1,000, and to Henry Digby he bequeathed his four 'leasehold messuages at 11, 12, 13 & 14 New Church St, Bermondsey' and the £1,000 he owed him.

Charles Henry's personal estate amounted to £3,436 9*s* 10*d*, somewhere over £1 million in today's money. Quite an estate for the grocer from Cable Street.

5

CHARLES DIGBY TAKES OVER

The early 1860s was the start of a dramatic change in the direction and speed of travel for the Harrod shop, and Charles Digby Harrod was the architect of this change. It is quite difficult to know where to start in trying to describe the man. Although his father had done some of the hard work and had laid the foundations for the Harrods shop that we know today, there is little doubt that in the thirty years after taking over, Charles Digby took the business into overdrive and changed the shop into a store. He had the personality, the energy and the vision to make it happen, and was helped by being in the right place at the right time. That his father, having decided to retire after forty years in business, had the confidence to leave the whole thing in the hands of his 20-year-old son, says a lot for his capabilities.

As we shall see as we progress, although Charles Digby was a hard taskmaster, he never expected his employees to work harder or longer hours than himself. He had enough drive for several men. He was an enthusiastic man who managed to infect his staff with his enthusiasm and the will to follow his example. He was brimming with new ideas and not afraid to try them out. In addition to all of these business traits, he had an engaging personality and managed to retain his common touch with his customers, who vied to be served by Mr Harrod in person.

After 1863 Charles Digby and his wife, Caroline, and later his growing family, progressively filled the living quarters at the back of the Kensington shop. The story of the shop has been gleaned from a variety of sources, including Tim Dale's books about Harrods, which are full of useful information, and an account by Gilbert Frankau written in the 1940s. I have, thanks to successive Harrods archivists, been granted access to the same information in the Harrods archives as was used by both Frankau and Dale.

Other information came from the book, *Modern Men of Mark*, in a section about Sir Richard Burbidge, Charles Digby's successor, and from the newspapers of the time, now available online. British History Online is a wonderful resource and provides a wealth of material.

CHARLES DIGBY TAKES OVER

An example of what was available to me in the Harrods archives is an original script, full of information, entitled, 'The Story of Mr C.D. Harrod'. Importantly, it is a first-hand account of events. This document is the transcript of a talk by Miss Conder to the Harrods staff on 26 January 1932. She was Katherine Emily Conder, an unmarried granddaughter of Charles Digby who was born in 1898 and died in 1989. She was alive at the tail end of Charles Digby's Harrods tenure and worked in the shop herself for some years, so had invaluable direct information and a lot of fresh second-hand information. Katherine Conder had been 7 years old when her grandfather died. I am sure both Frankau and Dale took some of the personal details of Charles Digby from this source.

Her account of the early days of Harrods differs somewhat from other observers, attributing little of the vision of the future shop to her great-grandfather, who she calls 'Henry Charles' rather than Charles Henry Harrod. He must have called himself Henry at some time as the sign in the windows of his early shop was 'H.C. Harrod'.

Although she denied bias, she was obviously a fan of Charles Digby Harrod. The start of her talk began thus:

The task of preparing the 'Story of Mr C.D. Harrod' has been considerably more difficult than I anticipated when I cheerfully accepted Mr Lawe's invitation to come here and tell it. During his lifetime, and he died a little past middle age, the significance of his achievement had scarcely begun to be appreciated so that, while there are of course, records of the development of his work, there are but few records of the man himself. The two, naturally, are inseparably bound, and the best I have been able to do is to piece together the records of the development of Harrods Stores with personal reminiscences of those who had intimate personal contact with its founder and so to sketch a portrait that I hope is in due proportion and likeness to the original.

I must ask you throughout the narration to dissociate me as far as possible from the bias of personal relationship. My grandfather died when I was only a small child and I have but few, though very happy, memories of him. Ancestor worship forms but little part of the modern creed, and so I hope you will regard me as quite detachedly interested, as I feel myself to be.

At the same time, I must admit that I have been able to discover very few faults recorded against him.

In his case it seems that the Shakespeare dictum has been reversed; the good that he did lives after him, the evil, if any, was interred with his bones.

The first Harrods shop in Brompton Road was founded by my great-grandfather, Henry Charles Harrod, in 1849, a small but 'select' grocer's shop which he had thought little of extending. Charles Digby Harrod left school at about 16 years of age, and entered a wholesale grocery business in the city. He very soon began to dream dreams and see visions of the possibilities for the development of his father's business, but he was not then allowed to put them into practice. However, he cherished them secretly and used those years of minority to exercise his own powers of observation, to watch the ways and means of current trade and commerce and to think out schemes for making his visions into practical realities.

In 1861, Henry Charles Harrod withdrew from the business and Charles Digby, at the age of 23 reigned in his father's stead. [He would in fact have been aged 20 when he took over in 1861].

For five years longer he continued his observations, meanwhile consolidating the business as it stood, winning and extending the favour of his clientele with reliable goods, attractively displayed, and by unfailing personal attention to the personal requirements of his customers.

Like most young men, Charles Digby was bursting with new ideas and I suspect his father would likely have advised restraint. It says something about the success of the shop that in those early 'consolidation' years between 1861 and 1864 Charles Digby was able to pay back his father at the end of that three-year period.

Charles and Caroline's first child, Fanny Elizabeth, was born in 1865, just over nine months after their marriage, and their second child, Grace

Miriam, followed soon after in 1866. The growing family soon began to put a strain on the accommodation, at the same time as Charles Digby wanted to expand the store and its products. A move elsewhere for the family was inevitable. Returning to Miss Conder's talk:

> By 1866 his plan of attack was ready. He had observed that West End shops were charging exorbitant prices, mainly because they were forced, on the one hand to allow their customers 2 or 3 years credit, and on the other to give large bribes to the servants in order to retain the patronage which their employers left to a great extent in their hands.

The family moved out in 1868. He started adding his first new sections to the shop and building a new shop front. He stepped up the pace of expansion, adding 'departments' selling furniture, perfume, china, and glassware.

He decided to take a gamble, hoping for increased trade by curtailing the ridiculous and exorbitant prices being demanded by the old established businesses in the West End.

The changes that took place were not aimed at the upmarket trade which has characterised the development of the shop in the last century, but were intended to increase the volume of sales, with good quality and value for money.

He did not employ 'barkers', as some shops did, but sent out discreet circulars to the better-class houses, listing his offerings. A barker was an employee who stood in front of the shop or walked the local streets to solicit customers by shouting out his loud sales spiel.

The key to this growth was his adoption of the 'co-operative' method of retailing, whereby the shopkeeper was able to charge low prices by taking cash only and refusing credit. He advertised his shop and selling methods, pointing out good things were to be bought on his premises at a small cost for a strictly cash payment.

At around the same time, the Post Office Supply Association was formed using similar methods, 'for the purpose of supplying officers of the Post Office and their friends with articles of all kinds for domestic consumption and general use, at the lowest wholesale prices'. It became the Civil Service Supply Association in 1866 and with membership exceeding 3,000, presented a real threat to Charles.

Charles Digby was not going to take this challenge lying down. He had seen the possibilities of publicity, and he hit back. In that year, he placed announcements in the *Times*, *Morning Post* and the *Pall Mall Gazette*, London's newest evening paper, and other papers. They proved a great success. The adverts proclaimed such bargains as 'Harrods sells 7 pounds of rice for 1/-.' He announced the installation of new plate-glass windows in late 1866 and that became reality in 1867, quite a novelty at that time. In the window behind there were no goods displayed, just the slogan 'Co-operative Prices'.

Crowds came to test the value for cash, and the business grew by leaps and bounds; so rapidly that it became necessary to build on to the premises every few years. The takings increased and the staff numbers were gradually expanded from the five in 1866. He later built a two-storey extension and opened new departments. By degrees, most of the shops down the same side of the street were bought and swallowed up by Harrods, beginning with Nos 101 and 103 Brompton Road in 1874.

Charles Digby saved by keeping the business in personal ownership rather than forming a company. The local co-operatives put up the fiercest of battles, but not for long. His methods meant he was able to compete keenly on price and success followed. After his brother, Henry Digby, left Brompton Road and went to live and work in Old Compton Street, Charles realised he needed additional management help, and preferably from within the family. In 1868, Charles Digby was joined by his cousin, William Kibble, who would have then been aged 16. William was the fifth child of James Kibble, a baker, who was Caroline Godsmark's uncle. James and Charles Digby were first cousins by marriage.

William Kibble was born in 1852 in Camberwell and went to school in Guildford. He is said to have learnt the trade at the Clapham Stores, with owners Walter and Mary Viney, although this has proved difficult to confirm. William went to Covent Garden each day and bought fresh fruit and vegetables. They were the best in the area. He proved to be a great asset.

William worked in Harrods as a manager for many years, retaining the role of grocery buyer until 1920. He was still working there when the book, *Modern Men of Mark*, was written, as he is mentioned there, 'It is interesting to note that some of those working for the firm then [the 1860s] are working for it still. William Kibble, the grocery buyer being one, and under his control grew other departments, patent medicines, perfumery and stationery.'

William is shown in the 1871 census working as a 'shopman' at Brompton Road. Some of the living accommodation had obviously been retained as he was living at the shop with two other young men, also listed as shopmen. Kibble subsequently married and lived in Lewisham, but later moved to Ovington Street, just behind Harrods. They had three children but sadly his wife died a year after the last child was born. The children went to live with William's unmarried brother and sister in Lewisham, whilst William continued working at Harrods and living close to the shop. He was obviously unstintingly faithful.

William became close to the family and was known as 'Uncle Willie'. Having devoted much of his life to Harrods, at the cost of not living with his children for some time, when Harrods was no longer in the family he moved back to Clapham to live with the Vineys.

An article appeared in the July 1935 edition of the *Harrodian Gazette* (the in-house staff magazine) describing William Kibble's early days. Mr Kibble was visited by the writer in Clapham Common, where he then lived aged 83. The article gives a unique insight into the shop of 1868. William was described as 'the oldest, and one of the most notable of our pensioners'. The article continues:

> Although it is as long as 68 years since he started working with his cousin Charlie Harrod, today Mr Kibble, who was then known as 'William', is alert and cheerful; in fact it does not seem possible that he has been living in comfortable retirement for 15 years. Going back to his early days with the Firm, Mr Kibble has some

delightful tales to tell. Imagine Harrods being one narrow shop in Brompton Road instead of occupying a whole block as well as 3 other buildings in the vicinity! The shop front was built on to the house where Mrs Harrod lived with her 2 children, and there was a tidy piece of garden but no back door. When William started work, at the early age of 16, the chief trouble was lack of space. There was no room for storage – all the goods had to be delivered at the shop door, even when customers were waiting to be served. The vans belonging to the manufacturers caused such serious traffic blockage that the policemen from Hyde Park Corner would walk up to settle it. By the way, Brompton Road was an extremely busy thoroughfare – one bus passed each way every half hour. Now for the staff. There were four counter men as well as Mr Harrod himself, and one odd job man whose duties were legion. He unpacked the goods, kept the stock, wrapped parcels for customers, cleaned the floor and last but not least, made the deliveries. On a busy day he would have to hire a barrow from a neighbour at the rate of 2*d* an hour! The men, including William, lived over the shop and had their meals with Mr Harrod. The hours were 8 a.m. till 9 p.m. except for Saturday, which was an extra busy time and the shop stayed open until 11 p.m. Mr Kibble remembers there being trouble one Saturday night, because one by one the men, who had their tea at 5 and worked until 11, left the shop during the evening to get refreshment. The following week, Mr Harrod anticipated them and provided a pint of beer all round at 9 p.m.

By 1867, Charles Digby had hired the five employees mentioned above to help sell the widening variety of goods featured at the store. In 1868, the store's payroll jumped to sixteen employees and turnover had risen from about £200 per week to £1,000 per week. The weekly wage bill was £15, including 10*s* each to two boys in white aprons who delivered goods.

During the 1860s and 1870s Charles Digby must have been a well-known figure in the area. He was great friends with some local men: young Mr Tattersall, of Tattersall's horse dealers' fame, who had re-sited their premises close to Harrods; and James Chatten, a general dealer and hansom cab owner. All three were noted for their sartorial elegance and were referred to in an article in the *Punch* of the times, as 'the three best-dressed young blades of Knightsbridge'.

In 1870, the first Harrods catalogue was published – the *Harrods Grocery Book*. It was a small booklet advertising 'Best Articles at Co-operative Prices'. Finest Teas were 2*s* 8*d* per lb, 5*s* for 2lb, Huntley and Palmer's biscuits were 6*d* per lb and Pears Transparent Soap 9*d* a ball. Charles Digby was reputedly the first person to import tinned fruit into this country. The catalogue stated, 'Prices for cash Only'.

The rate of change in the premises became almost maniacal. In 1872 Charles Digby built over the garden of No. 103. He bought a shop in Queens Gardens to act as a warehouse and then found it was not enough. Around this time, he acquired his first van to allow Harrods to match the delivery service that the Co-op stores already offered. In 1873 he added a two-storey extension at the back, in what had been his garden, and continued to build up its range of goods. This provided additional space for flowers, fruit and vegetables and cooked meats, and importantly a second-floor counting house! Probably in 1874, he acquired the leases to Nos 101 and 103 Brompton Road, adjacent to the east boundary of the shop, from Mr Stewart, a milliner. He faced the whole lot with new plate glass and above this appeared the name of the shop, 'HARRODS STORES'. This extension allowed perfumery, medicine and stationery departments to be added, and later confectionery, china and flowers.

Another *Harrodian Gazette* article, from May 1925, documents life at the shop in 1873. This edition noted the retirement of two faithful employees. One of these was Mr William Ball who left after thirty-four years of interrupted service. In the article he stated:

> I started work for Harrods in 1873. At that time Harrods was a very small shop and I occupied the position of errand boy, having to push a heavy truck about the roads, which in those days were none too smooth. After a time business began to improve and Mr Harrod realised that the work was getting too heavy for the truck boy, and

he hired a horse and van. I was then given the job as vanguard; in this job I soon learnt the way to drive a horse. As the business improved, so Mr Harrod hired another van and numbered them 1 and 2. Our first stables were at Walter Robertson's Yard, Paradise Walk, Queens Road, Chelsea [just north of the Embankment]. My first horse was named 'Razor', (a beautiful creature), and he was the start of horse power at the Stores.

As years went by the number of horses and vans increased and we stabled at our own stable in Turks Row, which is now Sloane Court [just south of Sloane Square], I then had a horse named 'Kitty', better known in those days as 'Mother Ball'.

The year 1874 was celebrated as the store's silver jubilee year. To put the date into a historical perspective: this was the year Disraeli came to power and passed eleven major Acts of social reform in the following two years – the Factory Act introduced the reduced fifty-six-hour week; Prince Alfred, son of Queen Victoria, then the Duke of Edinburgh, married Maria Alexandrovna, daughter of the Emperor of Russia; Hardy wrote *Far From the Madding Crowd*; and Verdi wrote his *Requiem*.

Stories of Charles Digby's business methods abound. He expected the same dedication from his staff as he himself gave. Reputedly, he installed a removable staircase at his employees' entrance and took it away at 8 a.m. whether everyone had arrived or not. Store employees who arrived later could not get in and lost their pay for the day. He would fine employees who were late at the rate of 1½*d* per quarter of an hour. This sounds hard-hearted, but he did use the carrot as well as the stick. Contrary to the usual practice, from 1882 he would pay 1*s* an hour for overtime, and half a sovereign was produced from his long silk purse for employees going on holiday. They were given one week's holiday after eighteen months' service.

Despite his harsh methods, he retained the respect and trust of his staff, and although he displayed an apparently abrupt manner from time to time, his kindness was to be seen on many occasions. It was recorded that once he pulled aside an assistant who was serving a poor woman and said, 'Let her have anything she needs in reason. Charge my account. Tell her it's a present.'

During this period, when Charles and his family were living in Ditton, near Esher, he would leave home at 6 a.m. and arrive at Harrods at 7 a.m. He stipulated that staff should arrive for work with clean faces. His formula for engaging a new assistant was abrupt and direct, something like, 'Start next Friday – 7.30 a.m. in the grocery – bring clean smock – ditto face – nine shillings per week.' It was accepted that employment could be terminated at a minute's notice from either side. It was often said by employees about Mr Harrod, 'at least you know where you are with him.'

According to his great-granddaughter, Jean Pitt, every morning he lined up his delivery men and made them sing 'Lead Kindly Light' before they set off for the day. Despite the increasing numbers of staff, Miss Conder in her talk points out:

> C.D. Harrod made it his business to know each and the work of each, down to the youngest and humblest worker. In this way he was accorded a loyalty which was to stand him in good stead in the Crisis of the House of Harrod.

Having started his revolution with selling volume cheaply, as success continued Charles Digby tried to encourage more wealthy people to visit his store and provided a personalised service for important customers. They found him 'so handsome, so honest and so obliging' that he soon built up a fine reputation for himself in the neighbourhood. He abolished 'cook's perks', the traditional prerequisite for servants who bought their masters' provisions at the store. He managed to increase trade by introducing his own-brand groceries, patriotically packaged in the colours of the Union Jack (this *may* have been copied since!). He attracted custom by delivering all goods free of charge. His decision not to employ barkers to attract custom, preferring to circulate lists of the produce on offer to local houses, led to the production of lists like the 1870 *Grocery Book*. His merchandising skills would not be out of place today.

By the late 1870s, the continued success of the business prompted a further move for the family to the leafy suburbs, and by the end of that decade the store boasted more than 100 employees. Considerable rebuilding followed and further departments were added. By 1883 the number of employees had risen to over 150, and there were numerous separate departments. According to the *Chelsea Herald*, Harrod's business, 'which at one time was a purely local one, is now worldwide, and his clients – or customers – rank from the "Peer to the peasant"'.

On 8 January 1880, Charles Digby used the first full-column advertisement in the *Times* to publicise the shop and the goods on offer. It consisted of dozens of mini adverts taking up the whole of the last column. Charles Digby was keen on detail. In the June 1923 edition of the *Harrodian Gazette*, the retirement of a Mr Clancy was recorded after forty-two years of service. He had started working there in 1881. After a presentation, he replied with:

> … much emotion, said how sorry he was to go. Through the generosity of the Company, he was retiring on a very good pension. He spoke of the happy times he had had whilst at the Stores. He said, 'I entered the business in 1881. In those days, the Stores consisted of Grocery, Provisions, Ironmongery, Turnery, China and Patent Medicines. There was only one entrance, where the Perfumery door is now. The Office lay at the end of the long Grocery shop. Here worked the Governor, one Mail Order Clerk and one Porters' Cash Clerk. One Country Ledger was kept, one Town and one To Pay Ledger. The Governor kept the Bought Ledger himself. Hours were from 8.30 a.m. to 9 p.m …
>
> The Country Orders were copied into a quarto sized book with pen. Any Country Orders with addresses of which the Governor was not conversant were made 'pro forma' (in those days it was called 'Label', because a label was stuck on the bill asking for payment).

Tallis map of London 1838–40, showing 228 Boro' High Street and the entrance to Maidstone Buildings.

Photograph of Charles Henry Harrod in mid life. (Harrods)

Ambrotype of Elizabeth Digby between 1850 and 1860. (Harrods)

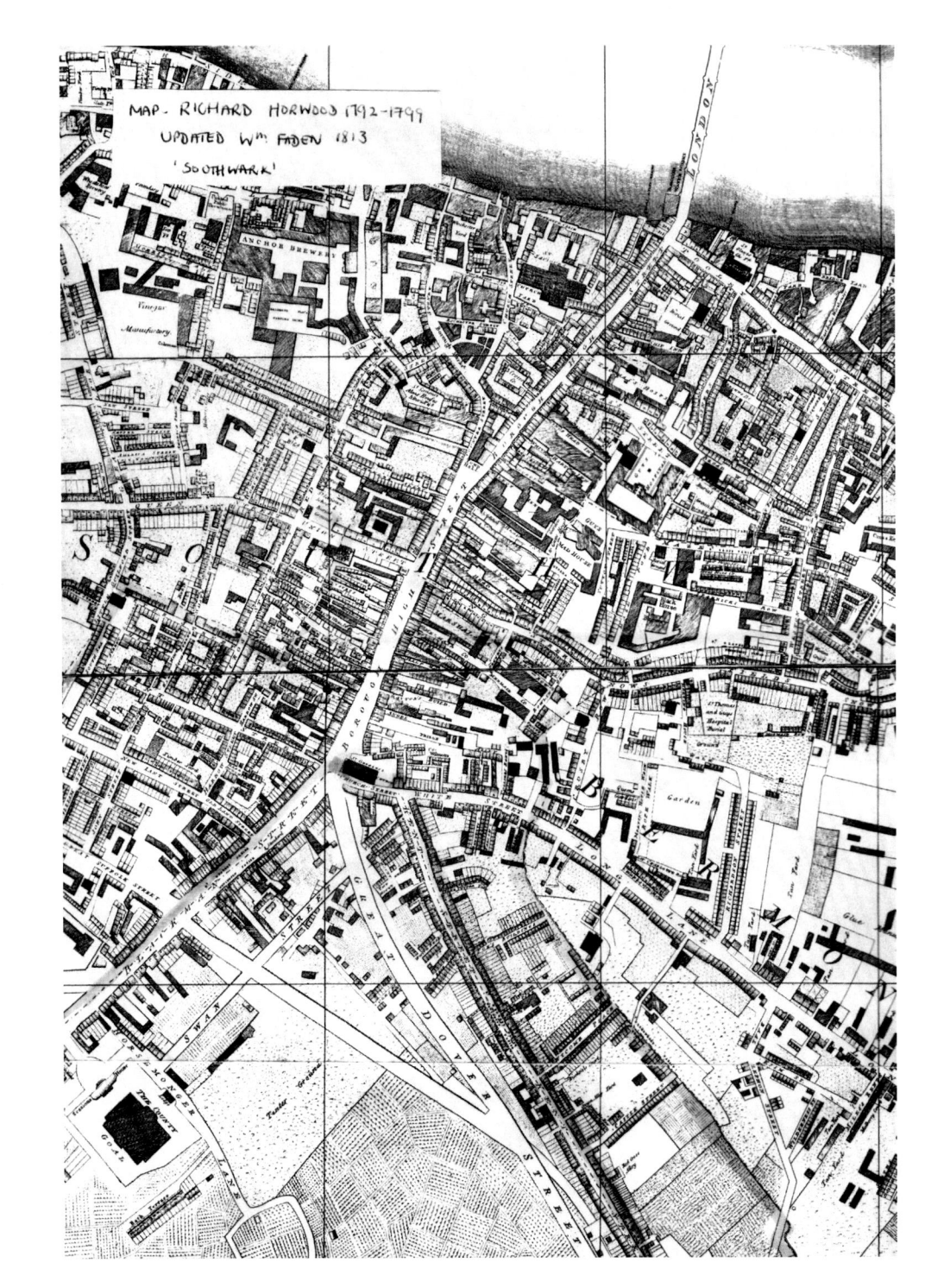

MAP- RICHARD HORWOOD 1792-1799
UPDATED Wm. FADEN 1813
'SOUTHWARK'

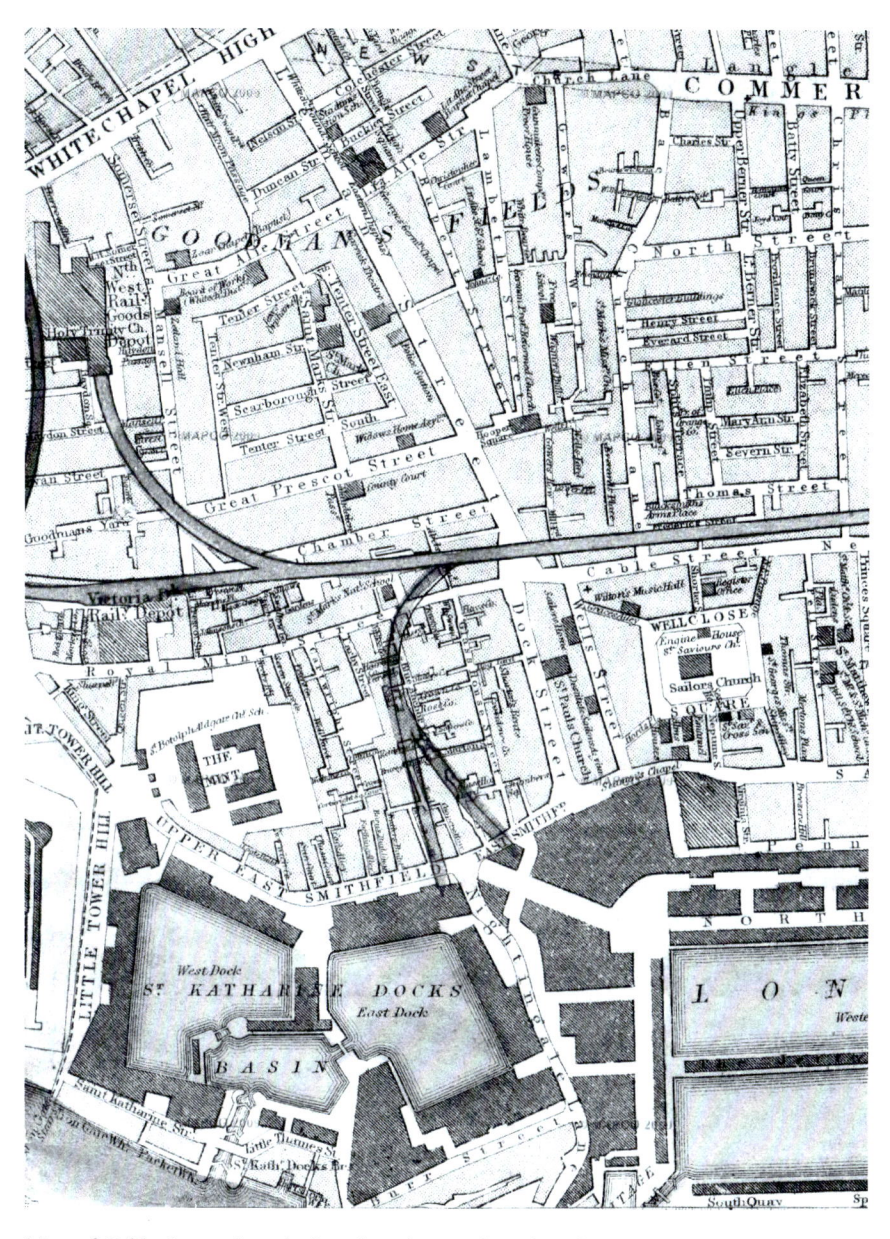

Map of Cable Street Area in London, from Edward Weller's map of London, 1868.

Opposite: Horwood's map of Southwark, 1792–99, updated by Wm. Faden in 1813.

Artist's impression of Harrods shop in 1849, produced for the Harrods centenary in 1949. (Harrods)

Copy painting of Charles Henry Harrod. Date and artist unknown. (Harrods)

Photograph and copy painting of Elizabeth Harrod née Digby. (Harrods)

Possible photograph of Elizabeth Harrod née Digby in old age. (Harrods)

Portrait of Charles Digby Harrod in his prime. (James Weightman)

Photograph of Caroline Harrod née Godsmark, wife of Charles Digby Harrod, and their four eldest children in about 1872. (Natalie Oliver)

Photograph of Caroline Harrod – disputed whether née Godsmark or Wade – in mid-life. (Jean Pitt)

Artists impression of the 1883 fire. (Fred Taylor / Harrods)

December 6th, 1883

Map of Brompton Road in 1885 showing the site of the new Harrods. (British History Online)

Harrods frontage in late 1890. (Harrods)

Harrods frontage about 1901 showing Queens Gardens entrance. (Harrods)

HARRODS' STORES, Ltd.
BROMPTON ROAD, LONDON, S.W.

1889   **1890**

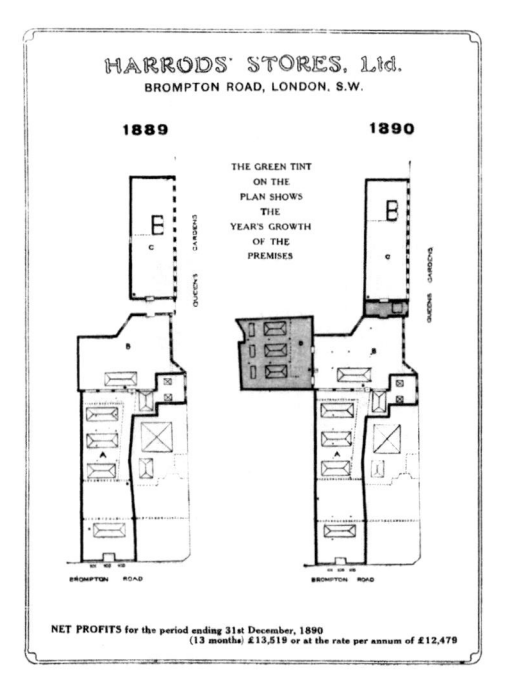

THE GREEN TINT ON THE PLAN SHOWS THE YEAR'S GROWTH OF THE PREMISES

NET PROFITS for the period ending 31st December, 1890
(13 months) £13,519 or at the rate per annum of £12,479

HARRODS' STORES, Ltd.
BROMPTON ROAD, LONDON, S.W.

1891

THE GREEN TINT ON THE PLAN SHOWS THE YEAR'S GROWTH OF THE PREMISES

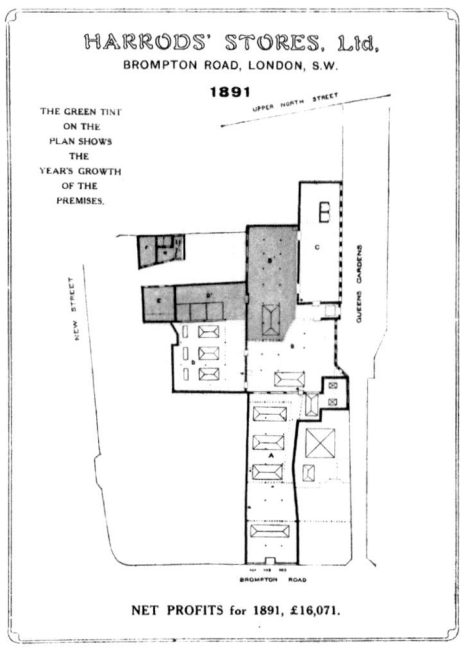

NET PROFITS for 1891, £16,071.

HARRODS' STORES, Ltd.
BROMPTON ROAD, LONDON, S.W.

1893

THE GREEN TINT ON THE PLAN SHOWS THE YEAR'S GROWTH OF THE PREMISES.

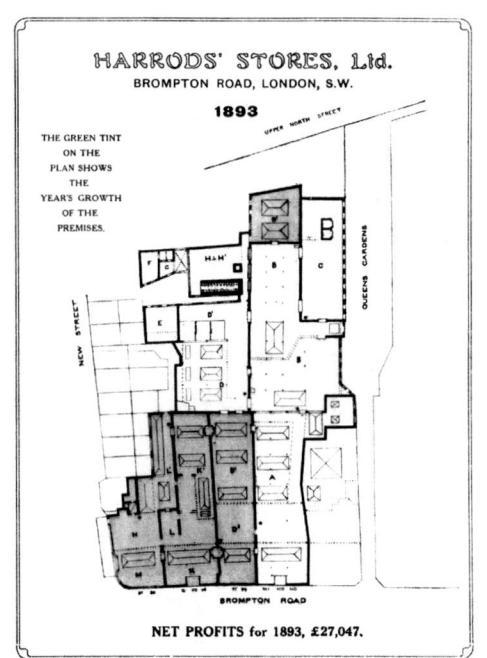

NET PROFITS for 1893, £27,047.

HARRODS' STORES, Ltd.
BROMPTON ROAD, LONDON, S.W.

1895

THE GREEN TINT ON THE PLAN SHOWS THE YEAR'S GROWTH OF THE PREMISES.

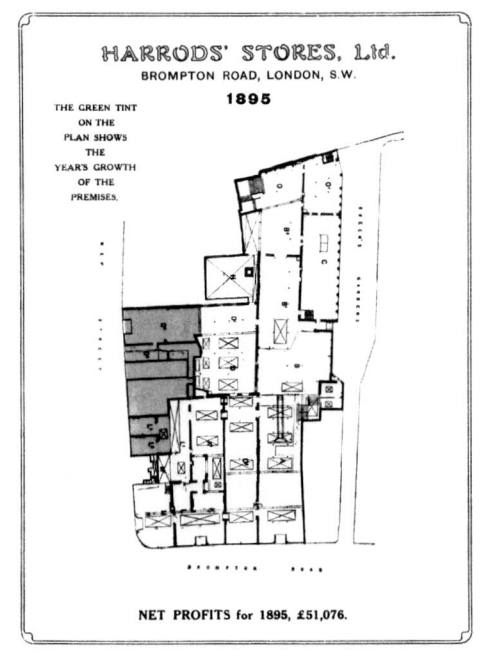

NET PROFITS for 1895, £51,076.

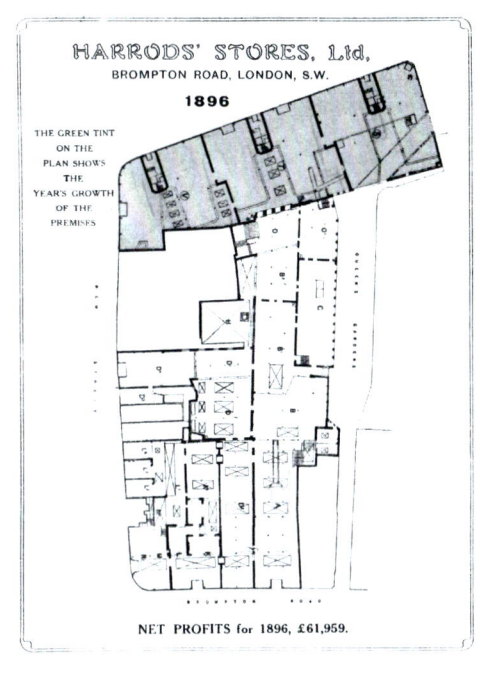

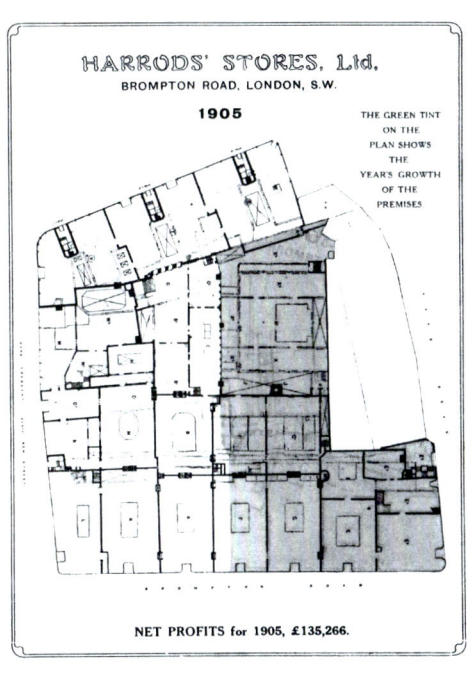

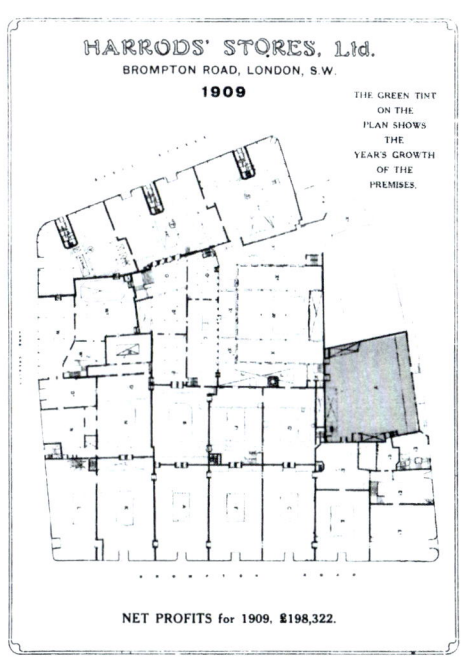

The series of floor plans showing the growth of the building from 1889 to 1909. (Harrods)

Beatrice Martha Harrod and daughter at the 1949 Centenary set of Charles Henry Harrod in his shop. (Harrods)

Photograph of William Kibble 1903. (Harrods)

Morebath Manor interior in the early twentieth century.

The front entrance to Morebath Manor in the early twentieth century. A coach is waiting and is thought to contain Charles Digby Harrod and some of his family. (Jean Pitt)

Culverwood House before 1945. (Mobbs Pitcher)

Edgar Cohen and his brother in Greece in the 1870s. (Harrods)

Richard Burbidge and his wife on honeymoon in 1868. (Harrods)

Richard Burbidge in later life. (Carol Samuel)

CHARLES DIGBY TAKES OVER

Charles Digby's dedication to his business was legendary. His youngest daughter Eva told her relatives the story of her father being thwarted in an attempt to get to Harrods one day by the thick fogs which, in those days, often enveloped parts of London. Having failed by cab, he set off walking to the store preceded by footmen with lanterns – he got there.

In 1883, Harrod bought a large piece of land at the back of the premises and began building again. This was almost completed by Christmas 1883, which promised to be the best Christmas ever. By early December the store was overflowing with merchandise in readiness for the rush.

Everything that Charles Digby could have wished for was coming to pass. The store was successful; probably more successful than he could have dreamed was possible. It had grown in size and prestige, and the profits had allowed him and his family to live a very comfortable existence in increasingly grand accommodation. It was all going so well. When the family moved out of Brompton Road to make room for expansion, Charles and Caroline's two daughters were 3 years and 18 months old. They moved initially to a sequence of houses in the London area, and then later into 'the country'.

Charles Digby's family life can be followed by using the births of the other six of their eight children in order to trace the moves to their various residences. Neither the records, nor any information gained from existing family members, have revealed what sort of parents Charles and Caroline proved to be. The impression I have gained is that Charles Digby was a loving father and much respected by the family. During the children's early lives, at least until Charles Digby retired later in the century, the children can only have caught fleeting glimpses of their father as he built up the business and worked long hours, six days per week. He left home at 6 a.m. and might not be back until 9 p.m., although Sunday would be the family day.

The Harrod family's circumstances gradually became more comfortably and Caroline had more help in the form of servants. In this way, the Harrod family probably did not differ much from many affluent middle-class Victorian families. Their first new home was 2 Hill Street,

Knightsbridge, and soon after their move in 1868 a further daughter had arrived, who they called Emily Maud. They would have been very pleased to have three healthy daughters, but I suspect Charles Digby might have wondered when his son and successor would be born.

Hill Street no longer exists, having changed its name to Trevor Place in 1936. It was just south of Knightsbridge and Kensington Road, opposite the west end of Hyde Park Barracks and north of Brompton Road. The house would have been about 200 yards away from Harrods, so a short walk to work for the man who had so recently lived above the shop and liked to start early. It was part of a terrace of brick houses, four or five storeys high. A photograph from 1993 found on British History Online shows the east side of Hill Street, or Trevor Place, and No. 2 can be identified. The house is three windows wide with a much lower building on the north, which was originally the stables, and a row of slightly lower terraced houses to the south. It was a grand town house for the family

In 1870, whilst still living at Hill Street, Charles and Caroline's next child was born. At last it was a boy. They named the son and heir Henry Herbert. Hence, in the 1871 census the household consisted of the four children and their parents. There were also three servants, comprising a cook, a housemaid and one general domestic servant. There are a few photographs of Caroline and the children, one showing the four children including a baby Henry Herbert. It was probably taken for Henry's christening in December 1870. There are no known photographs of Charles Digby with his wife or children. He may have been camera shy, or just too busy.

Charles Digby, by now 30 years of age, must have been relieved to have a boy, hopefully his successor for the business. Perhaps this relief slowed down the reproductive drive for a while – having had four children in almost six years, there followed a gap of four and a half years with no children. The family lived in Hill Street between 1868 and 1874, although an 1876 directory still lists Charles Digby there, and an electoral register list his name there in 1885. It is likely, then, that he retained the house or the lease after the family had moved out, and continued to use it as a pied-à-terre.

CHARLES DIGBY TAKES OVER

By the time of the birth of their fifth child in March 1875, the Harrod family had moved again, this time 'out of town' to Esher. It was another girl, their fourth, and they called her Amy Caroline. Amy's birth certificate actually gives the address as Ditton Marsh, Thames Ditton, but this is just on the eastern border of the parish of Esher, very much in the countryside. Although now not within walking distance of his shop, Esher was probably a very convenient place to live, as it was both on a main road and had a railway station with a good service.

The family only remained in the Esher area for a year or two, and by 1877 they were in Sydenham, which became the family home for the next fourteen years. Their new house, Armitage Lodge, in Wells Road, Sydenham was one of two detached houses (the other, The Woodlands, was also called Claverhouse) built in Wells Road in the early 1850s for Edward Saxton, a local solicitor. They were of high specification and 'state of the art' for the era. Though I tried to take a look, I found that the house was demolished some years ago. With the aid of the local studies librarian in Lewisham, the site was found at the Sydenham Hill end of the road, which is now called Wells Park Road.

Sydenham Hill itself was above and behind the house, which had superb views across the countryside southwards. The road winds down round the north side of the hill to become Wells Road as it descends on the other side. Less than a mile to the south, the family would have been able to see the famous Crystal Palace, which was moved there from its original site in Hyde Park. It was built originally for the Great Exhibition in 1851, when Charles Digby would have been 10 years old, and it is likely he would have been taken there with his brothers whilst they were living in Brompton; he might now have taken his own children to the Crystal Palace site.

Sydenham Hill Station was opened in 1863 to cope with visitors to the Crystal Palace, but was not convenient for that attraction. It would initially have been the nearest station for the Harrods on Wells Road. When Upper Sydenham Railway Station was opened in 1884 by the South Eastern & Chatham Railway, this was even more convenient for the family. It was just below the house and across the Wells Road, with the rail tunnel running under the hill. Charles Digby would then have been able to linger at home until the last minute before crossing the road for his train. The ticket office was on the Wells Road just above the tunnel entrance. The trains ran into Victoria Station, a brisk walk away from the store. The station was never financially successful, but despite that, apart from spells closed during both wars, it remained open until 1954.

Some years later, the name of the house was changed from Armitage Lodge to Greyfriars, and when demolished in around 1970 it was replaced by several blocks of flats that were given the same name. I found no trace of the house on a visit to Wells Park Road in 2009. A search below the Wells Park Road revealed the remains of the station with the original booking office, which still stands on the road at the top of a steep flight of stairs.

Armitage Lodge was apparently a grand nineteenth-century villa and very modern in its day. It had airy nurseries, a bath with running hot water and ample stabling. It was a house to suit a man of means with a growing family. The 1911 census shows the house had sixteen main rooms. Charles and Caroline's sixth child, another girl, was born in Sydenham in 1877. She was Beatrice Martha – my grandmother. Their last two children were also born in Sydenham, and Charles Digby was doomed to one boy and a house full of girls. Olive Mary was born in 1880, and Eva Marguerita in 1881. According to her family, Eva was named after 'Little Eva', a character in the popular novel *Uncle Tom's Cabin*.

There is a family photograph of the nanny or nurse in the Harrod household holding a child in a long christening dress. She was probably Harriet Pocock, who appears in the 1881 census staying with the family in Sydenham. The baby could be any of the last three girls, but I suspect it would have been Eva, as Harriet is listed as aged 42 in the census and looks at least that age in the photograph. Together with the four children and the nurse in that 1881 census were two other servants.

During the family's stay in Sydenham, in 1887 the eldest daughter, Fanny, was married in a Nonconformist church in Upper Norwood, whilst their second daughter, Grace, was married in 1889 in a Nonconformist church in Kensington after they had moved back into London. Both girls had married into families containing Nonconformist preachers.

Frankau lists 1882 as the date that Charles Digby became a Congregationalist. Certainly he came from a Nonconformist family background, but after retirement in the last decade of the century he frequented local Anglican parish churches rather than Nonconformist alternatives. He seems to have switched his allegiance several times, like his father, depending upon the availability of places of worship and perhaps just going with the flow. He was a man for all seasons …

6

OUT OF
THE ASHES

In 1883, Harrod bought a large piece of land at the back of the premises and began expanding again. This was almost completed by Christmas 1883, which promised to be the best Christmas ever. By early December the store was overflowing with merchandise in readiness for the rush. However, tragedy was just around the corner.

Harrods was still traditional in many ways, and the window displays in the store were lit with gas jets which burned all night, both to illuminate the goods and put off the local burglars. The second half of 1883 had seen some remarkable atmospheric and weather events after the major eruption of Krakatoa in Java in August. It had been cold and windy, and it was a foul winter's night on 6 December 1883, with temperatures that fell below freezing, wind and snow.

William Kibble was the last to leave the shop that night, together with another faithful servant of the company, Mr Gearing, the despatch manager. Whether the curtains blew into the gaslight jet because of the high wind or whether workmen in the basement had left a candle burning which caught alight is not known. What is known is that Mr Gearing was woken at midnight to be told that Harrods Stores was burning. His account in the archives tells us that he went round at once, and on seeing how serious the fire was, despatched Mr Gamble, another assistant, in a hansom cab to fetch Charles Digby from Sydenham. This journey would have taken about two hours.

In 1883, neither Harrods Stores nor Charles Digby in Sydenham were on the new telephone system. Alexander Bell had demonstrated the telephone first in 1876, and by 1880 the new device was spreading rapidly in the British Isles. It was not until 1886 that 'C.D. Harrod' was first listed as having a telephone at Brompton Road with the number 8542. The entry changed to 'Harrods Stores' after 1891.

Mr Gearing watched the fire all night; Charles Digby arrived at about six in the morning. Allegedly, on being told of the fire, his first question was 'is anybody hurt?' He sent 'every expensive delicacy the store could provide, and a dozen bottles of Martell Brandy' to an employee who had been hurt whilst saving stock.

At a blow, all his hard work and hopes seemed to have been wiped out. The newspaper reports were legion, and detailed the events at some length. It was reported in local London newspapers, national newspapers and even in the local press elsewhere in the country, from Nottingham to Aberdeen. Although the amount of cover amounts almost to overkill they do give quite an insight into the problems of urban fires in that era. One report read:

Fires. The men and engines of the Metropolitan Fire Brigade were busily engaged for several hours yesterday morning at the West-end in endeavouring to extinguish two fires which broke out within a short time of each other. The more destructive of the two was discovered a few minutes after 1 o'clock at Nos 101, 103 and 105 Brompton Road, the premises of Mr C.D. Harrod, general stores proprietor. The building was soon burnt out; and a second building of three floors, about 45ft by 27ft, which became involved, and which communicated with the building first mentioned, was also destroyed. The premises numbered 107, adjoining, occupied by E. Jeffcoat, brushmaker, were next attacked, and the back rooms on the first, and second floors, and the front portion of the shop, were greatly damaged by fire. Most serious damage was caused to No. 109, occupied by C. de Costa, Silk Merchant, and by M. Myhill, lodger. The outbreak, the origin of which is unknown, was not finally subdued until 7 o'clock yesterday morning. All the sufferers are insured.

Another report in the *Chelsea Herald* of Saturday 8 December reported as follows:

Tremendous Fires in West London.
Burning of Harrod's Store. Partial Destruction of Ransome's Factory.
　　It is many years since Brompton and Chelsea has been the scene of such conflagrations as those which broke out on Thursday night, and extended far into yesterday [Friday] morning.
　　Most of the residents in this part of the metropolis are familiar with Harrods in the Brompton Road. Situate on the southern side of

the road, near the Knightsbridge end and embracing Nos 101, 103 and 105 in that thoroughfare, they extended back to the cottages in Queens-gardens in the rear, and had been enlarged from time to time to meet the ever increasing volume of business attracted by Mr Harrod's adoption of the Civil Service store system of dealing, until the establishment had grown to enormous dimensions. Within the stores there were separate departments for groceries, provisions, confectionery, wines and spirits, brushes and turnery, ironmongery, glass, china, earthenware, stationery, fancy goods, perfumery, drugs, &c. The provision department was the leading feature of the Stores and during the present week it was being enlarged and further subdivided to cope with the special demands of the coming season.

It is particularly unfortunate that, just at the moment when these gigantic stores had been literally stocked to overflowing with Christmas goods – cosaques and cards and more elaborate presents, to say nothing of the hogsheads, and boxes of comestibles – an outbreak of fire should have occurred.

In the mid 1800s, the first Christmas crackers were quite small, about 6in long, and fairly plain. They were known as *'cosaques'*, French for Cossacks, because the noise they made reminded people of the cracking of the Cossacks' whips as they rode through Paris during the Franco-Prussian War:

Harrod's Stores are now a heap of ruins, and with those buildings other establishments which adjoined – those of Mr Jeffcoat, brushmaker, and of Mr C. DeCosta, draper, have been much injured. Had not a narrow thoroughfare intervened between Mr DeCosta's and the next house leading to the Queens-gardens the fire would have undoubtedly spread further down the road. As it was the Northumberland Arms, which occupies the corner of the other side of the narrow street, was in imminent danger of destruction, and was terrible scorched.

The alarm was raised shortly before midnight, and at half-past one in the morning the fire was at its height. From the raised pavement on the western side of Brompton Road a considerable crowd watched a scene of a splendidly terrible character. Only the skeleton of the three large shops and the stores at the back remained; but the fire raged in a seething mass shooting high up in the air from the inner portion, whilst the flames clung tenaciously to the window frames, mouldings, and other woodwork, thus outlining the structure as if by an intentional illumination. The steam fire engine and hose from the hydrants were pouring tons of water upon the burning mass; but for a time with no apparent effecting even checking the conflagration.

Meantime, in the rear, the scene was of a most exciting character. The wind blew the sparks in clouds, and at length the flames, right over the cottages in Queens Gardens, and across North Street, and even as far as Hans Place. The occupants of the cottages in Queens Gardens were so terrified that some of them removed their goods into the street, whilst women and children were running about excitedly and crying in their terror. Shortly before two o'clock, there was a terrific rush of flame from the rear of the stores, cause apparently by the ignition of a quantity of spirits or other inflammables. The fearful heat thrown out by this caused a general stampede of all who were near the fire, which at that moment seemed to threaten with destruction the whole of the range of private dwellings. Fortunately, however, this was averted. Enormous quantities of water were poured upon the part which connected the business premises with the cottages and thus the latter were saved. The water, moreover, soon had a perceptible effect upon the principal seat of the fire, for by half past two the Fire Brigade had obtained complete mastery over it. Between three and four o'clock it was difficult to approach the ruins owing to the smoke and steam which rose up in clouds from the smouldering mass.

The effect produced in the sky by the fire was most remarkable. Heavy snow clouds hung over Western London, and the reflection of the flames upon them, as seen from the Strand resembled in its brilliant grandeur some of those phenomenal sunsets which have lately excited general attention.

Engines from the following stations combined in their attack upon the burning mass:– Relton Street, Brompton, Paddington, Kensington, Baker Street, North Kensington, Hammersmith, Chandos Street and Southwark Bridge road headquarters. Large crowds of people were to be seen opposite the scene of destruction during the whole of yesterday [Friday]. A more complete wreck could scarcely be imagined; and up till after mid-day firemen were engaged with stand-pipes in soaking the ruins, which were still smouldering. Mingled with the charred remains of the timber and party-walls were remains of wine cases, potted meats, and provisions of every description.

The amount of damage cannot yet be estimated, but it is supposed to be between thirty and fifty thousand pounds [about £4 million today]. On the most prominent part of the ruins, fronting the Brompton Road, printed notices have been posted stating that arrangements are being made to carry on the business.

Mr Harrod will resume business in a few days on the opposite side of the road.

Superintendent Hambling, Inspectors Cronin, Jordan, Collins and Denton, 13 sergeants and 250 constables were present at the fire, the latter under their officers doing valuable service.

Mr Jeffcoat's shop and premises are almost wrecked. Mr De Costa's are also greatly injured at the back. Both shops are closed and barricaded at the front. Mr Pring's premises on the other side are slightly injured at the rear, and Nos 1 and 2 Queens Gardens have also been somewhat damaged.

Despite the mayhem caused by this fire, Harrods' customers received a letter from Charles Digby the following day, headed with the address of 101/103/105 Brompton Road, and dated 7 December. It read:

Madam,

I greatly regret to inform you that, in consequence of the above premises being burnt down, your order will be delayed in the execution by a day or two. I hope, in the course of Tuesday or Wednesday next, to be able to forward it to you.

In the meantime may I ask you for your kind indulgence.

Your obedient servant,

C.D. Harrod

PS All communications to be addressed to 78 Brompton Road.

No. 78 was exactly opposite 101 Brompton Road and Queens Gardens and on the corner of Lancelot Place where Charles Digby had premises for stabling his horses. Lancelot Place is these days the site of a very prestigious development. It was used during this emergency as the office, and a temporary shop space was found at No. 83.

Charles Digby posted an advertisement in the *St James's Gazette* of 7 December. It read:

FIRE NOTICE – HARROD'S STORES. 101/103/105 Brompton Road.
Arrangements are being made for RECOMMENCING BUSINESS which C.D. HARROD hopes will be completed in a day or two.

Some of the reports in country newspapers were very short, but gave different details. The *Exeter Flying Post* of 12 December stated that the fire had been spotted by a passing cabman, who alerted a policeman. The policeman called out the Ralton Mews Fire Station which was just 200 yards away. The paper reported that there were several thousand spectators for the fire.

There are many different accounts of the event and the aftermath, each based on the perspective of the witness. Some seem to have been trying to maximise their part in the rescue operation. Mr Clancy, in his retirement article quoted earlier, gave a description of his part in the fire:

> I arrived at business one morning to find the place in ruins. There had been a fire, the place was gutted, and nothing saved except the safe containing the Ledgers. Number 88 Brompton Road [does he mean no. 83?] was immediately opened as a Grocers and we carried on in a back room for the Office. Subsequently Humphrey's Hall was taken. This was a large Hall in the High Road opposite the Barracks. This Hall eventually became the Japanese Village, which a few years after, curiously enough, was destroyed by fire with loss of life

Humphreys Hall consisted of a large iron structure, and was well known to the late Victorian public as the venue for a series of exhibitions. The roller-skating rink which became the first Humphreys Hall probably originated within premises used for manufacturing bicycles and sports equipment. Thomas Sparrow and the firm of Sparrow & Spencer occupied these premises for several years in the early and mid 1870s. The skating rink, known as Dungannon Rink, was set up in about 1876 during a brief mania for the sport. Like many others, this rink had fallen out of use by 1880 when it was refitted for a supplier of cut-price food and general produce. In 1882 Dungannon Hall, as the premises had become known, was taken over by James Charlton Humphreys, the iron buildings manufacturer, who adapted and rebuilt it for public use. It hosted many exhibitions, including the Food Exhibition of 1882.

After use by Harrods in 1883, the longest running and most remarkable was the 'Japanese Native Village' which ran from 1885 to 1887. The exhibition employed around 100 Japanese men and women in a setting built to resemble a traditional Japanese village. Whilst Gilbert and Sullivan were writing their opera, *The Mikado*, in 1885 W.S. Gilbert visited the exhibition and engaged Japanese people from the village to teach his cast aspects of Japanese behaviour. The hall was destroyed by fire in May 1885 and a new hall was rapidly built and opened again later that year. It was later extensively reconstructed as the Prince's Racquets and Tennis Club.

William Kibble, in an interview with him for an article in 1935, which was also quoted earlier, was described as:

> … throwing new light on the happenings of that Friday morning … it was he who went across the road to rent another shop and supervised the fitting of shelves. He then had to 'step into a cab' and make for the City, so that the stock could be replenished. Instead of giving large orders to each wholesaler, Mr Kibble bought in small enough quantities, for delivery of all the goods to be made by Monday morning without fail. So it happened that, even without the aid of telephones and motor cars, Harrods was open to the public after the weekend, and, to the outward eye, it appeared very little worse for wear.

It is apparent that the Harrods staff, and William Kibble in particular, acted superbly after the fire and were a great source of support for Charles Digby, who must have been devastated.

Tim Dale reports in his book an item from *The Draper*, which was sent in a letter to William Kibble by a contemporary employee, Mr Wallace Fraser of Fulham. It suggests a different version of the aftermath:

> One day in 1882, Edgar Cohen [then in the sponge business – Cohen & Co.] was going home in an omnibus when a stranger asked him to lend him half a sovereign, saying he had lost his purse and giving him his card, which bore the name of Charles Harrod, and when Cohen obliged, asked for one of his. Charles Digby had been travelling to visit his solicitor in Bloomsbury, and had found he had boarded the horse omnibus without any money.
>
> When the money was returned the next day, Cohen forgot the incident until several months later, a woman's voice spoke to him on the telephone saying she was Mrs Harrod and imploring him to come over and see her husband, who was heartbroken because his store had been burnt down.

Harrod, who was almost prostrate with grief, asked Cohen to take charge. Cohen went to the Haymarket Stores and asked them to deal with all of Harrods' orders, putting Harrods labels on the parcels, and otherwise doing the business as though it were their own.

Then going to the site of a Japanese market which had just closed down near Harrods in Brompton Road, he rented it and opened there a temporary Harrods until the real store was rebuilt.

Well, this is a different story to that given by William Kibble, who didn't mention Edgar Cohen, so it is difficult to know how much credence to give this report. It certainly does not fit in with the 'strong man' and indefatigable image of Charles Digby, but may reflect his need to get as much help as he could after the fire.

There are a few parts of the story that make me wonder about the rest of the report. With the lack of a personal telephone, Mrs Harrod must have used another phone to contact Cohen, and would Charles Digby have taken an omnibus from Bloomsbury rather than a cab? Omnibus services of the day were in the form of mostly double-decker buses drawn by two or three horses abreast. There were numerous services, but they were expensive, overcrowded and relatively slow. They were faster than walking, perhaps a problem for Charles Digby, and much less expensive than a hansom cab. The detail of the solicitor in Bloomsbury rings true; many of the legal profession of the day were located in that area. The jury must remain out.

The *Daily Mail* Harrods centenary issue in 1949 reported another story – although the reader might feel it would, wouldn't it?:

> While others stood watching the final scenes of destruction to the premises, Charles was sitting at a table in a public house nearby organising a new, temporary Harrods, to handle the Christmas trade his competitors thought he had lost.

Was it Charles Digby, William Kibble or Edgar Cohen who saved the day? There was probably some truth in each of the versions.

Haymarket Stores *were* used and Cohen certainly became more deeply involved in the story, as we shall see later. Charles had just seen his life's work destroyed in one night and may have had a reaction to the event after a day or two, and sought help then – he was human, after all.

Soon after the event, in the manner which we might expect of him, Charles Digby proceeded to turn a disaster into a triumph. He was feeling better. Despite the fire, Harrods' trade that Christmas of 1883 was the best Charles Digby had ever achieved. He couldn't wait to get started on a new five-storey building which was to be built on the same site.

Clancy described in 1923 how the work had been continued after the fire:

> The Hall [Humphreys Hall] during our tenancy resembled a huge bazaar, with the departments arranged around the sides, the centre being reserved for stock, and just enough room for customers to move about.
>
> During this time we were executing the Town Orders, but the Country [orders] were sent to the Haymarket Stores, to be debited and executed by a number of Grocers [ours] sent there to work.
>
> I should like to mention that this hall held a Music Licence, and to retain that licence a band performance had to be given once annually. This occurred during our tenancy on one Saturday evening, and you can imagine the excitement and distraction felt, as we were working until 9 p.m.

One can imagine the carnival atmosphere that must have been created with the band.

Whilst the temporary premises continued to trade, the new premises were well on the way. British History Online records:

> In 1884 the old site was hastily reconstructed to the design of Alfred Williams, assistant district surveyor for Kensington, who had been Harrod's architect since at least 1881. The rebuilt store

was little more handsome than its predecessor and perpetuated the single-storey extension towards the street, but it stretched back to embrace many of the old cottage sites on the east side of Queen's Gardens and was of course built on a 'thoroughly fire-proof principle'. General provisions, meat, flowers and fruit were sold at ground level. In the 'warehouse' above were silver goods, lamps, china, saddlery, turnery, ironmongery and brushes. On the second floor along with games were the departments 'sure to find favour with the gentler sex', namely perfumery and patent medicines, while in the attic were beds and bedding. At an intermediate level was a large furniture department. Rebuilding began immediately and the new premises were opened in September 1884.

Remarkably, this was only nine months after the fire. Mr Clancy's report of 1923 continues:

Eventually we got into the new building. This of course was up-to-date, and had all the facilities for new departments, such as Meat, Poultry, Vegetables, Fruit, Confectionery, Wines, Cigars, etc.

The *Chelsea Herald* of 30 August 1884 reported the transformation brought about by the new build, once again at some length, in a piece attributed to a journalist with the nom de plume 'The Baron'. He is rather given to flowery language and long sentences, which identifies him as the likely author of the previous piece. However, the language and detailed description of the shop at that time makes it worth reading:

One of the most noteworthy instances of what energy and perseverance will do is to be found in a visit to the stores that are to be thrown open to the public on Tuesday next, September 2nd.

They are built in the Brompton-road, and are number 101, 103 and 105, and although the absolute frontage is not great, they run back a long distance, and spread over ground in Queens-gardens that but a few months ago was covered by small and dilapidated tenements [the shop frontage was about 180ft].

We have great pleasure in being able to chronicle the result of our lounge over these extensive premises which owe their origin to the father of the present proprietor, and are the outcome of a business started in the most unpretentious manner in Brompton some thirty or forty years ago, at which period the trade was of such limited dimensions that one or two employees were ample, but as the neighbourhood increased – which it did very rapidly – Mr C.D. Harrod grasped the opportunity (which has luckily for him turned out to be a golden one), and finding that so-called Co-operative 'stores', started by government officials, were underselling the retail traders, he resolved to drop the 'shop' and enter the competitive field against those formidable rivals who had already created quite a scare amongst the shop-keeping classes of the community.

He saw clearly that the true system of co-operation meant the entire wiping out of a credit business, and that if he could but secure a cash trade, he could sell in most cases at the same price, but in many, much lower than the newly fashioned establishments, for he would be directly untrammelled by any Board of Directors – a costly article – entrance fees or share liability, three items in a retail business which in themselves mean a large charge on first cost of the articles sold.

As a further thorn in the sides of his opponents he determined to deliver all his goods free, thus serving his customers as they should be served, and not leaving them to carry their parcels away, or be put to the expense of paying an account for carriage; he had clerks to make out the order sheets, and so save customers the annoyance of having to be their own bookkeepers, and above all he guaranteed that his staff should be 'civil', a word only applicable in one sense to many of the employees at the government 'stores'. In other words he wiped out anything like red-tapism, a Gordian knot, which it has been impossible to cut in any matters in which the governmental element is introduced. How far these plans have succeeded, and his ideas have been appreciated, is best shown in the enormous – and we use the word advisedly – business he has got together, in fact, it speaks for itself when we record that at the present time his employees number close – very close – upon two hundred, and a business which at one time was a purely local one, is now worldwide, and his clients – or customers rank from the 'Peer to the peasant'.

But while Mr Harrod has had what the world is pleased to call 'luck' (an ill-natured way of admitting that he, having worked hard, has reaped the reward of his labour) he has assuredly had a share off ill-luck in his business career, for on the night of December 6th, 1883, his premises were attacked by the demon 'Fire', who, during his absence, gained a complete victory.

At first it looked as though the toil and trouble of years had in a few short hours been utterly destroyed, but here again his energy saved him, and being fetched in the dead of winter's night from his residence many miles away, he never rested until a temporary office was opened with a small stock, just enough to supply his customer's immediate requirements, a notice sent out asking indulgence for a few hours (not days or weeks) and all this was the work of twenty-four hours.

At the end of three days great changes had come about. Humphreys Hall – luckily just roofed in – was hired, fixtures, desks, counters and offices were in their respective places and most of the departments in good order. We think, therefore, this feat is worthy to be classed as one of the 'local' wonders of the world more particularly when it is taken into account the thousands of articles that had to be got together to avoid customers being in any way inconvenienced.

The public, every ready to acknowledge merit, responded to his call and whether from selfish motives or from sympathy the result is that the nine months working in the temporary building has been in no way the worse for the customers and certainly none to the proprietor, than if the fire had never taken place.

It was but the work of a few days after the fire that the ground was cleared and the contractor for the rebuilding was hard at it, and the new building Phoenix-like began to rise from the ashes, the result being the rapid completion of a warehouse considerably larger, and in every way more convenient than the old one, for where departments were once crowded, ample room is now provided for the display of goods that must of necessity be inspected before being purchased, and there is room for branches that are now added to the already imposing list.

It would be a work of time to fully describe this 'store' and would encroach too much on the limits of our lounge, but we may mention that the new building is an erection of somewhat imposing exterior and we are informed is put on a thoroughly fire-proof principle so that although this precaution is somewhat like 'shutting the door after the steed is stole' it will be readily admitted to be a wise one.

As we enter from the street we are struck by the vast area that opens to our view, but we proceed at once to the basement and here we find strong rooms where the silver goods kept in stock can be placed safely after closing hours; here too are cellars built purposely for the storing of sugar, others for provisions, and bins by the score for the varied assortment of wines and spirits. There are also tea rooms piled up with chests from the lowly 'mixed at two shillings per pound' to the aristocratic 'scented pekoe' and another 'all the sweet perfumes of Arabia' containing the spices and other condiments of an appetizing nature.

Ascending, we are in the 'shop', and in the centre we see a large circular counter where orders are to be written out and instructions given to a staff of clerks specially appointed for the purpose. On the left there are the wines, and we find a stock assorted to suit the tastes of all opponents of total abstinence. There are clarets from 'ordinaire' to high class Château productions, ports of the vintages sacred to those who have no dread of the gout, and selected from the best shipments of Cockburn, Kopke, Graham, Morgan and others. Champagnes from that bearing the very broad description "superior" up to such luxurious drinks as Giesler, Mumm, Perinet, Piper or Pommery, while for those of smaller means or semi-abstainers there are the exhilarating but somewhat saccharine liquors that owe their origin to fruits grown on British soil. Then there are spirits called not 'from the vasty deep' – for water is a matter that when Gin, Brandy, Rum or Whisky are concerned

Mr Harrod prefers to leave to the discretion of his customers – but there those of the mineral class from soda to the medicinal Carlsbad, Schlossbunnen, Taunas and some which are bottled for the fair sex namely, Mesdames and Celestines.

Stretching from here for a long way into the distance is the tea and grocery counter where pyramids of tea and sugar, mountains of coffee are mixed up with tins of biscuits, breeches' paste, blancmange, glycerine, lobsters, plate powder, sugar candy, boot top powder, wax vestas, salt, prawns, phosphor paste, oysters, milk, knife polish, house flannel, dog biscuits, mustard and a thousand and one other articles of a heterogeneous nature but all of which meet in the store room of any well-ordered household.

Next on the right comes the fruit and flower department and here is to be a collection that will hold its own against any of the Covent Garden shops, while in flowers there are to be daily supplies of shrubs and blooming plants, not are the beau, and belles' requirements in the shapes of bouquets and 'button holes' to be forgotten.

Beyond this is the 'stall' where poultry and game are to be on view, and we are informed that arrangements have been made for a constant and daily supply direct from the country so that the handling, packing and repacking which is so objectionable but which it is impossible to prevent with ordinary market-bought produce will be entirely avoided, and to complete this side of the place there is a long counter where cheese from America and the foreign Gruyère, Chapzugar Camembert, with the delicious productions of Wilts are to be found. Here too will be seen the goods comprised under the heading 'general provisions' such as Australian meats, bacon, butter – not bosch – and hams from York, Ireland, Canada or Westphalia.

As we look around this ground floor we are quite surprised at the enormous quantities of each article that it appears necessary to keep ready but it is to be explained that often, and more particularly at holiday times and on Saturdays, there is such a rush of customers that unless this precaution was taken it would be impossible to serve quickly enough to keep the place even moderately clear.

In the middle of this floor is a grand staircase wide enough for 5 or 6 persons to ascend or descend abreast and this takes us to a spacious warehouse where we find an amazing show of sterling silver and electro goods, and being all perfectly new and freshly unpacked the effect is somewhat more than one would expect to find in any retail establishment of ordinary dimensions.

There are spoons and forks of all sorts, tea services, trays, biscuit boxes, soup tureens, kettles, and stands, but a very noticeable feature is a splendid assortment of the goods that are now somewhat the rage, namely jugs, flagons, salad bowls, trays, &c, made of oak and mounted in electro. These of themselves are worth seeing, and will, we doubt not, attract a good many people to take a lounge on this floor.

But this is not all that is to be found here, for there is a big show of lamps, from those burning benzoline and costing a few pence, to the delicately painted china varieties for the drawing room or boudoir, and as a direct contrast there are lanterns for stable use and the burglar's bull's-eye.

Around the wall are cases for saddlery, and the stock comprises everything from the donkey's pad to the racing saddle, or from a halter to a set of four horse harness, while further on there are boxes, portmanteaux, overland trunks, hat cases, in fact travelling luxuries of every conceivable shape and size. To the left there are the modern brass goods comprising high class fenders, fire-irons, coal boxes, and beyond are kitchen requisites and turnery, mats, brushes, &c. The whole of this spacious floor is under the management of Mr Smart, and he is to be congratulated on having produced a show that being almost unique in this class of business deserves to be fully patronized by all who visit his employer's new premises.

One flight higher and we are in a portion of the building that is sure to find favour with the gentler sex, for here are displayed all sorts of fancy requisites for the toilet, perfumes from the laboratories of Atkinson, Plesse, and Rimmel together with the countless odds and ends in the way of cosmetiques that are eagerly sought after by those who indulge in 'paint, powder, and patches'. Then there comes a stock of articles equally or even more necessary, but not quite so much sought after, namely, patent medicines, and arrangements have been perfected with a competent dispenser in the neighbourhood so that prescriptions at store prices can be made up without delay.

After all this realism, turning to something of a lighter character, we find ourselves surrounded by games of all sorts – croquet, billiards, chess boards and the racing game, and another bearing the somewhat wild title of go-bang. There are also coupelette, magic skittles, targeteer, la poule, knock-'em-downs, and last, the dear old soul for whom we have such affection at holiday times, 'old Aunt Sally'.

On the third floor we find iron and brass bedsteads and bedding, suited for high, low, rich or poor, but on the way down we are passed through a pair of iron doors, to find ourselves in an immense place set apart for the exhibition of furniture, and thence into a huge reserve store of all the goods that are in daily requisition in the different departments.

Descending once more we are shown over the stables, where there are stalls and loose boxes for a large number of horses, together with standing room for carts, vans and hand-trucks, in endless variety, and with this our tour of inspection ends.

We then had handed to us a copy of the list of everything that is to be obtained, and setting aside the matter of price we must notice how complete the book appears to be in every particular. The extraordinary assortment of qualities in every article shows that no stone has been left unturned to provide for the wants of not only all the present customers, but of the numberless new ones that will doubtless give their support to such a well-arranged mart for every-day wants.

Though not wishing in any way to disparage the so-called co-operative societies, with our strictly conservative ideas, we think we may venture to point out that money earned in this borough should be spent in it, but we do not ask this, if it can be shown there is a better market elsewhere, all we say is; follow our example, take nothing for granted but go and just for yourselves, flock there in your hundreds, and thousands, nay millions if it so pleases you on Tuesday next, lounge round the place, particularly visit the show on the first floor, and when your tour of inspection is completed, take a price list home with you, compare it to the one issued by the Rifle and Rudder Supply Company, and then if you find all we have said to be as true as we believe it to be, you will make your way again to the Brompton Road, and your second visit will no doubt be as interesting to Mr C.D. Harrod as your first will have been to yourselves.

THE BARON

Well, what an endorsement! Harrod had no need of advertising with articles like that. Despite the difference in size, the shop of 1884 does not sound as far removed as one might have thought from that of today. The shop had many new departments and a staff of over 200. Charles Digby attracted 'celebrity' clients of the era, and Lily Langtry, Ellen Terry and Oscar Wilde were amongst those that were allowed the first weekly accounts.

In March 1885, Charles Digby's father, Charles Henry Harrod, died in Chiswick, aged 85. His address was close to that of Charles' brother, Henry Digby. Charles Henry had been on his own for some time, with only a housekeeper as company. He may have moved to Chiswick to be closer to family and it is interesting that he chose to be nearer to Henry rather than Charles. Charles Digby may have been too busy, perhaps his wife did not get on with his father, or perhaps Charles Henry did not want to be in the 'country' at Sydenham, so far from his old shop.

Also in 1885, after a lifetime of prejudice against the idea, Charles Digby finally relented and employed his first female assistant. She was Ida Annie Fowle, the 27-year-old daughter of a local chimney sweep, and she was employed as a clerk in the counting house on the third floor.

Later that same year, a newspaper report of the annual dinner at Harrods Store showed that social life had continued despite the fire disaster. Certainly by this time, the 'family at Harrods' concept was apparent:

> On Wednesday evening, the Annual Dinner in connection with this establishment took place in what is designated the Town Delivery Room. In the evening the room certainly presented a pretty appearance, it was draped with cloth, and flags were flying from the ceiling, while the gas burners were assisted in their work of illumination by several pretty oil lamps. The tables were tastefully decorated, and were a credit to the floral department of the store. About 90 of the assistants sat down to the dinner, which was well served in every respect. The dinner itself was also managed entirely by the Store, for this summer a new department for catering with dinners, luncheons, &c., was added to the already multifarious sections of the business carried on by Mr Harrod in the Brompton Road, and is, we understand, meeting with a good deal of support.
> Mr W. Kibble [the same] occupied the chair, and Mr W.G. Smart the vice-chair.
> After the cloth had been cleared, the Chairman proposed the health of Mr C.D. Harrod, which was drunk with musical honours and much enthusiasm, as was also the health of Mrs Harrod and family.

Charles and Caroline had completed their family of eight children by this time and they were aged from 3 to 20 years old! It is odd that Charles Digby himself was not at the annual dinner. He may have been away, or inconvenienced, or have just given up going. It is known that in the late 1880s he started to suffer from health problems due to hardening of the arteries. He was only 44 years old in 1885, and might have needed the toast to his health more than he thought:

> The Chairman in proposing the toast of 'Prosperity to the Employer and Employees' said this was the third dinner that they had had, and this one was held a little earlier than usual so as to be held near the anniversary of the opening of these new premises. He trusted that this year would be as prosperous as the last one had

been. (Hear.) If they went on extending their business as they had in the past, the premises would have to be extended still further, and, instead of having 200 men in the firm, 300 would have to be employed. He might mention that the whole expense of the dinner, &C., was defrayed by Mr Harrod. (Cheers).

Mr Smart replied on behalf of the assistants to this toast, and proposed the health of Mr Kibble and Mr Hillman. These gentlemen he thought had been connected with the store the longest of any present, and he felt sure that without their aid, and the aid of the assistants who were there then, the business could not have increased by such leaps and bounds.

Mr Kibble briefly replied, and the rest of the evening was spent as a smoking concert.

Mr Clancy [the same man who wrote the article in 1923] opened the programme with an excellent rendering of the 'Little Hero', this gentleman also gave the 'Yeoman's Wedding'. Mr Arnold gave 'Too Late' and Mr W.G. Smart sang 'The Village Blacksmith' with feeling … and the evening was brought to a close by the singing of 'Auld Lang Syne'.

There were a dozen or so employees singing that evening. It looks as though William Kibble, as a family member, despite being listed just as a 'buyer', acted as the recognised deputy to Charles Digby.

Another *Harrodian Gazette* article, written by Mr W.A. Mercer in 1928, throws light on life in Harrods in 1885. In 1928 he was the employee with the longest service and reflected on 'the good old days', when Charles Digby was still very much in control:

Mr Charles Digby Harrod, son of the founder, was a 'live wire' and you had to jump to it or else get out. Many of us, however, were lucky to have the experience of such a good chief.

I 'joined up' on 14 November 1885, as the sequel to an interview, somewhat terse, and lasting about five minutes, concluding with 'Start next Friday in the Grocery at 7.30; bring clean smock, ditto face – 9/- per week.'

This being my third job, it did not come very rough, but it was soon 'What about that 7 soda, 14 jam and dozen hearthstones?' from four or five of our old grocers, Norrington, Fraser, Weed and Bell, until 9 p.m. and 11 on Saturday, then sweep the shop and the rest of the day to yourself.

Saturday meant going strong, right up to closing. Quite a number of customers had overlooked the Sunday joint or other necessary item, owing to having started shopping in the afternoon at 'The Buttercup' or 'Friend at Hand', one at each end of Queen's Gardens, which was a narrow road that used to exist between Harrods and Hans Road.

By just after the turn of the century both of these public houses had been demolished and incorporated into the expanding Harrods Store, which by then was well on its way to occupying the whole of the site that we see today. To give you some idea of the geography, the Buttercup was situated about halfway along the front of the store as it stands today, and the Friend at Hand was at the back where the Hans Road turns into what was Upper North Street and is now Basil Street. Mr Mercer continues:

We juniors had to fetch the beer for our sections, and if the can was not full – look out!

Often we had to take to a suburban house an overlooked Sunday dinner. This meant a run with the black or roan pony and trap, and getting back after closing time.

The office of C.D.H., or 'the Governor' as he was called, was erected in the centre of the shop, and through the glass panels he did not miss much that was doing.

All goods were paid for at the time of purchasing or sent C.O.D. No easy line of resistance was offered until some of our older clients requested credit. After a time a few accounts were opened, and rendered in book form weekly, being taken by a boy on Monday and settled promptly each week.

C.D.H. gave me the job of memorising these accounts and marking the carman's sheet, my status being raised from Grocery to the 'Order Counter' with dear old Dan Blyth.

This counter was next to the office, and manned by the smartest order clerks in London.

A word regarding our recreations may not come amiss.

Derby Day caused some envy to a few of us. Some of the lucky ones went off from the front door in a fine turn out, driven by Mr Harry Pike of Chelsea. Complete with white silk hat, he could handle four of the best, to say nothing of a well-stocked hamper in the boot of the coach! ...

... It may interest some of our young ones to learn that a lot of fun could be had for a very little money. Does anyone remember the Collins at Clerkenwell, near the Sadler's Wells, where a seat could be obtained for fourpence in the 'Pit' with a glass of ale given in? Six of us used to have our night a week at a shilling a head. Eight till twelve-thirty and perhaps a cigar on a birthday!

Collins Music Hall was a famous venue in its day and could hold up to 800 people. It is now a Waterstone's book shop, 10 Islington Green:

Reverting to business: Stock was taken on Good Friday [!] and the day was finished at 3 p.m.

Saturday's orders, post, etc. were getting heavier and we had to 'Line up' at 6 a.m.

C.D.H. arrived promptly on horseback from Sydenham.

'No humbugging – get on with it' – his usual expression, and Mr Blyth, assisted by his staff – Wright, Greenaway, Nicholls and Billy Weston (late Confectionery Buyer) got on with it! ...

... Although rather abrupt himself, the chief was insistent on politeness to himself and the customers.

The present holiday list just rendered to Headquarters, reminds me that after one year and six months I got my first holiday of one week. Managers, more fortunately, got two.

On this memorable occasion Hillier and I went to Ramsgate, leaving our main entrance at 4 p.m. in a 'Growler' like a couple of Rothschilds, our finances having been strengthened by ten shillings each from the long silk purse of 'The Governor'. [The growler was a four-wheel, enclosed carriage with a coachman drawn by two horses and the precursor of a hackney carriage, that is, as a vehicle for hire. It could accommodate four people in rather cramped circumstances.] 'And,' he remarked, 'as you have been a good boy [sic] remind me about a rise on your return,' I did not forget, and – it came off. Our neat little single-horsed vans were quite attractive, lined up at Brompton Road, six or eight abreast. They had to be away at 9 a.m. sharp, or a Walton Street policeman would come along with threats of a summons for obstruction.

Differences of opinion were seldom taken to the Head, and a rough and tumble in Queen's Gardens, which was our National Sporting Club, made many a shortened dinner hour worthwhile. Our first floor, Hardware Section, consisting of Ironmongery, China and Turnery, was doing very well. Carpets occupied the floor above, on one side of which was our Counting House.

There is a further account of life at the store at this time, regarding Mr Cole. It was probably an interview with him and was published in the *Harrodian Gazette* of 1930:

In 1886 Mr Cole of the Jewellery Department joined up as a boy. It was then a very small department of four small enclosed counters, and the stock consisted of cheap fancy jewellery. A young lady – Miss Sturgiss – was in charge. After she left, Mr Kibble [another relative, but not the same one], a nephew of Mr C.D. Harrod, who was a practical jeweller, was appointed, and he filled the dual roles of assistant, repairer and shopwalker. Mr Cole was then put in charge as Salesman, and a stock of real jewellery being obtained, the section as a jewellery department proper began its career. Optics were added at our friend's suggestion, rimless folders at sixpence a pair and ordinary steel folders at three and sixpence. Mr Cole

OUT OF THE ASHES

speaks to-day of Mr Harrod as a man who never spared himself, he having seen him pushing a truck so heavily laden that only a strong man could move it. He expected the same ungrudging service from all under him. The hours were long, the wages were small. There was no weeks' notice, dismissal came on the instant, with pay up to the moment you were told to get your money, but with it all there was a certain camaraderie. A good fellowship, that united for good work, and there was one great feature, the food was good and there was plenty of it.

For in those days breakfast, dinner, and other necessary meals were provided by the Firm, so that if wages were low, the stamina of the Staff was ensured.

The interview with William Kibble, quoted earlier, also deals with this period after rebuilding, telling the reader:

After the rebuilding was completed, Mr Harrod lived out in Esher and was in the habit of taking a few days' holiday from time to time. When he was away, 'William' was left in entire charge, buying goods, paying accounts, and managing the whole business. Until his retirement, Mr Kibble was the Buyer in the Grocery Department of Harrods, and has purchased over £7,000,000 worth of goods on behalf of the Company.

Mr Kibble's memory must have been letting him down, as by this time Charles Digby had not lived in Esher for ten years!

After Harrods was no longer in the Harrod family hands, several years later William Kibble was still working there and was held in such high esteem by Richard Burbidge, the new managing director, that he was given a 'gold watch, massive and handsome', with the following inscription inside:

Presented to Mr W. Kibble by Mr Richard Burbidge, Managing Director of Harrods Ltd, in recognition of the valuable assistance rendered by him in making the record increase of a Quarter of a Million Sterling upon the trading (Grocery Department) of the previous year, Brompton Road, February 21st, 1903.

A much more recent article about an employee who joined at this time was written by the present Harrods archivist, Sebastian Wormell. It was published in the *Harrods Bulletin* of 14 March 2013. It was headed, 'Kent's Way':

> If you work in the Knightsbridge store you must have noticed the curious names given to the basement corridors. Intended to help employees find their way through the bewildering maze of passages, these seemingly bizarre names actually have quite straightforward origins. 'Frosty Way' is near cold storage, 'Wine Cellar Close' adjoins the old wine cellars, but one name has even puzzled our archivists – 'Kent's Way'. We had no idea how this name was derived, until all was revealed in a letter we received recently.
>
> Herbert Kent came from a family of blacksmiths and farmers in the village of Allerford on Exmoor where, in the 1880s, Charles Digby Harrod had a holiday home. When in 1887 Harrod offered Herbert a job in his London store, the young man boldly accepted his offer and set off for a new life in the capital. He must have found work at Harrods congenial, as he stayed with the store until his retirement in 1929.
>
> For more than 30 years Herbert was the clerk in charge of receiving all goods coming into the store.
>
> Not surprisingly, the receiving bank became known as 'Kent's Bank', and the passage leading to it was named 'Kent's Way' – as it has remained ever since.
>
> Interestingly, the Kent family's connection with Harrods did not end there. His son, Herbert John Kent, worked in the Furniture department, rising to become Buyer of Bedsteads and Bedding, until he retired in the 1950s. Herbert John was a prominent figure in Harrodian sports and social activities, a keen member of the Bowls Club and Chairman of the organising committee for the big annual garden parties. The family's link with Harrods even

continued into the third generation: Herbert John's son Bruce worked at Dickins & Jones, J.F. Rockheys and D.H. Evans when they were all part of the Harrods Group of stores. And it was Brenda, Bruce's wife, who recently wrote to help solve this fascinating puzzle in Harrods' history.

It is impossible to know what made Charles Digby decide to sell the business and retire late in the 1880s. Tim Dale wondered if the building of the new store had taken a lot out of him, and this could be correct. Ill health is often quoted as the reason why he took the decision. This may well have been the case, though there is little written evidence to back this up apart from a reference to his health in the sales prospectus, which is significant. He survived for many years after retirement and led an extremely full and active life in those years, which would suggest that if he did indeed suffer with poor health, it was partially stress related and that retirement proved to have been a very good idea.

My reading of the evidence is that by the late 1880s, in addition to a background illness, he was tired of running the show. Although he was only 50 years old, he had been working continuously in the business since his early teens, developing the business his father had started, working hard to buy his father out and working as long hours as the lowliest of his employees.

He had created his empire and, in modern parlance, he had 'been there and done it'. His father had recently died; his brother William was settled permanently in New Zealand, and brother Henry was ploughing his own furrow elsewhere. Perhaps of most significance, although he and Caroline had eight children, seven of them were girls. In 1890, the girls ranged in age from 9 to 25 years. His two eldest daughters were already married, but neither of them had married anyone in 'the trade' who could, or would want to, continue to run the shop.

His only son, Henry Herbert, then aged 20, was at Cambridge University. He was training as a solicitor but, as we shall see in the next chapter, by this time it would have been obvious to his father that not only was he very unsuited to taking over the Harrods Store dynasty, but he was also very unlikely to marry and have children of his own. He did not seem to want to work at all. This could easily have formed the basis for disagreements between father and son.

Charles Digby would have been sad and angry that his lifetime's work was not to be continued within the family. Why go on? At around the same time, in 1889 or 1890, whilst Charles Digby made decisions about retiring and leaving Harrods, he was also making decisions about where the family would live in the future. His eldest daughter Fanny had married in 1887 whilst the family were still living in Sydenham, and Fanny and her husband then moved out to South Norwood, between Bromley and Croydon. His second daughter, Grace, was due to get married in late March 1889.

Sometime between 1887 and 1888 Charles had moved the family into 1 Evelyn Terrace, Cranley Gardens, and Grace married from that address. It is unlikely that he kept on the house in Sydenham for any length of time as, by the 1891 census, Armitage Lodge in Sydenham had other occupants.

Although Evelyn Terrace was a 'smaller' property, it was big enough for a couple and seven children. It looks as though their previous residence in Hill Street, opposite Harrods, which had been kept on after the family had moved to Esher, was sold when they moved into Evelyn Terrace. The exact date for the move to Evelyn Terrace is not clear. James Weightman, who is a Harrod cousin, owns a Bible which belonged to Charles Digby, and which was signed and dated by him in December 1888, giving his address as Evelyn Terrace, Cranley Gardens.

No. 1 Evelyn Terrace is in Kensington, now between the Old Brompton Road and Fulham Road, and about 1 mile from the shop. It would certainly have been well-placed for him to use during the handover of Harrods, and was intended as a temporary house pending their move further away from London. The house was kept on for some time after he retired and was used by successive members of the family as a town house.

All of the houses in Evelyn Terrace are built in the red-brick, Anglo-Dutch, Domestic Revival style typical of the area. It was part of a new build at the time; constructed in 1886 and 1887. The name of this block of houses was changed later and 1 Evelyn Terrace became 31 Evelyn Gardens. The floor plans for 31–44 Evelyn Gardens and a photograph of Evelyn Gardens in 1990 appear on British History Online.

Large as these houses may seem by modern standards, the houses in Evelyn Gardens were modest by comparison with those previously built in nearby De Vere Gardens, which did not sell so well, or the later Italianate houses in Onslow Gardens and the rest of Cranley Gardens. They had a relatively narrow frontage (21ft) and three main storeys. Rents ranged between £170 and £210 per annum (about £15–20,000 today).

Charles Digby and his family were the first occupants of No. 31, and they occupied the house between 1888 and 1894, although by the latter date most of the family were living elsewhere. Charles was certainly living there as the process of selling Harrods began.

As well as the London house, Charles also took on a seaside property, Allerford House in Allerford, near Selworthy on the north Somerset coast. This cannot have been a random choice and I suspect the family must have holidayed in the area prior to the purchase. This theory is supported to some extent by the story about Herbert Kent and Kent's Way, included earlier in this chapter. Herbert was offered a job by Charles Digby and joined Harrods from his home in Allerford in 1887. As Charles Digby did not take over Allerford House until 1888, he must have known Herbert from previous visits.

Allerford is a village located within the Exmoor National Park, and is part of the parish of Selworthy, 1 mile from the coast, and 4 miles west of Minehead. It is very picturesque and appears in the Domesday Book as 'Alresford – forda Ralph de Limesy Mill'. The village has many thatched Exmoor cottages and was used for the filming of *Lorna Doone*. The higher ground in north Allerford would have had some splendid views of Porlock Bay to the north. One of the village's main attractions is the much photographed Packhorse Bridge. Built as a crossing over the River Aller, it is thought to have been constructed in the eighteenth century.

Allerford House dates from the sixteenth–seventeenth century, but was enlarged in the late eighteenth century and is typically Georgian, with a symmetrical three-storey, three-bay frontage. It was the childhood home of Admiral John Moresby (1830–1922), who explored the coastline of New Guinea – Port Moresby, the capital city of Papua New Guinea, was named after him. The 1911 census, which gives the number of rooms in a property, shows that apart from minor rooms, it had twelve rooms. The house was initially acquired by Charles Digby as a holiday home and was used as an alternative to the London house for a few years The house was extensively refurbished in recent years and now has six bedrooms, four bathrooms and two staff flats..

A postcard was shown to me by Jean Pitt, granddaughter of Fanny, Charles and Caroline's eldest daughter, and her husband, Rennie Conder. It was written by Rennie to 'Miss Conder', one of his daughters, in Eastbourne on 8 May 1916. He wrote:

> I bought this from old Mrs Chapple of Allerford. She then soon recognised me quite well. You can just see half of Hill Cottage right in the middle of the picture. It is simply lovely here this evening. Love from Father.

The postcard suggests the family had a longer relationship with Allerford, and that the children and their families used Hill Cottage at an earlier date. Rennie knew the shopkeeper Mrs Chapple, and she can be found in the 1911 census, five years earlier, when she was the 49-year-old post office assistant.

Jean's mother, Margery, was born in 1890, so she would have been very young at the time that Allerford House was in use, and this memory must have referred to holidays in the area after that time, perhaps at Hill House.

Allerford was not an easy place to get to. Road travel would have been almost impossible from London, and the family must have used the train. The Great Western Railway or GWR – called by some 'God's Wonderful Railway' and by others the 'Great Way Round' – was the holiday line taking people to English and Bristol Channel resorts in the West Country as well as the far south-west of England, like Torquay in Devon, Minehead in Somerset and Newquay and St Ives in Cornwall. There were direct services from London Paddington to Taunton, and then a change was needed on to the Minehead Railway line which terminated at that town. The Minehead Railway was itself absorbed into the GWR in 1897.

The 5-mile coach trip to Allerford would have been reasonably easy, travelling along a fairly flat section of what is now the A39, rather than up or down along the very steep hills in the area which are west of Allerford.

With his housing requirements sorted out, Charles Digby would have been ready to sort out the sale of the shop.

7

HARRODS GOES PUBLIC

Whatever Charles Digby's reasons for retiring at this stage of his life, retire he did. In November 1889, Charles Digby sold out and Harrods was floated as a limited liability company.

Tim Dale tells us that Edgar Cohen, whom Charles Digby was purported to have met on the bus prior to the fire, and who had allegedly lent him the fare and helped organise the recovery, advised him on the sale. This part of the Cohen story can certainly be corroborated. Cohen bought the business and floated it, advising Charles Digby to take his money in shares. Charles replied, 'If I sell I retire. If I own shares I shall worry about the business, which will not be retirement.' This was a decision he came later to regret.

It is said that the price Charles Digby received was £120,000, probably about £10 million by today's prices. When Charles Digby did eventually at a later date buy founder shares, he had to buy in at a much higher price. The prospectus is printed in Tim Dale's book and the original has survived. It is available online as an advertisement in newspapers in November 1889, including the *Morning Post* and *Western Daily Press*, and on Find My Past and British Newspapers Online.

Applications were invited to be received before Tuesday, 26 November 1889. The prospectus lists the directors, none of whom are related to the family, the solicitors, and the bankers. Edgar Cohen did not appear in the list of directors. Six years later, a newspaper advertisement for a new sale of preference shares showed Cohen was by that time a director. (Of note, the auditors were Messrs. Deloitte, a well-known name to this day.)

Part of the 1889 prospectus follows:

HARROD'S STORES, LIMITED
CAPITAL – £141,000,
DIVIDED INTO
140,000 Ordinary Shares and 1,400 Founders' Shares of £1 each
After payment in each year of a dividend at the rate of 8 per cent on the Ordinary Shares, the surplus profits, subject to the provision of a reserve fund, will be divisible in equal moieties between the holders of the Ordinary and Founders' Shares.

The whole of the Founders' Shares and £75,000 of the Ordinary Shares have already been subscribed at par, in accordance with the terms of the prospectus, and will be allotted in full, and subscriptions are now invited at par for the balance of the Ordinary Shares payable as follows:

5*s* on Application, 15*s* on Allotment

PROSPECTUS

This Company is formed to take over, carry on, and extend the well-known Harrod's Store, in the Brompton Road.

The business, which was originally established by the father of Mr C.D. Harrod, the present Vendor, has steadily and of late years rapidly developed; the sales for the year ended Good Friday 1889, amounted to £492,548, and except for the state of Mr Harrod's health, which makes this step imperative, the opportunity of acquiring this business would not have presented itself.

The Company acquires the valuable and extensive leasehold premises in the Brompton Road, which are chiefly held for an unexpired term of 47 years, at the aggregate moderate rent of £1,635 a year; also the extensive warehouses on the east side of Queen's Gardens, Richmond Gardens and New Court, embracing a large area. These premises, a portion of which are sublet at about £400 per annum, are not only sufficiently commodious to carry on the present business, but afford simple accommodation for a large increase in the volume of trade which may confidently be looked for.

The Stores are admirably situated, having an extensive frontage to a most important thoroughfare, and adjacent to perhaps the largest residential neighbourhood of London.

Mr Harrod's business is mainly in provisions and articles of daily household use, and not, therefore, liable to the fluctuations attending a business which is subject to the influences of fashion.

The books of the Vendor have been examined by Messrs. Deloitte, Dever, Griffiths & Co., the well-known Accountants; and in their report ... showed ... net profits for last year £17,244.

The turnover for the current year has again increased by over £400 a week, and, with the evidence of increasing trade before them, the Directors consider that an annual net profit of £20,000 may soon be anticipated ... suffice to pay the 8 per cent dividend on the Ordinary Shares ...

The price to be paid by the Company for the entire properties, including plant, machinery, horses, vans, harness, fixtures, fittings, furniture of every description, the extensive leasehold, premises above mentioned, and the goodwill, is £100,000, while the stock is to be taken over at cost ...

The business is acquired from 2 December, and from that date until taken over it will be carried on by the Vendor for the benefit and on account of the Company.

Arrangements have been made with the Vendor's present Manager, Mr Smart, by which his services as Manager have been secured to the Company for a period of seven years ...

Mr Smart was mentioned earlier in the 1884 newspaper article as 'Manager of the new First Floor or Warehouse Floor', and later as vice chairman at the 1885 annual dinner:

... No promotion money has or will be paid. The purchase is made direct from Mr Harrod, and the Company will have the very unusual advantage of commencing business without having its undertaking weighted with the profits of an intermediate Vendor ...

James Clancy's article of 1923 talks about the period leading up to the sale of Harrods, and immediately afterwards, inevitably with details of the accounting process:

In course of time the Chartered Accountants came along, and we had instructions to commence dissecting the debits. This was the commencement of the Dissecting Dept – one clerk. Shortly after this the Store was turned into a Liability Company.

The extra work meant more Staff for the Office. The Governor gave up the Bought Ledger, and engaged Bought Ledger, Town ledger and Mail Order Clerks.

At this time the coming of Lady Clerks commenced, Miss Fowle being the first. [There is evidence she had started earlier, in 1885, during Charles Digby's time.]

The starting of the Company was immediately successful. The trade increased so much the Counting House could not cope with it, and got into a hopeless muddle. The clerical staff was considerably increased, some working all night, but to no purpose, until that strong man came along [the late Sir Richard], when the new System began to assume signs of success, which carried the Good Ship into Calm Waters.

This account does not match completely other accounts of what happened after the start of the company, for things did not go well for the store under Smart's management. Mr Mercer also discussed the same period in his article. It certainly sounds as everything was not so well ordered as previously:

For some years there was no change, except slightly earlier closing.

In 1891 [he may mean 1889] Mr Harrod turned the business into 'Harrods Stores, Ltd'. Mr Smart was appointed general manager, having been in charge of the hardware section for some years. He was a fine handsome man, but, I think, lacking the necessary temperament of a tactful G.M.

Having some clerical work to do for C.D.H., my office consisted of – a couple of cwt cube sugar boxes covered with brown paper, and on this pretentious desk I wrote quite a number of 'applications' for shares, including one for myself. Probably some are held to-day by those lucky applicants.

Soon after these events 'the ship began to roll', to use a nautical expression. The feeling of safety was replaced by one of uncertainty and business began to suffer in consequence.

Following a difference of opinion with the general manager one Thursday I was told to take my money, and that evening was paid accordingly by Mr Strutt, chief cashier, who seemed astonished at such a turn of policy.

I had been told to see Mr Smart on the following morning, and turned up – at eleven a.m., having been to Kensington Stores, the predecessors of Cadby Hall, to see about a job.

This interview with Harrods general manager resulted in my receiving another week's pay, in addition to an increase in salary, as compensation.

Things were getting somewhat mixed up in the Counting House owing to a new system, and accounts had got muddled with P.O.D.'s to such an extent that no accounts were rendered for a fortnight.

The chief clerk was getting sixpence an hour to stay all night, and after better monetary inducement by Mr Oxboro, the chief accountant, I put in a couple of nights, i.e., in continuation of day work and we managed to straighten things out.

The coming of Mr Richard Burbidge was the saving of a nasty situation and he, followed by Mr A.J. Naughton as chief accountant, soon put us on a sounder basis, as they brought many items of the system introduced by the late Wm. Whiteley, that pioneer of solid West End business methods.

Omitted from this article was the last involvement of Charles Harrod's family in the store. As business and profits fell after the sale, the board of directors dismissed William Smart as manager. His seven-year contract may have been expensive to terminate. They asked Charles Digby to return and run the shop until a new manager could be found, which it is said he did for a further eighteen months. The profits for 1890 had fallen by 27 per cent to £12,479.

The new directors had no detailed knowledge of retail, which is presumably why they fell back on Charles Digby – in addition they must have considered the fact that his presence would steady the ship and attract old customers back. Harrods archives gave me access to a transcript of the company secretary's letter to Charles Digby, dated

7 November 1890, taken from the minutes of the board meeting of that day:

> Dear Sir:
> My Directors having dispensed with the services of Mr Smart as General Manager as per the enclosed copy of notice, they will feel greatly obliged by your attending and assisting in carrying on the business of this Company until such time as they can make other arrangements. I am especially requested by my Directors to thank you in anticipation for your valuable assistance.
>
> I am Dear Sir,
> Yours obediently,
> Edwin Howell, Secretary

The unpublished story by Gilbert Frankau gives a more fanciful, romantic and unsubstantiated account of the events. This extract starts with Charles Digby in Selworthy, north Devon, where he had moved in 1890:

> And down to Selworthy in Somerset – at least according to the legend, for all records of those early days except Richard Burbidge's diary have been destroyed – goes Edgar Cohen, bearing Newton's S.O.S. Once again, the sober historian must refuse to confirm a legend. For all we know, Charles Harrod may still have been living in Evelyn Gardens. The only certainty is that he responded to that S.O.S instantaneously, thus providing us with the final proof of his integrity, of his sense of honour, of his respect for his father's name.
> As a rich man, he could easily have refused without giving a reason – or pleaded, with complete justification, the state of his health – or pretended to hesitate before demanding an extortionate salary.

Frankau wrote that there is 'a living witness to the state of affairs the governor found that first morning [i.e. when C.D.H. returned to the store]', and he seems to be using information from this eyewitness when he paints a colourful picture of no-nonsense Mr Harrod sorting the place out, paying bills, chasing creditors, tidying the horses harnesses etc.. Charles Digby had a look at the two new departments, one for boots and one for hosiery:

> Harrod found them too small, their stocks second rate and their buyers little to his liking. He gave both the rough edge of his tongue; and sacked a poultryman, whom he heard being impolite to a customer, on his way back to the office.
>
> He worked all through September, with the strain now beginning to tell; all through October, with one witness after another reporting to Alfred Newton, 'Search parties to look for the old man, whom the assistants often find collapsed and insensible when they come in of a morning'; and all through November; right on until the last of the Christmas stocks had been ordered and that eight per cent dividend promised by the prospectus was as good as certain for the first thirteen months' trading of the new company.

At which point, Frankau seems to suggest, Harrod suffered a complete breakdown and the directors had to go off and find a new manager. Certainly if he had been in poor health, coming back to rescue the store he loved might well have exhausted him.

During his time back in charge, Charles Digby entrusted Mr Cohen with the task of finding a new general manager. Cohen recommended Richard Burbidge, who had just left Whiteley's, which was the largest department store in London at the time. Burbidge was then working at West Kensington Stores. Cohen first approached Burbidge on 16 December 1890. Three weeks later, on 6 January 1891, as Burbidge says in his dairy, Cohen has been to see him 'for about the 5th time on behalf of Mr Newton, chairman of Harrod's Stores', but he is still declining the managership of Harrods. The diary explains that Cohen and Newton eventually managed to persuade him, and Burbidge's resignation from the West Kensington Stores was accepted on 18 February 1891.

On 26 February, Cohen introduced Burbidge to Charles Digby at the National Liberal Club. Burbidge then attended the Harrods board meeting on 2 March 1891, 'meeting Mr Harrod and other directors who introduced me to different buyers'. On 2 April 1891 Richard Burbidge, having been appointed, started work and was now in charge. It is likely that Charles Digby would have worked in tandem with him for a short time to make the introductions and show him the ropes. Assuming that Frankau's account is accurate, which may be doubtful, and that the dates of these meetings in Burbidge's diary are correct, which is very likely, it would seem that Charles Digby returned to work for seven months from September 1890 to March 1891 inclusive, and not the eighteen months mentioned earlier. His health had again played a part.

The only problem with these dates is that the Harrods management did not write to Charles Digby asking him to return until 7 November 1890, so even if he had responded immediately, he could not have been working to the point of collapse through September, October and November as Frankau suggested. The census, taken in early April 1891, and details of which are given later, shows that Charles Digby had already returned to Allerford by this date. So the longest he could have worked back at Harrods was about twenty weeks between early and mid November 1890 and the end of March 1891. Unless you know differently, of course …

Whiteley's store of the time was bigger than Harrods and, like Harrods, started from humble beginnings. The rise of William Whiteley not only mimics closely that of Charles Henry and later Charles Digby Harrod, but was achieved at some pace.

His father apprenticed him in 1848 to a draper's shop in Wakefield. He spent seven laborious years learning everything he could about retailing, importing and wholesaling. In 1851, Whiteley, visited the Great Exhibition in London and was inspired by the range of goods all displayed under the same roof. He returned home to finish his apprenticeship and was determined to start a store doing just that.

At the age of 24, he left his home to seek fame and fortune in London. He had only £10 in his pocket but he had a dream in his heart – to create a store such as London had never seen before, a store that could offer the shopping public everything and anything. He worked in London learning the trade and scrimped and saved until he had amassed £700. With that, in 1863 he opened a small shop in a little known and unfashionable part of London called Bayswater. Whiteley's department store started as a drapery shop at 31 Westbourne Grove, not long after Charles Digby was taking over the shop in Brompton Road. In the next four years Whiteley's expanded to a row of shops containing seventeen separate departments.

By 1875 he had become an entrepreneur of note – buying up more shops in the area, cutting prices, offering vast ranges of goods and services, from clothes and kitchenware to estate agency work. 'The Universal Provider' became one of his slogans; 'Everything from a pin to an Elephant' was another.

His competitors, and presumably that included Charles Digby, naturally disliked him as much as his customers loved him, but nothing could stop him. In 1885 he achieved his ultimate dream – the most comprehensive department store of its time, with a staff of 6,000 people by 1890. Most of the employees lived in company-owned male and female dormitories, having to obey 176 rules and working 7 a.m. to 11 p.m., six days a week.

Whiteley bought massive amounts of farmland and erected food-processing factories to provide produce for the store and for staff catering. In 1896 he earned an unsolicited royal warrant from Queen Victoria – an unprecedented achievement. It was 1913 before Harrods received one, from Queen Mary, although many royals shopped there, including the Russian royal family who bought the sailor suits often worn by their children there.

The parallels with Harrods continued. Whiteley's was devastated in an enormous fire in 1897, one of the largest fires in London's history. The store was rebuilt and continued trading in Westbourne Grove for a few years.

William Whiteley came to an untimely end. On 24 January 1907, he was shot dead by a young man called Horace Rayner, who claimed to be his illegitimate son by a former shop girl named Louie.

Mr Rayner shot Whiteley twice in the head, and then attempted suicide. He failed, but was hanged after a trial that lasted just five hours. Whiteley's two sons took over, but my impression is that they never had their father's enthusiasm.

There was a surprise when his will was read. In addition to various small bequests, Whiteley had specified that the (then considerable) sum of £1 million be used to purchase freehold land '… as a site for the erection thereon of buildings to be used and occupied as homes for aged poor persons'. The Whiteley Village Foundation was established, and still flourishes in Surrey caring for the elderly.

When the Westbourne Grove lease expired, the Whiteley brothers opened a splendid new shop in Queensway in 1911; the Lord Mayor of London performed the opening ceremony. It was the height of luxury, with a theatre as well as a golf-course on the roof. The store appears in a number of early twentieth-century novels, and Shaw's 1913 play, *Pygmalion*, when Eliza Doolittle is sent there 'to be attired'.

The Whiteley's store was sold to Gordon Selfridge in 1927, but declined in the decades thereafter, suffering bomb damage in the Second World War. The store closed in 1981, but re-emerged in 1989 when the building became incorporated into a shopping centre on the west side of Queensway. It has not been wonderfully successful. It is no longer unique, containing shops that can found on most high streets. It also has a lot of local competition.

In contrast, under Burbidge, Harrods went from strength to strength. Richard Burbidge was born in 1847 in Bradford upon Avon, Wiltshire, and was the fourth of nine sons of a local farmer. When his father died in 1861 his mother wrote to ask Mr Jonathon Puckeridge, a grocer and wine and provision merchant in Oxford Street, if he would accept 100 guineas to teach her 14-year-old son the retail trade.

He moved to London as an apprentice and worked there for five years. In 1881 he joined the Army & Navy Auxiliary Store, shortly before he moved to Whiteley's. He left Whiteley's after having apparently fallen out with them over money. He then worked for two years at the West Kensington Stores before joining Harrods.

Whiteley's loss was Harrods' gain. He proved to be a talented administrator and manager, enabling Charles Digby to retire with confidence to the West Country. The new management team soon got on top of things, and as the size of the establishment and the number of employees grew, Harrods developed more and more the 'family of employees' attitude. By the between-the-wars period, Harrods, like Whiteley's, had something like 6,000 employees. They had dozens of different sporting clubs and societies.

The Burbidge family was able to build on the solid base developed by Charles Henry and Charles Digby Harrod, and took Harrods to a new level altogether

To close this part of the story, the end of the era when the Harrods were involved in the store, there is one more quote from the *Harrodian Gazette* of 1926. William Ball returned to his story in the year 1885:

> In 1885 I left the Stores to go cabbing, but in 1891 I resumed work again for Harrod Stores, being employed to drive a horse and van delivering in the Fulham District, at the same time going to Smithfield Market for the Poultry Department every morning. I held this job for 30 years.

He retired in April 1926, after forty-seven years of service, and ended his article saying, 'I am sorry I could not say good-bye to everybody, because Harrods Limited is a little bit bigger than it was fifty years ago.' How very true!

Richard Burbidge took on Harrods with the same enthusiasm that Charles Digby had forty years earlier. As British History Online puts it:

> Almost immediately a more forward-looking phase of expansion began. Further new departments opened, adjoining properties were secured, and a depository was acquired at Barnes. Following a further surge in trade the board determined in 1894 on erecting premises of very substantial character.

By the turn of the century Harrods had taken over the title of the largest store from Whiteley's.

In 1895, another public share offer was made to raise capital for this further development. Premises had been bought, leases acquired, refurbishment undertaken, and the Barnes Depository land was purchased. The advertisement in the *Pall Mall Gazette* now showed the name of Edgar Cohen in the list of directors.

The decision to expand substantially involved rebuilding on the whole of the quadrilateral area now occupied by Harrods. Back to British History Online:

> ... the main site of Harrods lay on the freehold estate of John Goddard and William Watkins, whose long-delayed rebuilding plans for the whole of their Brompton Road frontage were afoot by 1892. Behind this, the equally decrepit south end of Queen's Gardens and the whole of North Street came in 1892 into the hands of the Belgravia Estate Limited, which co-operated with Goddard and Watkins on a mutual plan of reconstruction. One of the directors of this syndicate, Herbert Bennett of Marler and Bennett, estate agents in Sloane Street, was also a director of Harrods. This connection enabled Harrods to negotiate an arrangement whereby the Belgravia Estate Limited rebuilt this portion of North Street (subsequently Basil Street) on a line further south and Harrods took most of the new street's northern frontage, thus extending its premises southwards into Chelsea and stopping up the old south end of Queen's Gardens.
>
> As yet, however, the company does not seem to have thought generally of expanding west of Queen's Gardens, where they held no leases. The presence here of a small but quite recent London board school, erected in 1874 ... constituted one difficulty. This school never proved popular, ... but despite rumours of its demolition as early as 1892, Harrods did not secure the promise of a sale until 1897 and entered into possession only in 1902, when the school was finally amalgamated with another ... A graver problem was that from 1893, under the rebuilding plans of Watkins and

Goddard, good new houses were being erected all along the east side of Hans Road.

The architect chosen for the reconstruction of Harrods was C.W. Stephens, and his reputation was wholly local. He had been involved in the redevelopment of Hans Place.

... His buildings here and elsewhere in the district were of a banal Queen Anne character, but presumably he was a competent businessman and an effective planner ... In 1892 he designed a new chimney shaft for Harrods, having also worked recently for the store's nearby rival, Harvey Nichols of Lowndes Terrace, Knightsbridge. But 1894 was the annus mirabilis for Stephens, bringing him not only the prospect of reconstructing Harrods but also the huge and fashionable commission of Claridge's in Mayfair ... But Harrods, bulging expansively out of its rich casing of Doulton's terracotta, is unique among them.

The transformation of Harrods into the vast department store known today was a piecemeal business, since sites were acquired only gradually, business had to be kept going, and building regulations required that such large undertakings had to be divided into several structurally separate entities. Generally speaking, the rebuilding proceeded anti-clockwise from 1894 until 1912, from Basil Street and Hans Crescent round into the Brompton Road and so finally into Hans Road. Throughout, it was Stephens' arduous task to combine the requirements of each individual sector with a semblance of unity.

A notable publicity coup was that in 1898, Harrods introduced the first 'moving staircase' to an amazed public, a notable event. This was not an escalator in the modern sense of a moving staircase, but literally a moving slope. Attendants were stationed at either end to help the anxious public on and off this new-fangled mechanical invention.

The meteoric growth continued and over the period of a couple of decades the Harrods we know today emerged, with the purchase of surrounding premises to produce the present building footprint. The rebuilding of the frontage awaited purchase of all the relevant sites in 1897. The general lines were agreed with the LCC in 1901 and it was built in stages, being completed in 1905.

At this point, the floors above the ground-floor shop were given to storage showrooms and flats, the most elegant facing the Brompton Road, and:

> ... had at least fifteen rooms and a superficial footage of over 5,000 square feet each, and rented at £400–500 per annum. They enjoyed ample space for circulation and were arranged around large light-wells, which descended to illumine skylights over the first-floor showrooms. Beneath these skylights were well-holes allowing light to the ground floor ... For the gentry, access to the flats [which were named Hans Mansions] was from lifts or staircases within entrances in Hans Road and Hans Crescent, but by a makeshift device the service staircases rose from a dingy sub-basement through the store itself, from which they were entirely enclosed. The original finishing of the shop interiors was very lavish, too greatly so for Joseph Appel, who in 1906 caught himself 'admiring the fixtures and really not seeing the goods ... Mr Burbidge says they get the land so cheap – ground rent – that they can afford to spend money on luxurious fittings. But really it is because they are among such elaborate surroundings in London, beautiful public buildings, elaborate castles and private homes, and so on, that they have to decorate more luxuriously than we do.'

During the rebuilding of Harrods, trade was continually expanding. The cost of the works doubtless exceeded a million pounds ... but this was amply justified by returns. Between 1890 and 1910 yearly profits rose steadily from £13,500 to just over £210,000, and turnover in 1906 was put at £2,100,000. So many new departments were opened that before reconstruction was complete there was already pressure for further expansion.

All this building and expansion paid off. Harrods, under Burbidge and later his son's care, gained international renown and became the most famous department store in the world. The Boer War, and later the First World War, provided enormous stimulus to the growth. The store received the royal warrant in 1913. At the time of Burbidge's death in 1917 Harrods had 6,000 employees. He was succeeded by his son, Woodman Burbidge.

Over the ensuing decades, Harrods has held many celebrations of the anniversary of the beginning of the store, always using the date for the start of the shop as 1849, the year that Charles Henry Harrod was thought, erroneously, to have moved to Brompton Road. The Diamond Jubilee celebrations in 1909 were contrived to maximise publicity. It is interesting to note that whilst Harrods were celebrating their Diamond Jubilee in 1909, in the same year Harry Selfridge opened his London store on Oxford Street.

Harrods' celebrations concentrated on the store's support for the Territorials. They were trying to emphasise its Britishness and patriotism, in contrast to the American-style store which Selfridge had launched. The store frontage is recorded in a photograph from about this time, probably in 1901. The narrow entrance to Queens Gardens can be seen between the last blind on the store window and the lamp post across the alley, in front of the Buttercup public house. The adjacent shops look as though they are empty and will be incorporated into the extending building, an event which occurred by 1902.

I am grateful to the Harrods Limited Company Archive for access to the anniversary records. There is a lavishly produced guest list and seating plan for the 1909 luncheon, together with the menu. Harrods has a copy of the guest list which belonged to Lloyd Chandos, who was one of the singers who performed in the free concerts that Harrods laid on that week for the jubilee celebrations. He was a sober tenor, in marked contrast to the 'Dolly Sisters' of Selfridges fame. It can be seen that despite only twenty years having elapsed since Charles Digby retired and sold out, the only representative of the Harrod family present was his son Henry Herbert Harrod.

The event was reported in the national newspapers of the day, including the *Times* and *Daily Express*. According to the *Times*, the celebrations lasted a week, from 15–19 March, and included the luncheon and a concert. A morning meeting was held to promote interest in the Territorial Force. The concert hall held 1,500 people and Harrods had received 50,000 applications for tickets. There were about 500 guests at the luncheon. The concert featured the London Symphony Orchestra and many individual artists, including Miss Margaret Cooper, a well-known pianist and singer who married one of my great-uncles the following year.

The *Daily Express* commented, 'The whole commemoration week will be arranged on the most lavish scale, no expense being spared to make it into a phenomenal success.' In a later edition the *Daily Express* eulogises about the store at some length:

> The ordinary conjuring trick of producing tables of food is done daily at Harrod's. Its restaurant is one of the largest and most elegant in London, with reading and retiring rooms for ladies, and a smoke room and lounge for men. Many London women might find it hard to realise that Harrod's never existed, or to imagine how they would shop if Harrod's ceased to be. But few people who shop at Harrod's know that the business, which now ranks among the world's leading stores, was growing gradually out of obscurity for forty years until it burst into bloom as 'Harrod's Stores Limited' and became one of the wonders of the shopping world … Harrod's can house you (in one of the comfortable flats over the stores), feed you, clothe you, furnish you, fit you out for an Arctic voyage (it equipped the *Discovery* for the Antarctic exploration), or for a military expedition, book you to anywhere, sell your stocks and shares, bank your money on the premises, dress your hair in the latest fashion, supply you with books, put your advertisements in any paper, dress a theatrical company for you (as it recently dressed 'Our Miss Gibbs' at the Gaiety), provide your children with cradles, take you out in motor cars, keep your jewels in strong rooms and your firs in a cold-air chamber, and when you have exhausted every other pleasure, provide you with a comfortable coffin!

In 1949, there was a Centenary Luncheon, attended by the great and good. This time, many more of the Harrod descendants were invited, including my grandmother, Beatrice Martha. The information and documents for this event come from the Harrod family and their descendants.

To illustrate the paperwork, mock-ups of the original 1849 shop were constructed and artist's impressions of the shop reproduced on postcards. They were what they say, impressions giving a rather glossy image of a shop which was, certainly initially, rather more basic at the time. A report in the *Daily Mail* covering the celebrations stated that originally the shop had a 30–40ft frontage, it employed two assistants, and the turnover was about £20 a week.

A splendid photograph of Beatrice Martha, together with her daughter, Bridget, was taken in the mock 'back parlour', with an actor playing Charles Henry, her grandfather and my great-great-grandfather. It is probably the best photograph I have of my grandmother.

The Harrod family members invited to the Centenary Luncheon on 2 May 1949 were the following: Beatrice Martha and daughter Bridget; Frank Henry Harrod, a son of Henry Digby Harrod; five members of the Conder family, Eustace Reynolds (Rennie) Conder, then aged 91 and rather frail, John Reynolds (Jack) Conder and his second wife Eileen, Margery Caroline Morfey and Katherine Emily Conder. Fanny Elizabeth (née Harrod), Rennie's wife is on the list as 'Mrs Reynolds Conder', but had actually died seven weeks earlier, after the lists had been produced; two Weightmans, John Walter Weightman and Mrs Mary Dolleymore, respectively the son and daughter of Amy Caroline Harrod; and two Rodgers, Eva Margarita (née Harrod) and husband, Dr Frederick Millar Rodgers.

The menu that I have had access to was illustrated with the artist's impression of the store in 1849 on the frontispiece. On the back page, many members of the Harrod family group had signed this particular copy. Apart from the above, the signatures also included that of Digby Milward Weightman, the eldest son of Amy Caroline Harrod, who is not listed on the guest list but was obviously present as a replacement for Fanny Elizabeth.

8

RETIREMENT

On 2 April 1891, Richard Burbidge took over the reins at Harrods. At long last, Charles Digby Harrod could leave his beloved shop in safe hands and take a well-deserved retirement. The 1891 census, taken on 5 April, shows that three days after the official takeover Charles Digby Harrod was at Allerford House in Somerset, with his wife, Caroline. They were both 50 years old. With them were two of their daughters, Amy Caroline, then aged 16, and Beatrice Martha, my grandmother, aged 13 years. The two eldest daughters, Fanny and Grace, were married and living with their families in south London. Henry Herbert, their only son, was a student at Cambridge but was staying on this day in Croydon with his sister Fanny. Of the other three daughters, Emily Maud, aged 22, was obviously acting as the 'babysitter' for the two remaining daughters, Olive Mary, aged 10 years, and Eva Marguerite, aged 9. They were staying in the house in Evelyn Gardens with just the six servants – I guess the house remained fully staffed in case the whole family needed to stay. All the servants were single women, aged between 20 and 36 years old.

Rather surprisingly, also present in Allerford House that day with the family were Charles Digby's nieces, Edith Caroline Elizabeth Harrod, aged 17 years, and Kate Emily Harrod, aged 16 years, the two eldest daughters of Charles's brother, Henry Digby.

I say surprisingly for two reasons. Firstly, with all that was going on in 1891, the retirement and the move from London, the family probably had enough to keep them busy without visitors. However, no doubt the cousins would have been good company for each other. It is likely that the rest of the family were already in Allerford when Charles Digby arrived back from London after his handover to Burbidge, and there were three servants at Allerford to help the family: a cook, a parlour maid and a nurse maid. Secondly, despite what in times past had been a difficult relationship between their fathers, the cousins had remained good friends. Henry Digby and the rest of his family were at home in Chiswick in the 1891 census.

Charles Digby had not moved to north Somerset to settle down at Allerford. This would prove to be just a stepping stone to finding a more permanent and prestigious residence. It looks as though he might have already found a suitable place, and was using Allerford as a base in the area whilst work was done elsewhere. On 10 August 1891 he bought a large country house in Morebath, north Devon, quite close to the Somerset border and a few miles to the south of Allerford.

When Charles Digby purchased Morebath House it was owned by the Bere family, who had been in continuous occupation for 230 years. The parish records give the purchase price as £37,000. Using relative price calculators, this would have been the equivalent of about £3 million today.

The Morebath parish records show that on 7 January that year, there was a village entertainment for Mrs Bere and her family. The locals sang a 'Parting Song', to the tune of 'God that madest Earth and Heaven' (*Hymns, Ancient and Modern*). Sadly, no record of the words remains. The census for Morebath House, taken in April 1891, shows in residence only the gardener and his wife, perhaps acting as caretakers, and their two daughters aged 10 and 23, so the Bere family seem to have left by then.

Morebath is on the southern border of Exmoor in sheep farming country. According to 'Parishes: Maker – Musbury', *Magna Britannia*, Volume 6: Devonshire (1822):

> Morebath was in the hundred of Bampton and in the deanery of Tiverton, it lies about two miles from Bampton, and nine from Tiverton. The manor of Morebath was in the crown at the time of taking the Domesday survey [1086]: Warin de Bassingbourn gave it to the abbey of Berlinch or Barlynch. After the Reformation it was granted, with other possessions of that monastery to Sir John Wallop, by whose family it was sold, in 1658, to Thomas Bere, Esq., of Huntsham. It is now the property of his descendant Montagu Baker Bere, Esq. The old manor-house is dilapidated.

It was dilapidated in 1822, so heaven knows how bad it would have been in 1891.

Kelly's Directory of 1893 tells us more about the village. It had a population of between 300 and 400. St George's Church in Morebath had been restored in 1874 at a cost of nearly £2,500, and had several windows dedicated to members of the Bere family. It had a station on the Devon and Somerset branch of the Great Western Railway, which had opened in 1873 (and of course is now closed).

The branch to Morebath was completed in 1884. I suspect that the rail connection may have played a part in Charles Digby's choice of property. It was 180 miles from London, albeit by a rather convoluted route. A branch to link the Exeter line to Tiverton in Devon meant that a second station was needed, and Morebath Junction Halt was built. It had a more frequent service than at Morebath Station and the halt was much nearer the village, but could be reached only by an often muddy footpath across fields.

Railway mythology recounts that in 1890 the GWR appointed a Mrs Town as signalwoman at Morebath Junction, and she was said to be the only recorded example of a signalwoman on any railway in Britain in the nineteenth century. This fact was linked to the statement that the traffic was relatively light, as there were only fourteen trains per day! An assiduous researcher of railway history called Helena Wojtczak investigated this lady thoroughly, so wanting her to be the first lady signalman. Despite examining many articles in railway magazines and entries on line, she was unable to find Mrs Town anywhere in the historical records. She eventually found an entry and details. Mr Down had been the 'gatekeeper' at Lodfins Crossing, just south of Morebath. He died in 1886, leaving her with six young children and potentially no home and no income. In an act of generosity, GWR allowed his widow, Sarah, to take over the role. There is still argument as to whether her tiny house next to the line was actually a signal box. Thanks to Mr Beeching, the nearest railway station is now Taunton.

Morebath House, as it was called originally, lies less than a mile to the north-east of the village, off the present B3190. It was in a poor state when Charles Digby bought it, and whilst he and the family lived in Allerford, he demolished the house and built another, calling it Morebath Manor. The house came with a 2,000-acre estate containing a number of farms. Charles Digby brought 100 workmen from London and they worked there for two years. No expense was spared and the finish was superb.

Whenever the question is asked about what happened to the Harrod money, it is probable that quite a lot of it went on Morebath Manor. The building cost was about £10,000, which in addition to the purchase price would account for £47,000 of the £120,000 received from the sale of Harrods.

It was not until 1893 that Charles Digby and the family moved into Morebath Manor, almost two years to the day after the date of purchase. The parish records state that on 6 August that year the bells were rung to welcome them into residence at Morebath. In the 1893 Kelly's Directory, Morebath Manor was listed as the residence of 'Charles D. Harrod, Esq.', and he is named as lord of the manor, a title which presumably came with the property.

The house was apparently splendid. There are several first-hand accounts of the house in recent times. There is an account by my Uncle Michael, who visited with his wife, Anna, in 1989; a visit by my brother Peter a few years later; a very glossy sales brochure produced by Knight Frank in 2003 and passed on by Harrods' archives; and my own visit in 2004.

When Michael visited, the house was in the hands of twin brothers called Handy. After failing to gain admission on turning up at the house, they were able to make telephone contact and arrange an appointment for tea the following day. The Handy brothers were very pleased to have made contact with a relation of the Harrods. Michael's own words give the best description of the event:

> The large manor house was on the side of the hill with huge wrought iron gates at the beginning of a long drive ... The nearer we got the more spooky it became. One of the reasons for this was probably due to the fact that all the windows had long, and rather unkempt, lace curtains hanging. It is an absolutely fascinating place and apart from internal decorations it is exactly as Charles Digby left it. The brothers collect antiques of all sorts and the total value in the house amounts to a very large sum of money. Hence the ever drawn lace curtains and no visitors without an appointment ... The

rooms are magnificent, the billiard room still having the billiard table made for Charles Digby. The entrance hall and staircase are very impressive, the staircase having been made from mahogany especially imported for my grandfather.

Dennis Handy told Michael he was writing a history of the house and would send on a copy, but this never arrived. He had some odd ideas about Harrod genealogy. He told Michael that his grandfather's grandfather (William Harrod) was either a Russian or Polish Jew who came to England, bought a small shop in the Mile End Road, East London, and sold tea. His source for this information was apparently a Penguin paperback, name unknown. Well, it is an interesting theory, but there is no evidence to back it up and the book has never been traced. Michael was given a postcard sketch of the house complete with peacock.

Jean Pitt, the Conder relative quoted earlier, has sent me copies of family photographs of Morebath in its heyday, which are splendid and show the interior soon after the reconstruction, members of the family at the front of the house and various scenes from the grounds. The interior photographs reveal the heavy furniture and distinctive décor of the late Victorian era. Morebath Manor became a listed building in the mid 1980s.

Country life of August 1967 shows the house and estate up for sale or auction via Knight, Frank and Rutley. No price is stated, but the estate at that time had reduced to 8,442 acres.

In 1994, Harrods archivist Nadene Hansen was approached by Clive and Christine Miller of Bognor Regis, who were prospective purchasers of Morebath Manor. They asked for a search of the archives for information that might help them restore the house, including plans, a biography of Charles Digby, paintings or photographs. They requested a loan of 'artefacts or miscellanea' to allow them to stage a permanent public exhibition. They also asked if Harrods would be prepared to support the project with grant aid! Nadene replied to them with some details of the family and history of the store. She passed the letter on to me in case we might want to help.

Whether they went ahead with the purchase is not known, but by 2003 the house was on the market in a very well-restored state. A brief description in the Knight Frank brochure describes the house as Grade II listed, with a commanding elevated position, ten bedrooms, nine bathrooms, including a self-contained flat and two-bedroom cottage, stables and outbuildings, gardens and land of 21 acres. The house was bought the following year by actress and comedian Caroline Quentin.

Somewhere between Charles Digby's occupation and this sale the estate had reduced from 2,000 acres to 21 acres! All of the associated farms had been sold off along the way, and the only trace found of these sales is a document in the National Archives, which lists three farms and several cottages being sold off in 1963 from the 'Outlying Portion of the Morebath Manor Estate' by Jackson Stops. It would seem that much of the estate remained intact for some years, being sold to finance restoration.

The beautiful photographs in the brochure bear comparison to the Victorian ones, only they are in colour. The quality of the fittings and décor is superb. The billiard table is still the original one. The plan shows that there are three floors and a cellar. The kitchen area includes a butler's pantry, scullery, laundry room, boot room, larder, housekeeper's room and gun room. The brochure price then was £2 million, but it may have sold for more in those heady pre-crash days.

Jean Pitt, one of Fanny Elizabeth's granddaughters, wrote in a 1989 letter:

> He [Charles Digby] also had a holiday home at Allerford, the one that shows in all the pictures of the Packhorse Bridge – mother used to tell wonderful tales of taking the coach to Allerford up Countesbury Hill, quite a hairy experience … Mother used to talk a lot about Allerford and Morebath where she spent many happy holidays.

The Harrods must have travelled back and forth between Allerford and Morebath during 1891 and beyond. There would have been trips associated with the purchase and then the building of the new house, and afterwards the family must have made trips to the seaside from time to time.

Any journey from between the two places, over Exmoor, would have involved a tiresome, lengthy, hilly and winding journey by coach. The most direct road, using the present A396, looks very convoluted but is by far the most direct and shortest route. Travelling via Countisbury Hill, which is just east of Lynmouth and about 10 miles west of Allerford, would have entailed a triangular route of about 30 miles, which seems unnecessarily devious, unless this was the better road for a coach in those days. It is possible her mother meant Porlock Hill, which is nearer Allerford, but again not a direct route from Morebath. A YouTube video of a modern double-decker bus descending Countisbury Hill in 2008 can give some idea of the journey. If you can bear to watch the seven-minute video you will understand what a frightening and difficult experience it must have been to ascend and descend this hill in a coach and four (http://www.youtube.com/watch?v = C7rQe4aPRbc).

All the hills in the area are steep and have narrow bends. A horse and cart, or coach, remained the most effective form of transport long after the invention of the car, as early cars did not have the power to make the climb. It was not until 1920 that charabancs were able to make the journey. The only reasons for using that route might have been if the family wanted to go to the coast at Lynmouth, or if a coach service only ran by that route. Jean Pitt, talking about travel from London in her letter said, 'Mother ... told the tale of how the horse-drawn vehicle came to meet them at Lynton and then had to get up the notorious Porlock Hill and how they had to get out and push!' They must have used this route on occasions in later years, perhaps just to visit Allerford.

The move to the West Country must have been a shock for the family. They had lived all of their lives in central London or the suburbs; Charles Digby had worked all of his life in his shop and had probably had little time for leisure. Now they found themselves living in a palace in the middle of rural and quiet Devon.

The story written by Miss Conder in 1923 continues with her

grandfather's life after retirement, giving a glowing account of his achievements, and explaining how Charles Digby filled his time:

> After such a strenuous business life he withdrew into the heart of the country, living first at Morebath, on Exmoor, and later at Heathfield in Sussex. Here he devoted his energies to the welfare of the country folk, and manifested quite a different set of interests. He took up very keenly the question of adult education and the wise use of leisure. He founded and guided Village Institutes and Social Clubs. He took a keen interest in politics, and promoted Liberal Associations ... He was fervent in support of anything that concerned the welfare of children and was a true fairy godfather to the village schools and to the children's section of the local Workhouse.

He threw himself into the local community and church. There was a 'Harrod' pew at St George's Church, Morebath, and he was nominated by the vicar as church warden in Easter 1896. According to the parish records, he regularly contributed to the local charities. In 1895 he contributed a guinea, £1 1*s* (about £100 in today's value) to the voluntary church rate. He gave the same amount to the organ fund; £3 16*s* 1*d* to the Clothing Club; £2 2*s* to the Morebath Church of England School and £1 6*s* 3*d* to the St Thomas Day Fund for the poor of the parish. The poor fund was distributed amongst fifty-four families, at the rate of half a crown, 2*s* 6*d* (about £13 in today's value) for a man and his wife and 3*d* each (about £1.25) for each child not of an age to work. These contributions seem very small considering his wealth, but he gave freely of his time.

Charles Digby became a Justice of the Peace and his name features in this role in the local newspapers. He was an active member of the local Liberal Party, to the point where the Liberals wanted to put him forward as their next parliamentary candidate. He declined.

My cousin Vanessa has unearthed several documents in the Devon Records Office in Exeter, which relate to Charles Digby's stay in Morebath. There were a number of references in the archives relating to proposed road changes to the entrance to Morebath Manor drive planned in 1890. A series of council documents and reports in the *Tiverton Gazette* record the progress of the proposals through the legal process in 1897 and 1898, when permission was finally confirmed. The number and complexity of the documents makes today's planning consent applications look simple.

Charles Digby became chairman of the Morebath Parish Council in 1898, as reported in the *Tiverton Gazette and East Devon Herald*. The article also lists those responsible for the flowers in the parish church, most of which were donated by Charles Digby.

A more recent article in the *Somerset Free Press* of 1980 gives us some further insight into Charles Digby's local involvement at that time:

> Some 90 years have elapsed since the name [Harrod] was brought down our way by Charles Digby Harrod, son of the founder of the store, through his purchase of the manor of Morebath. He lived at Morebath House for some years, having converted it into a typical late Victorian mansion and re-named it Morebath Manor. C.D. Harrod 'reigned' there as a beneficent squire and gave much help to the agricultural improvement of the district. It must have been a life far removed from that of the fashionable shopper's Mecca in the Metropolis. It was C.D. Harrod who had turned the little 'village' store in Kensington into the great Harrod emporium.

A lovely story about Charles Digby's stay at Morebath has survived and was told to me by an ancient relative. Timekeeping was an absolute fetish of his, as we know from his working years:

> He was always 'on the dot', believing that being minutes early was as bad as being minutes late. And so ... one evening, his coachman turned up at the front door to drive the master to a dinner appointment. Aware that Mr Harrod was not likely to appear until dead on the minute, the coachman went in to the servants' quarters, settled himself down with a glass and a bottle ... and lost himself. On the dot, out came Mr Harrod and seeing no coachman, mounted the box himself and drove the coach off to his dinner. He returned

again later as his own coachman. As he pulled up at his house the butler, knowing nothing about the missing coachman, opened the coach door and peered inside. No Mr Harrod to be seen! Looking up at the dark figure on the box, the butler called out, 'Hey, what have you done with the old —er?' Came the shattering reply, 'The old —er's up here on the box, and you'll be hearing from him indoors presently.'

I wonder what happened to the butler and the coachman …

Charles Digby's concern for the less advantaged of society is highlighted in a report in the *Western Times* of 6 January, 1899, recounting a gift to the poor of the parish at Christmas, 'Mr C. Harrod J.P. had a bullock killed and cut for distribution in the Parish. The School treat and Christmas tree was a great success, and thanks are due …'

I suspect that whilst Charles kept himself busy with 'good deeds' in north Devon, he kept half an eye on what was happening in London. We know that he and the family used the house in Evelyn Gardens for some years after they had left for the country. His father had left some property in Bermondsey in his will and Charles would have dealt with this. Charles Digby also retained some other business interests in London after his retirement.

A chance finding in the *London Gazette* confirms this. In the edition of 18 April 1899 notice was given of the dissolution of a partnership from 30 January, between Walter Robertson and Charles Digby Harrod. They had been carrying on business together at 42 Queen's Road West in Chelsea, as wholesale and manufacturing confectioners. Walter Robertson was born in 1847, in Chelsea, and worked in the confectionery trade all his life, like his father William and several of his brothers. Walter carried on the business after the dissolution, but no other details are known. I have searched for, but have not found, any other businesses in which he might he have been involved.

After ten years of the bucolic life, Charles Digby and the family started to get itchy feet. On the date of the 1901 census, 31 March,

Morebath Manor was occupied only by servants. Those in residence were Anna Radley, aged 50, a parlour maid, and Maud Beer, aged 23, a housemaid. Allerford House was, by this time, occupied by Mr Frere and his family, a retired solicitor from London, and the Harrods obviously had no further involvement with this property.

The Harrod family and all the children are easily traced in most of the censuses, apart from that of 1901, from which several members of the family are missing. Two daughters of the family, Fanny and Grace, were living with their respective husbands and families in south London. A third daughter, Emily Maud, unmarried and aged 32, was staying with her sister, Fanny. Henry Herbert, the son, now aged 30, was a single man and living in a residential hotel in Knightsbridge. But missing were Charles Digby and Caroline, and their four youngest daughters, Amy, aged 26 years, Beatrice, my grandmother, aged 23, Olive, aged 20, and Eva aged 19 years.

Where were they? They do not appear in the census records for England or any other part of the United Kingdom, and they do not appear in any shipping records to suggest travel abroad. A simple explanation could be that the particular census record is missing. That situation is not uncommon. Some records were lost during bombing in the war, others in various moves and reorganisations of the records. But if the family were somewhere in the UK, where were they staying? They were not at any of their known residences, nor with any of their relatives.

Whilst searching, I began to wonder if they had gone abroad. Distant intercontinental travel would almost certainly have been by boat, but the available shipping records showed no sign. Travel to Europe, however, was different. This was almost exclusively undertaken by cross-Channel ferry and the railways. These boats were not recorded in the shipping records unless the boat was also travelling further afield, and passports were not compulsory for travel abroad until 1914.

Meticulous travellers, regular travellers, those going to exotic parts or those on government business sometimes carried passports, and these were complex and large documents signed by the Home Secretary, and carried folded into small packs. They were a form of 'safe conduct' document and, amazingly, were written in French until 1858. Some years ago the Find My Past website digitised an index for passport applications from 1896 to 1901, and later the years 1853 to 1903 became available. This list is not complete and I came across this facility by chance.

A search revealed some interesting results. On 22 January 1901, Mrs C. Harrod, and the Misses E.M., A.C. and B.M. Harrod applied for passports. (Coincidentally, that was the very day that Queen Victoria had died, aged 81 years, and after sixty-three years on the throne. A momentous and sad day for Britain.) Did Charles and the last missing daughter not go with them, or did they already own a passport? A foreign trip now looks a distinct possibility. A wider search a few years later in 2010, when the range of years for passport searches had been extended, showed that Charles Digby had applied for a passport on 8 June 1892, followed almost exactly a year later by Emily Harrod and H.H. Harrod.

So, most of the missing family were in possession of passports. They did not travel far by boat, so must have crossed the Channel and used the railways. They are more than likely to have been doing the Victorian equivalent of the 'Grand Tour', visiting several European countries and cultural sites. (The fact that my grandmother was missing in 1901 became of some importance to me when trying to track down her early life. This story forms part of another tale!)

Charles Digby and Caroline decided to sell up and move from Morebath, which they did in 1902. I think the decision had been taken the previous year, and a prolonged European tour may have covered the gap between houses whilst their next house was being prepared. The reason for making a move is not definitely known. My Uncle Michael was told that Caroline was very lonely there and wanted to go back to London. Charles Digby seems to have become well embedded locally during his short ten years in occupation, but perhaps Caroline was not. The single daughters may have missed the social life of London, they did not have the same chances to meet new friends in Morebath and for the five unmarried girls, aged between 21 and 34 years of age, this would affect their marriage prospects.

Charles Digby must have left his Devon friends with a heavy heart, and they certainly told him he would be missed. Charles Digby was so well liked and admired by his tenants, fellow parishioners and friends that he and his family were given a scroll on his departure, listing their names and thanks. The scroll was shown to me by James Weightman, a Harrod cousin. It reads:

TO CHARLES DIGBY HARROD ESQ., MRS HARROD & FAMILY
We being the Tenants of the Morebath Manor Estate and your Fellow Parishioners and Friends desire to express our regret at your leaving MOREBATH and ask your acceptance of the accompanying SILVER MONTEITH BOWL as a token of our regard and appreciation of the kind and charitable interest shown by you in all that concerned the welfare of those around you.
MOREBATH MANOR TENANTRY
[Below this, a list of twenty-nine names, and C.R. Morris Sons & Peard, Agents to the Morebath Manor Estate]
MOREBATH PARISHIONERS & FRIENDS
[There follows a list of 113 names followed by a block name for Morebath school children]

The scroll was dated 1902. It was presented in a black and gold frame and was beautifully illustrated. The monogram at the top is CDH, and the four miniatures at each corner are (from top left clockwise): Morebath Church; Morebath Manor; a rural scene with deer; and a rural scene with a pheasant. The silver bowl was itself engraved around the edge.

Morebath Manor sold for £50,000 in 1902, today's equivalent being about £4 million. The reader will recall that the purchase price was £37,000 and that £10,000 had been spent on building works. Considering what else he may have spent on the place, this may well have left him just breaking even.

The records available suggest that Charles Digby bought his next residence, Culverwood at Cross in Hand, near Heathfield in Sussex, in the same year and the farewell gifts confirm he had left Morebath in that year. Wherever the Harrods went in 1901, sometime in 1902 Charles Digby moved in to Culverwood and, as before, with his usual vigour he threw himself almost immediately into the affairs of the estate and the local community.

Why had he chosen to live near Cross in Hand, a small village 15 miles directly north of Eastbourne and 11 miles south of Tunbridge Wells? It was in the country, so he could continue the country squire routine, but not as isolated as Morebath. It was closer to London and the married family – Caroline and the girls probably liked that – and his son, Henry Herbert, was by this time already well embedded back in London. It allowed easy access to the coast if desired. Most important of all, it had good transport links from nearby Heathfield.

In the late 1870s an aristocratic newcomer to the Heathfield area, Lady Dorothy Nevill, described it as 'a remote old-world district which seems to have been wrapped in slumber ever since the furnaces of the old Sussex ironmasters were extinguished.' There had, in reality, been considerable change since the 1840s, but the pace of change was speeded up by the rather late arrival of the railway in 1880, which was followed by the expansion of the local poultry industry. The station at Heathfield was uniquely lit by gas from a local bore hole, the first natural gas deposit discovered in this country, fortuitously whilst searching for water.

Culverwood House stands in the triangle between Waldron, Cross in Hand and Heathfield. Heathfield Station was just a short distance away and was on a combination of train lines which eventually connected Eastbourne to Victoria and offered frequent services to London. It must have felt very much less isolated than Morebath.

The Cross in Hand name is believed to be based on the legend that the English Crusaders assembled here before sailing from Rye to the Holy Land, intending to join others hoping to return Jerusalem to Christian control. The Crusades, instigated and promoted by various popes, became a series of intermittent battles which spanned almost 400 years.

Culverwood is a large brick-built country house, probably erected in the early 1880s. It is situated on what is now the A267, running south from Cross in Hand to Hailsham and Eastbourne, and is just north of a hamlet called Little London. Although the nearest church is probably at Cross in Hand, the house is in the parish of Waldron. It was at St Peter's at Waldron that the Harrod family chose to worship. They became regular worshippers, and thus was forged an alliance with the family of the rector that was to influence my family history for the following generations.

During a visit to Waldron in 1989, an aged resident, Mrs Hogben, told me that Culverwood House was built two years after the coming of the railway, hence in 1882. There are residents in the house in the 1881 census, so it is likely that Culverwood was built in 1880 or 1881. It was not occupied by the Harrods until about twenty years after that, in 1902. A flyer for a later sale of Culverwood House is copied below. The date is not known, but it is probably from between the wars. It gives a good description of the property:

THE CULVERWOOD ESTATE, CROSS IN HAND
A Well Built Country House
Lounge, 4 reception rooms, billiards room, 8 principal bed and dressing rooms, 5 staff bedrooms, 3 bathrooms. Partial central heating. Mains electricity and water. Septic tank drainage. Garage premises. Entrance lodge and wooded gardens and grounds.
ATTESTED HOME FARM WITH HOUSE AND BUILDINGS
4 COTTAGES, FIRST-RATE GRASS AND ARABLE, VALUABLE WOODLAND
TOTAL AREA 188 ACRES. ALL WITH VACANT POSSESSION
For sale by Auction at an early date as a Whole or in 5 Lots (unless previously sold privately)
Price £8,750

Cheap at the price! It would be interesting to know the date.

It sounds like a house to suit Charles's style including, once again, a billiard room, and looks to be about the same size as Morebath Manor. A comparison of photographs taken between the wars and recently shows that the house today has changed externally. A two-gable wing on one side of the house has been demolished and much of the greenery growing up the house has disappeared.

Charles Digby once again became involved in local affairs and was a local benefactor. Considering the short time of his tenure, which we shall see, it is amazing how embedded he became in the community. He became a parish councillor, being elected in 1904, and also an East Sussex county councillor, and he was appointed a manager of the Heathfield Schools. He was involved in local politics and was known in the area as a strong Liberal Party supporter, as he had been in north Devon. The Liberal Party in the first few years of the twentieth century was undergoing a revolution. Having lost the 1900 and preceding elections, they made great progress and swept to a huge majority in 1906. It must have been an exciting time for a Liberal supporter. Sadly the 1906 victory was not to be enjoyed by Charles Digby.

Following an appeal for information in the *Waldron Parish Magazine* in 1989, a few interesting facts and stories came to light, one of which follows. A letter from a Mr Newnham, then living at Millers Lodge in Cross in Hand, came to me telling a story about Charles Digby:

> I was born in 1904 and remember my father talking about Mr Harrod and the field on the opposite side of the road from Culverwood …
>
> My father, J.B. Newnham and his partner, Jebez Ashdown took the Cross in Hand windmills on a six year lease in 1888. Not knowing if they would be able to renew the lease or buy the property, in 1894 they bought a field close by, on which it was their intention to build a mill if they were turned out.
>
> They were able to buy the windmills and so did not want the field.
>
> Mr A. Jarvis, the builder in Cross in Hand wanted to buy the field, but did not have the money. He owned the field opposite Culverwood which he wanted to get rid of, so that he had the cash to buy the other one. He knew that Mr Harrod took a morning walk down the main road, so he resorted to the following trick.
>
> He took about six labourers and started digging in various places

in the field and when Mr Harrod came along he stopped and said:– 'What are you doing Jarvis?', to which Jarvis replied, 'I am going to start a brickyard, Sir.' Mr Harrod then said, 'I do not want this Jarvis, how much do you want for the field?'

The result was that Jarvis sold the field to Mr Harrod and with the money bought the field from father and his partner. This is the field on which Jarvis built Beaconsfield Terrace and Salisbury Terrace which are still there today.

There cannot have been many men who put one over on Charles Digby. Checking the Jarvis records, there were several families of Jarvises in the Cross in Hand area, most of them were builders or bricklayers. The same Jarvis family also features heavily on the First World War memorial at Waldron.

Charles Digby held a regular annual party for the local children and teachers at Culverwood House. Waldron School (mixed & infants) had 150 children in 1909, the nearest year when figures are available, and there were two teachers, John Bannister, master, and Mrs Bannister, the infants' mistress. The average attendance at the school was 108. According to the *Sussex Express* of 12 August 1905, at Culverwood House Charles Digby and Caroline had entertained 290 children of all denominations, and thirty-three teachers from various local schools, at 2.30 p.m. on the previous day, Friday 11 August. There was cricket, swings and sports. Tea was held at 3.30 p.m. for the children and 4.30 p.m. for the teachers and helpers.

The following Monday morning, 14 August, Charles and Caroline went up to London and stayed at the Grosvenor Hotel in Buckingham Palace Road. This was their usual London hotel and was conveniently close to Victoria Station. According to newspaper reports of the event, he was apparently then in his customary good health.

However, early on the Tuesday morning, 15 August, Charles Digby Harrod died suddenly in the Grosvenor Hotel as the result of a heart attack. That evening Mrs Harrod, grief stricken, returned to Culverwood, and on Wednesday morning the body was conveyed by a special train to the Sussex residence.

His death certificate shows that the death was registered by E. Reynolds Conder, the husband of Charles Digby's eldest daughter, Fanny. Charles Digby was described as a 'retired general merchant, aged 64 years.' The death was certified by Dr John F. Broadbent, and the cause was given as 'Morbus Cordis (Fibrodegeneration – 6 years), Arteriosclerosis, Syncope'.

The list of causes is a bit confusing. Syncope describes the actual mode of death; literally, it means a faint, but here it is used to describe a sudden collapse. Arteriosclerosis is the word used for generalised hardening of the arteries, and morbus cordis is a catch-all term to describe degenerative heart disease. Fibrodegeneration is another cardiac term describing a slow degeneration over some years. In summary, it suggests the doctor was told by Caroline that Charles Digby had suffered with arterial disease for some time, and heart problems, probably something like angina, for six years. This would suggest that he started with his heart problems in about 1899, some ten years after his retirement. On the day of his death he had collapsed and the doctor felt this was caused by a heart attack.

He was buried at Waldron Church cemetery, the gravestone being engraved with a text from Ecclesiastes: 'Whatsoever thy hand findeth to do, do it with thy might.' That sounds very much like a Charles Digby Harrod choice of text.

There were numerous reports of Charles Digby's death and funeral in both the local and the national press. The *Sussex Express* of 19 August 1905 gave an initial response:

> A gloom has been cast over the Parish of Waldron and the surrounding neighbourhood by the painfully sudden death of Mr C.D. Harrod of Culverwood, Cross in Hand.
>
> Mr Harrod, who was the founder of the famous 'Harrod's Stores' in Brompton Road, was well known and respected in the locality in which he resided and the news of his death came as a great surprise and shock to the inhabitants.
>
> Mr Harrod left Cross in Hand for London early on Monday morning and with Mrs Harrod stayed at his usual hotel. He was

apparently in good health, but early on Tuesday morning he succumbed to a heart attack, the fatal attack only lasting a few minutes. Mr Harrod practically retired from business several years ago. He purchased Culverwood in 1902 and soon began to display an interest in local affairs. In 1904 he was elected a member of East Sussex County Council, representing the Mayfield division and was subsequently appointed a manager of the Heathfield Schools, he was also a Justice of the Peace for Somerset. In politics Mr Harrod was a Liberal, and did a great deal to further the cause of his party in the district. Since taking up his residence at Culverwood, Mr Harrod has been a great financial supporter to the various benevolent institutions in the neighbourhood. He was also a member of the Waldron Parish Council and Chairman of the Local Schools Attendance Council. The funeral, we understand, will take place today [Saturday] at Waldron Parish Church. It is requested of the family that there should be no flowers.

The funeral was also reported in several newspapers. Male relatives only were invited, which would have been quite normal for this time. The *Sussex Express* once again gave a full report:

The funeral of the late Mr C.D. Harrod took place at the Waldron Parish Church on Saturday.

Soon after half-past twelve the mournful procession left the deceased's country mansion, Culverwood, which nestles amongst the trees between Cross in Hand and Horsham Road, and journeyed through Cross in Hand to Waldron, a distance of about three miles. The glass panelled car containing the body was followed by several private carriages containing the chief mourners and personal friends of deceased. At the church gates the cortege was met by the Rev. W.J. Humble-Crofts (Rector), the Rev. C. Henning (the Incumbent at Cross in Hand), and a surpliced choir. The first named read the lesson appointed for the burial of the dead, and also the committal sentences at the graveside. Mrs Humble-Crofts was at the organ, and during the arrival of the congregation rendered Mendelssohn's 'O rest in the Lord' [from *Elijah*], and the hymn 'Now the labourer's task is o'er' was sung by the choir and congregation.

(As far as I can find, there were no motorised hearses in 1905, and the 'car' must refer to a carriage. The first motorised hearse was an electric vehicle which was used in 1907 in Paris. A combustion engine version appeared in America in 1909.)

Another newspaper covered the content of the address given by the Reverend Henning:

He based his remarks upon the text, 'Whatever thy hand findeth to do, do it with thy might' [as on Charles Digby's gravestone]. In the course of some telling observations the reverend gentleman pointed out that the text formed the keynote of Mr Harrod's life, for whatever he did he performed it thoroughly. He also alluded to the good work which the deceased gentleman had done in the Parish, and spoke of the high esteem and regard with which he was held by all classes and sects.

Only male relatives were present, amongst them being Mr Herbert Harrod [son], Mr .E.R. Conder, and Mr .J.H. Martin [sons-in-law], Mr H. Harrod [brother], Mr J. Conder and Mr W.H. Martin [grandsons, then aged 18 and 16 years old respectively].

There followed a long list of mourners, including the great and good of the area:

The grave was lined with greenery consisting of ferns, laurels, yew and ivy, and the coffin was of polished oak, with brass furniture ... Although the wish of the widow was there should be no flowers, there were a few floral tributes from sympathetic friends and relatives, including a beautiful harp with a missing string, 'from his loving daughters, Bee and Eva'. Others were inscribed: 'From Grace and Bertie'; 'From Emmie, Amy, Olive and Herbert'; 'With deepest sympathy from the maids at Culverwood'; and

'From Fannie and Rennie'.

As a mark of respect to the late Mr Harrod, a half-muffled peal of several changes was rung at Waldron Parish Church before Divine service on Sunday morning last.

The flowers were from close family and staff. Daughter 'Bee' was Beatrice, my grandmother; this was her name in the family.

Another newspaper report added a different slant:

It is no mere sentimental exaggeration to say that the whole countryside around Cross in Hand and Waldron, was in mourning on Saturday afternoon, when with that quiet simplicity which invariably characterises a funeral in rural communities, the remains of the late Mr Charles Digby Harrod, J.P., of Culverwood, Cross in Hand, were interred in Waldron churchyard. The cortege left Culverwood about half an hour after noon, and on every hand during the rather lengthy journey to the Parish Church the feelings of regret occasioned by the sad loss to the village found reverent demonstration. In the vicinity of the church a large crowd awaited the arrival of the cortege, all classes being represented in a sympathetic tribute of respect to the memory of one who was deservedly beloved throughout the district.

The rest of the report echoed the previous one.

Even allowing for the 'squire' status, it is quite astounding what an impact a man who had lived in the area for only three years had made on the community. The *News of the World*, quite obviously a different sort of newspaper in those days, reported, 'Mr Harrod's business career has been an exceeding interesting one, and forms quite a romantic chapter in the history of modern commercial enterprise in London.'

The *Daily Mirror* said:

Mr C.D. Harrod was among the pioneers of advertising as we understand it today. He was the first man, it is said, who had a full page advertisement in *The Times*. So successful were his methods that the business which, when he embarked upon a commercial career was only a small grocer's shop in a mean thoroughfare, now occupies four acres of land. 'Harrod's Stores', indeed, is known all over the world …

It was in 1864 that Mr Harrod, a young man of twenty-three, took charge of his father's business and sold grocery and provisions over the counter. The humble shop occupied a position on the same site where the present stores stand. When he had been in business for two years, Mr Harrod began to dream dreams, and then to realise them. The store trade was just being started, and the first stores had recently been opened in the Haymarket. Young Harrod saw his opportunity. 'I will fight the stores', he said. The fight was a long one. He advertised as perhaps no man had advertised before. People saw in the newspapers and in the windows of Harrod's shop such announcements as: 'We sell 7lb of rice for 1*s*.' He cut prices in every way possible and was not astonished when his receipts increased by leaps and bounds.

All the time he smiled. 'What is the use of always looking serious?' he said. Customers liked his cheerful air, and even when he was drawing thousands a year out of the business they used to ask for 'Mr Harrod to serve them.' His smile was a valuable asset.

Another report gave further details of his business career, some previously unrecorded:

Mr Harrod's father kept a grocer's shop in Cable Street, St Georges E., where there were opportunities of making money half a century ago. With under £500 capital, Mr C.D. Harrod came westward, and set up a small grocer's shop on a portion of the huge site now occupied by Harrods Stores in the Brompton Road.

He was a keen buyer, and worked all the day, and took his books home to make up at night. Even when he was rich, he never relaxed the careful supervision of his growing business, to which his success may be chiefly attributed.

Mr Harrod was a man of frugal habits, and when controlling the business, absented himself one hour only a day for lunch. He had a habit of inspiring his employees, and he often remarked that his proudest moments were when presiding at the annual dinner of his staff, not in a hotel, but in the store, after business hours, and served from choice viands in stock.

When he commenced business, Mr Harrod gave employment to a handful of men, but he lived to see his business develop, in the course of a few years, into one of the largest, if not the largest, stores in the world, employing nearly 4,000 people, and having an annual turnover of between two and three million pounds.

There is almost a touch of irony in the fact that when Mr Harrod opened his shop one of his main objects in view was to fight, in a modest way, the competitive stores, which were then beginning to spring up in London.

The report detailed the fire of 1883 which, it thought paradoxically, by his bold response to the disaster helped the store become an institution. The report went on to discuss his contribution to local life in Sussex. It seems he never forgot his and his family's humble beginnings:

While Mr Harrod resided at Culverwood he evinced considerable interest in the affairs of the district and was a warm hearted supporter of the poor in a kindly and charitable disposition, and ever ready to assist a deserving person or object. With the children of all classes, and irrespective of religious denomination, he particularly endeared himself, and never seemed happier than when they were enjoying festivities which he had thoughtfully provided for them. By these young people his loss will be deeply felt. The children in the Uckfield Workhouse were never forgotten by him, and for some years past he has brightened their lives by entertaining them at the seaside. His kindness in this respect was unrestricted, and there was never the least stipulation as to the amount the excursion was to cost. All he desired was that they should have thorough enjoyment.

His interest in the parish life of Cross in Hand was manifest in his endeavour to erect an institute wherein the adult portion of the residents could spend their evenings. He endeavoured to acquire land for this purpose, but up to the time of his demise a convenient plot had not come on the market.

In politics, Mr Harrod was an ardent Liberal, and while residing at Culverwood he did a great deal to promote the interest of his party. He was a generous supporter of Liberal efforts in the Eastbourne Division, and was, indeed, at one time regarded as the probable candidate for the Division. [Eastbourne finally acquired a Liberal MP eighty-five years later, in 1990!] Mr Harrod's ambitions did not extend in that direction, and so he declined when overtures were made.

He did not participate very actively in sporting pursuits, although he was very fond of shooting. The Heathfield Park Cricket Club found in him a warm supporter, and at nearly all the matches he was an enthusiastic spectator, closely following the fortunes of the summer game.

It continued later, 'one who during his comparatively brief residence amongst them, had won their affections by his kindly disposition towards those who not so fortunate in fighting life's battles'.

The *Drapers' Record* said:

Mr Harrod was a most energetic worker and his personality was so charming that many of his customers would not be served by anybody but himself. He had a smile for everybody, and took an immense interest in the well-being of his assistants, and it is to his indomitable energy and business-like enthusiasm that the success of the immense concern in the Brompton Road is, in a great measure, due.

It reported, contrary to what had been said elsewhere, that, 'He intended to stand for Parliament, but bad health put an end to his ambitions in that direction.'

The news reached Devon, and there were reports in the *Somerset Press* following his death. Headed, 'IN MEMORIAM', it read:

By the death of Mr C.D. Harrod, J.P., which took place in London on Tuesday, residents of Tiverton and the district have lost a sincere friend. It is about sixteen years since Mr Harrod sold the large commercial undertaking, now known as Harrods Stores, to a syndicate of businessmen, and came into the West of England to live. His first establishment was at Allerford House, Selworthy, where he took a keen interest in local matters. When in 1894, Morebath Manor came into the market he bought it, and shortly afterwards entered into occupation. From that day onwards, until 1902, when for reasons of health Mr Harrod left the district to live at Culverwood, Cross in Hand, Sussex, he threw himself heartily into all movements for the benefit of the community [the date of 1894 is wrong].

In various spheres, Mr Harrod made himself very useful during the time he lived at Morebath Manor. He represented the parish on the Tiverton Board of Guardians and Rural District Council; and was deeply interested in all social questions, spending much of his time in trying to find a means of checking the exodus from the rural districts. For several years he kept the Bampton, Morebath, and Oakford Ploughing Match in existence. After he left the locality the annual event soon fell through.

Soon after his acquisition of the Morebath estate Mr Harrod was placed on the commission of the peace for the counties of Devon and Somerset. He sat regularly on the county justices' bench at Dulverton, and also occasionally at Bampton and Tiverton. He was held in high esteem by his tenants and all who came into contact with him, and he was a generous supporter of local charities and philanthropic movements.

When the war in South Africa broke out [1899], Mr Harrod initiated a public subscription in association with the local branch of the Soldiers' and Sailors' Families Association, himself giving £100 [about £8,000 in today's terms], and devoting much time and labour to the administration of the fund. He paid the expenses of administration out of his private purse, in order that the whole of the sum subscribed [in total about £850] should go for the benefit of the wives and children of our brave defenders.

RETIREMENT

Mr Harrod was a firm believer in the advantages of education, and was ever ready to assist in efforts to spread the light. For some time he was Chairman of the Tiverton District Technical Education Committee. He was also a benefactor of the Tiverton Technical School.

Mr Harrod will be much missed in the Tiverton district by the Liberal Party. It was mainly through his help that the Tiverton Liberal Club was founded nine and a half years ago. Mr Harrod was elected the first President of the Club, and has each year since then been re-elected, taking the greatest interest in the club throughout. Mr Harrod was several times asked to become the Liberal candidate for the Tiverton Division, but always declined by reason of ill health. He was the means of keeping up the registration for several years, also of appointing a Liberal agent, and (to a large extent) of securing Mr W.H. Reed, J.P., C.C., as the Liberal candidate.

As a light token of appreciation of his services to the Tiverton Liberal Club, the club members on February 15th 1902, presented Mr Harrod with a silver salver. Mr Harrod was deeply touched with the gift, and shortly after leaving the town he made the members a return gift of a full-sized billiards table. When the news of Mr Harrod's death became known to the members of the Club on Wednesday last, they were deeply moved, and in the evening Mr John Searle (Hon. Sec. of the club) sent a letter to Mrs, and the Misses Harrod expressing sympathy with them in their bereavement and the regret of the Liberal Club at losing 'such a generous friend, so sterling a Liberal, and so true a specimen of an English gentleman.' The flag of the club remained at half-mast all last week.

Always a keen supporter of Sunday schools – he once acted as Superintendent of the Trevor Chapel School, just opposite his business – Mr Harrod took a prominent part in the religious life of his country home, extending support to the various Nonconformist places of worship in the Morebath district, as well as to the Church.

Mr Harrod's last visit to Tiverton was on the occasion of the presentation of the freedom of the borough to Mr John Coles in June 1904. He was present at the luncheon in honour of Mr Coles, and briefly responded to the toast of 'The Visitors'.

The change from Devonshire to Sussex does not appear to have done Mr Harrod the good he hoped it would. As a matter of fact his health became worse after leaving Devon, and he passed peacefully away on Tuesday at the Grosvenor Hotel, London ...

We understand that Mr Harrod had taken a house in the Minehead district for September and October, and was looking forward to a pleasant reunion of the members of his family.

Once again, confirmation of the family's visits to north Devon and Somerset after they had left Morebath, and many further accounts repeat the same respect and opinion.

So, that was the end of my maternal great-grandfather; Charles Digby Harrod was a remarkable man.

Rather surprisingly, Charles Digby seemed to be as rich at his death as he was when he retired. He left an estate valued at £147,494 gross, net £103,117 (about £9 million in today's spending power). His will, dated 7 December 1904, appointed wife Caroline, and children, Henry Herbert and Emily Maud, as executors. All the personal and household effects were left to Caroline, together with £1,000, (about £90,000 today). To Henry Herbert, he left £2,000. To his five unmarried daughters, Emily, Amy, Beatrice, Olive and Eva, he left £1,000 on the day of their respective marriages during Caroline's life, or at Caroline's death if they were still not married at that date.

The income from the residuary trust estate was to be divided as two-fifths to Caroline, and the remaining three-fifths divided equally between the eight children. The net residuary estate would have been £95,000, so the income would have been substantial. To try to make some sense of this in today's value apparently 6 per cent was a reasonable expected return on an investment in 1900, and inflation was a staggering zero per cent, so it is possible to calculate how much this would be today. Caroline would have had an annual income in excess of £200,000 and the children would each have had an annual income of about £40,000.

After Caroline's death, the residuary trust was then to be divided into eight equal shares. All eight children were alive in 1922 when Caroline died, so would have received about £12,000 each (about £600,000 today). Caroline Harrod decided to sell up and leave Culverwood sometime fairly soon after Charles Digby's death, although the date is not known exactly. She moved to Tunbridge Wells.

On 21 October 1905, there was a report of the Waldron Parish Council meeting: 'Note of condolence was sent to the widow of Mr C.D. Harrod who had served for a considerable time on the council.' On 18 August 1906 it was noted in the parish records, under Cross in Hand, that 'The death of Mr C.D. Harrod has deprived the children of their annual treat.' I think it is certain, therefore, that the remaining Harrod family had moved from the area by that date, a year after Charles's death, as I suspect Caroline would have otherwise honoured the school tradition started by her husband and held the annual garden party.

I think that Caroline probably moved to the Red House, Bishops Down, Tunbridge Wells, sometime in the early months of 1906, a few months after she was widowed. Tunbridge Wells is about 12 miles to the north of Cross in Hand, on the A267. The valuation records for the Red House show that Caroline took the house on a twenty-one-year lease starting in 1908. The rent was £230 per year. She may have rented temporarily before that.

In 2011, Mobbs Pitcher, the then occupier of Culverwood, responded to my appeal for information and sent me a copy of the conveyance document for the sale of Culverwood to 'Arthur William Ranken Esquire'. It was dated 8 January 1906, and signed by Caroline, Henry Herbert and Emily Maud, the other executors. The witness was Ethel Lungley, a housemaid at the Red House.

The Conveyance shows that the sale price for Culverwood was £13,500 (£775,000 today). The estate consisted of '76 acres, 2 roods and 12 perches, with 2 acres, 2 roods and 29 perches on the west side of the Tunbridge–Hailsham road containing a public right of way'. For Caroline it would have been a good move, it was just a little closer to London, and to her two married daughters who were living in Croydon and Penge. Henry Herbert had been living independently in central London since the turn of the century, so Caroline would have moved to Tunbridge with her five as yet unmarried daughters.

Caroline Harrod died in 1922 in a nursing home in Tunbridge Wells. She was aged 81. Her cause of death was given as 'Cerebral Thrombosis 6 months, Cardiac Failure 2 months'. So, six months before her death she had had a stroke, and two months before her death she had developed heart failure and, one presumes, died of this.

The executors to her will were her son, Henry Herbert Harrod; her son-in-law Herbert James Martin, a solicitor; and another son-in-law, Arthur James Weightman. Her personal estate was not huge – it was £10,944 11s 9d, or about £450,000 in today's value. The trust money would not form any part of her estate.

Caroline's death was the end of any generation of Harrods who were involved with the store. They had built a great foundation for some very competent people who continued to create the magnificent store we know today.

9

CHARLES DIGBY'S FAMILY

Any story about Charles Digby would not be complete without some details of his children. It is remarkable that there was no one in the family who was keen to take on and continue the family business. Having seven daughters and a single son who had no interest in the business must have been one of the reasons that led Charles Digby to make the decision to retire.

I have collected a large amount of information about Charles and Caroline's children, their families and descendants. I have tried to pick out some of the more interesting parts of it below. Sadly, there are very few photographs remaining in family hands. The Harrods Photographers' Archives seem to have disappeared. I will list his children in their birth order.

FANNY ELIZABETH HARROD AND THE CONDER FAMILY

Fanny Elizabeth was born in 1865, above the shop at 105 Brompton Road. The sign of a true Harrod she, like her father before her, was born within the sound of the cash registers! Fanny was the eldest of the seven daughters.

She married Eustace Reynolds Conder at the Congregational Church, Upper Norwood, in 1887. She was 22 years old, and he was 29. The marriage was celebrated by the Reverend George Martin, who was to become her sister Grace's father-in-law two years later. It is not known whether the family ever worshipped at this church, but Fanny and Eustace Reynolds may have met at church, and the Conders were staunchly Nonconformist.

The Conder family lived in Forest Hill in South London, about a mile away as the crow flies from Armitage Lodge in Sydenham, making a church meeting possible. It also suggests, as seen earlier, that at times Charles Digby hedged his bets and worshipped in both Nonconformist and Church of England churches.

The more prominent Conders are Josiah Conder, a bookseller, publisher and author; Francis Roubiliac Conder, the first son of

CHARLES DIGBY'S FAMILY

Josiah, who was a civil engineer and railway contractor in Britain, Ireland, France and Italy; the Reverend Eustace Rogers Conder, the second son of Josiah, one of a number of Nonconformist preachers who contributed to the *Leeds Congregational Hymn Book*; Josiah Conder, a grandson of Josiah, who was an Anglo-Japanese landscape architect; Major Claude Reignier Conder, the son of Francis Roubiliac, an explorer, mapmaker and biblical and Altaic scholar; Charles Conder, the British/Australian artist, who was born in India, worked in Australia and then France, where he was a contemporary of Lautrec – he died in an asylum in England from tertiary syphilis; and, more recently, Peter Conder, the naturalist and president of the RSPB; and Neville Conder, his brother, an architect.

In total numbers they are small family – there were 264 in the 1881 census, mostly in Northumbria, Lancashire, Hertfordshire and Cambridgeshire, and still only 318 in 1998.

The Conders have been very well researched by various members of the family. I have contacted many descendants: firstly Peter and Neville Conder, who were the grandsons of Eustace and Fanny, then later Jay Conder, who organised a reunion of all the branches of the Conder family in 2000. He told me:

> Neville and I are descendants of different branches of the family. We have to go 11 generations back to get to our common ancestors. Neville's line stems from an Adam Conder, born around 1520, who lived in a farmhouse near Kendal, on Westmoreland, and my line stems from his brother Richard. [The father of Richard and Adam was an Edward Conder, born about 1486. He was a Yeoman from Kirby Lonsdale in Westmoreland, and fought at Flodden Field in 1513 under Stanley. He lived for many years after and died aged 56.] Neville's Conders moved to Leeds and thence to Essex and London. My line remained northerners, continuing to live in the house named Terry Bank for 500 years. For a few generations my lot farmed in Dentdale, but when the primogeniture line of Terry Bank Conders faded out, it was passed to my father.

Fanny's husband, known as Rennie, was the first child and only son of the Reverend George William Conder. George Conder was born in his father's shop in Hitchin in 1821. His biographer, Edward Miall described a setback in early life:

> He must have been endowed with a strong natural constitution, seeing that a course of medical treatment, probably to a great extent unnecessary, certainly injudicious and severe, during the greater part of his childhood, although it left behind it deep and indelible traces in after life, did not prevent the development of a fairly manly and vigorous frame.

Photographs of him, albeit in later life, confirm the 'manly and vigorous frame'. Like us all in later life, it was not quite as 'manly and vigorous' as it had once been.

His father George had a thriving drapery business in Hitchin. Nearing retirement he was persuaded by his future son-in-law, Wilhelm Bremer, a shipbroker's merchant, to move to Hull and put his money into shipping. His grandson Rennie recorded that he lost all his money in this enterprise as a result of the Crimean War. By 1871, widowed and living on a small annuity, he moved further south to live with his son.

George's only son, George William Conder, attended the grammar school in Hitchin and did well enough for the principal to urge his parents, backed by an offer of liberal assistance, to educate him for holy orders. His biography describes his attributes, 'The extraordinary quickness with which he mastered the rudimentary knowledge usually accessible in such institutions etc … ', and his reaction, 'The advice was in accord with neither their judgement nor his own tastes.'

George and his parents initially ignored this advice and determined that he would follow his father into the drapery trade. It was whilst George was apprenticed to a firm of silk merchants, Morrisons in the City of London, that he attended the Kings Weigh House, a local Congregational church. Originally a seventeenth-century weighing house for taxation purposes, it was rebuilt after the Great Fire. The last site of the church is now occupied by the Ukrainian Catholic Cathedral.

George was an active worker in its school, the pupils of which were from some of the poorest areas. Under the influence of its famous minister, the Reverend Thomas Binney, who was not slow to discern George's capabilities, he decided to enter the ministry. Quoting again from the biography:

> His heart began to yearn after the ministry of the Word. His desire became so urgent, and was so persistently expressed, that his father's not unnatural reluctance to assent to so great a change in the direction of his son's future career was at length overcome.

Whilst working at Highbury College in 1845, George was invited to become the assistant to Reverend Judson at the Independent Chapel, High Wycombe. It was there that he met his wife, Maria Swallow. George William and Maria married in 1847 and 'went forth and multiplied' – eight times altogether.

After another post in the Isle of Wight, he was asked in 1849 if he would take up a post at the Belgrave Chapel, Leeds, to succeed the Reverend William Winter Hamilton, a noted preacher of those days. This was a huge compliment for a man of his comparative youth and inexperience. He remained there for thirteen years and became a legend. His teaching was evangelical and used rich illustrations and analogies. He wrote a great deal, published sermons, collated religious literature and was heavily involved in various charitable causes. In 1853, he assisted in compiling the *Leeds Hymn Book*, as it became known.

His preaching was fearless and renowned, a real fire and brimstone style. He wrote his sermons in shorthand which, as Edward Miall said, 'he read with surprising facility, and with fervent and appropriate emphasis. Not that he needed to confine himself exclusively to what he had written. When the fire burned within him, his utterance at times soared above all trammels.'

In 1864, shortly after the birth of their last child, George was beginning to feel the strain – not surprising in view of his energetic and enthusiastic involvement in so many ventures. He moved to what he thought might be a less arduous position at Cheetham Hill Church, Manchester. During his stay here, his eldest daughter Lucy died, aged 13. This loss devastated him. He lost heart and ran out of steam.

At length, George felt he was not suited to the damp and pollution and in 1870 he moved south to a small church in Forest Hill, close to some family and friends. It was there that he was to see out his days, and it was there that his son Eustace Reynolds would meet Fanny Elizabeth Harrod.

Whilst living in Forest Hill, George had a second wind and continued travelling extensively to give religious lectures. In 1871, whilst in Malvern, he wrote a postcard-letter to his youngest daughter, Florence. It is in rhyme:

Wednesday Afternoon.

Dear little Miss Florence, I hope you are well,
This letter from Pa comes merely to tell
of his journey safe and arrival at Stroud,
Where the plaudits last night were both long and loud.
As you know, I've to lecture at Worcester tonight
Outed as Malvern is only a wee to the right
off the proper straight road I've just turned aside
Not more than an hour or two here to abide.

I've climbed up yon hill – today covered with snow
And had on the top a magnificent blow,
And the view! – I have hardly seen any so grand
And the wind was so strong that I hardly could stand.

And now I am sitting here waiting for dinner
For fear that my walk should have made me much thinner
Tell ma that at Worcester it isn't the Bell
But the 'Star' is the name of the proper hotel.

But I'll call in the morning and ask at the Post
Office – take care that the letters ain't lost.
And have 'em sent on in the course of the day
To Cardiff – the next place whereat I must stay.

The salmon's a broiling – the chops are a frying
I'm hungry and thirsty and time is a flying
So I beg you'll accept these short lines from Papa –
My respects to the fleas, and my love to Ma.

GWC March 15 1871

Tragically, in 1874 George died suddenly of scarlet fever at the Hermitage, Forest Hill, aged 52 years. He had caught the disease from that same daughter, Florence, who was then aged 11. He had seemed to be making a good recovery, and then relapsed; Florence recovered. He had predeceased his father by three years. Edward Miall's version of the event is worth quoting, '… to the inexpressible grief of his little flock, he received his Master's call to the "everlasting rest".'

Eustace Reynolds Conder, who married Fanny Harrod, was known as Rennie and spent most of his working life in a shipbrokers' office, initially as a clerk, later as a manager. Rennie and Fanny had five children, all born in Croydon. Two of them died in childhood.

One grandson, Peter, the son of Rennie and Fanny's eldest, Jack, had an interesting Second World War. He developed an interest in birdwatching at school in Cranleigh. After capture at Dunkirk, in captivity he spent most of his time birdwatching, a cover whilst tracking the movements of the German guards prior to escape attempts. After the war, he later went on to be director of the RSPB. Peter's history has been well documented by his daughter, Sarah, and is available elsewhere.

Jack and Edna's other two children also led interesting lives. Their daughter Natalie married Vic Oliver, the entertainer prominent during and after the Second World War, and their third child, Neville, became an outstanding and acclaimed architect.

Fanny died in a home in Surrey in 1949, aged 84. Her husband Rennie outlived her by four years, dying in 1953, aged 95.

GRACE MIRIAM HARROD AND THE MARTINS

Grace Miriam was the second daughter of Charles Digby and Caroline Harrod. She was born in 1866 in Brompton Road. The family moved to Hill Street when Grace was about 3 years old.

In 1881, aged 14, she was staying with her younger sister, Emily, at Hill View Lodge, Dartmouth Hill, at the home of her maternal grandmother, Caroline Jones (previously Godsmark, née Kibble). By 1889 when Grace got married, aged 22, the family were living at Evelyn Terrace.

She married Herbert James Martin, a solicitor. He was 26 years old and had been born in Deptford. The ceremony took place in the Congregational Kensington Chapel, Allen Street, just south of Kensington High Street, and the service was conducted by Herbert's father, the Reverend George Martin. The two eldest daughters of Charles Digby Harrod had both married the sons of Nonconformist ministers.

Herbert Martin was the fourth son of the Reverend George Martin and Sophia Davis, both Londoners. He was known to the family as Bertie. There were eleven children altogether in the family. George Martin was the independent minister at Lewisham High Road Congregational Church.

I was helped with Martin family history by Deborah Martin, a descendant of William Carson Martin. He was one of Herbert Martin's uncles, and had emigrated to Australia with his wife and children. Deborah has supplied many letters written by relatives in England to family in Australia between 1850 and 1903, which illuminate the family life in the 1800s.

The Martin family are descended from Huguenots who originated in the Picardy region of France and came over to England to escape religious persecution, probably in the late seventeenth century. The earliest Martin I have found is Esai Martin, who was born in France in about 1632, but was buried at St Mary Northgate, in Canterbury, Kent, in 1702. Esai is a Hebrew/Latin name also used in Spain, which is variously described as meaning 'God is Salvation', and 'Gift'.

His son, also called Esai, was born in France, and his grandson, Jacques, born in 1683, was the last of this line to be born there, so they probably left sometime between 1683 and 1702. Many Huguenots travelled together crammed into small boats, refugees not unlike those now crossing the Mediterranean. They brought the silk trade to London, and quite a few, like this family, settled in Spitalfields. Some refugees were able to travel back and forth, and Jacques died in France in 1793.

David Martin, the great-great-great-grandson of the first Esai, was born in 1781 in Bethnal Green. He was a silk weaver and merchant in Spitalfields. He was Herbert James' grandfather. He and his wife, Mary, had eight children, the first seven were born over a period of fourteen years and were baptised at the same ceremony in 1824, at St Matthew's, Bethnal Green. Some of the children became involved in the silk trade, and one son became a Nonconformist minister. This latter individual was in 1851 the independent minister of Spitalfields Chapel. (Times change, though, and this building is now the home of the Brick Lane Mosque.)

William Carson Martin was the sixth of those seven children. He married Charity Church and they emigrated to Sydney, Australia, in 1849 with their two daughters. They had nine further children in Australia. Charity Sophia wrote a remarkable history of her complex maternal Rowley family for the benefit of her daughters. It reads like a Dickensian drama, it is full of orphans and wicked uncles.

After losing his wife in 1897, Reverend George Martin continued to work and look after a sizeable congregation well into his seventies. Many of those Australian letters were from George to his widowed sister-in-law in Australia, for whom it is apparent he had a very soft spot. Both of them were lonely and, I suspect, had it not been for the fact that they were getting older and were half a world apart in an era when travel was difficult and uncommon, they might have got together and solved their loneliness. George died in Lewisham in 1918 aged 90.

The Martin family was obviously given to writing, what with George's religious tracts and the Rowley family history by Charity in Australia. One of George's grandchildren, Christabel (1895–1982), also wrote her memoirs, detailing life as a Victorian child.

Herbert James, George Martin's son, was born in 1862 and became a solicitor. He married Grace in 1889 and they set up home in Penge. They had three children. William Harrod Martin, the eldest, was born in 1890 and died in 1916 on the Somme, a lieutenant with the London Regiment.

Amy Grace, the second child, was born in 1893. She married George Parr in 1918 when he returned from Rio de Janeiro, where he had worked as vice consul. They lived for some time in Chelmsford and then Northern Ireland, where his work in the Civil Service was as 'Northern Ireland Comptroller & Auditor General'. He remained there for the rest of his life. He was awarded the CBE for his work.

The third child, Dora Gladys, was born in 1896, married Alan Heath in 1927 and had two children.

Herbert James Martin worked in Queen's Yard in the City with the legal firm Martin & Nicholson. He acted as the Harrod family solicitor in much of their business. He is mentioned as executor for several of his sisters-in-law and their families.

Grace died in a home in Cheam in 1941, aged 74, and Bertie died in 1953, aged 90.

EMILY MAUD HARROD

Emily Maud was the third child and daughter for Charles Digby and Caroline Harrod. She was born in 1868 in Hill Street, Knightsbridge. She was known in the family as 'Emmie'. She remained single and lived much of her life in Purley, close to her sister Fanny. She died in 1933, aged 64.

HENRY HERBERT HARROD

Henry was the fourth child of Charles Digby and Caroline. He was born in 1870 in Hill Street, Knightsbridge. Most importantly, he was the first and only son. He was the most colourful character amongst their children.

Henry Herbert, like his siblings, had a privileged childhood. The family were very comfortable by the time of his birth, as Harrods was already an extremely successful and increasingly profitable business. As the only boy, he would no doubt have been spoilt, not only by his parents, but also by his sisters. However, being the only boy did bring with it high expectations.

He was educated at Merchant Taylors School between 1883 and 1889. He then went up to Peterhouse College, Cambridge and gained his BA in 1892. He qualified as a solicitor in 1897, but he never worked or practised. He remained a single man throughout his life, and spent much of his time writing fairy stories and collecting pictures and books. Jean Pitt remembers that he was 'sweet but dreamy, a poet but no businessman, which was sad for Charles Digby Harrod as he could not pass Harrods on to him'.

Henry Herbert's lifestyle certainly did not fulfil his father's expectations and he would have been a disappointment for his father. Charles Digby Harrod had spent his life working hard and developing Harrods, so having his solicitor son spend his life with fairy stories must have difficult to accept. Henry Herbert must have told his father he had no interest in the shop, and by the time he went off to Cambridge Charles Digby was already selling up.

After the turn of the century Henry lived much of his life in private hotels in West London, not an unusual style for young men of the day who were 'living on their own means'. From 1918 onwards, Henry Herbert lived exclusively in the area round the southern end of Earls Court Road. After the horrors of the First World War, London had 'loosened up' considerably and major social changes followed. Industry and population began moving out along the major arterial roads to the suburbs and those in London who could afford it were having fun.

Henry Herbert wrote and published his first book of fairy stories, entitled *The Lord of the Deer, and other Fairy Tales*, in 1907. The publishers were Lamley & Co. and the illustrations were by Gilbert Ledward, then a 19-year-old student, but later to become a prolific and renowned sculptor. Henry Herbert's bookplate was also designed by Gilbert Ledward, and was discovered during a visit to view Henry's book and picture collection, which is housed at the Victoria & Albert Museum.

Henry was fascinated by book illustrators and their works, and by sketches by well-known and less well-known artists, some of whom were contemporaneous. Over his life he built up an enormous collection of over 20,000 pictures, paintings, prints and illustrations, which he bequeathed to the V&A. Many of the illustrations were originally used in children's books and fantasia stories, so it is no surprise that when Henry eventually published his second book in 1923 he produced his own illustrations. This book was entitled *Nine Little Fairy Tales*, and was published by A&C Black.

After Henry's death in 1945, the V&A retained only those pictures which filled gaps in its collection, numbering about 1,600; the rest were auctioned to pay for death duties. Letters between the executors and the Revenue, detailing the bequest and the tax payments, can be found in the National Archives.

In 1958 the *Times* featured an article reviewing the V&A 1948 catalogue of acquisitions. These catalogues, usually produced each year, had been delayed by the war, and Volume II for that year is devoted entirely to the bequest from Henry Harrod. The article stated:

Mr Harrod ... was a collector on an omnivorous scale.

The drawings in the Harrod bequest include a few by old masters, but the majority consists of English drawings, many of them sketches, mostly of the nineteenth century, though some are earlier, or later, and some are by Continental artists. Among them are examples of du Maurier, Keene, Leech, Linley Sambourne, Phil. May and other *Punch* Illustrators; of Cornelli and other designers of theatrical costumes; and of draughtsmen as variable as Blake, Sir

Thomas Lawrence, G. Cruikshank, Burne-Jones, Wilkie, Beardsley and Rowlandson – to name only a few at random.

The value of this acquisition, which includes also examples of many minor draughtsmen, is clearly very great to an historical reference collection such as that of the Department of Engraving, Illustration and Design – and all the more so since the accent is on the nineteenth century, which so far has not been intensively cultivated by collectors.

Most of the pictures and illustrations collected by Henry were unframed, so were kept in folders and files. One hopes he might have had some of them on his walls to admire them, however, as I discovered later, the majority were kept in Harrods' depository. Further details of his collection can be found in the *Penrose Annual* of 1959, Volume 53.

The *Penrose Annual* was a London-produced graphic arts journal which ceased publication in 1982. In Volume 53 there is an article by Harold Barkley which gives a detailed critique and listing of the Harrod bequest. It reveals the huge range of pictures which had been retained, including three Charles Edward Conder drawings. These included his 'Imperia la Belle' from 1906 and a 'View of Porlock and Porlock Bay' by Francis Towne, 1785, probably acquired because of the family's interest in nearby Allerford.

There are pictures from eighteenth, nineteenth and twentieth centuries. There are drawings by Gustave Doré; Du Maurier drawings for *Punch*; 'pin-ups' by Coleman used by De La Rue on cards; designs for theatre and ballet costumes; and Max Beerbohm's drawings of pre-First World War celebrities.

I have seen many of the illustrations and books at the V&A and found many of the pictures were very attractive. I was blown away by the breadth and beauty of Henry's choices. I particularly liked some illustrations: those by Randolph Caldecott from 1883, used as illustrations for his book, *A Frog he would a-Wooing go*; Edmund Dulac's illustrations for 'Beauty and the Beast' from the 1910 book, *The Sleeping Beauty and Other Fairy Tales retold by Sir Arthur Quiller-Couch*, and the same artist's illustrations for 'The Snow Queen' from *Stories from Hans Andersen*, published in 1911. I was fascinated by sixteen drawings of 'Comic Birds' produced in Italy in about 1880 by the poet and artist Edward Lear, who was also famed for his very serious bird illustrations for ornithological reference books and the Zoological Society. Many of the pictures and illustrations can be seen on the V&A website, searching for 'Henry Herbert Harrod'.

Henry Herbert Harrod also collected a considerable number of nineteenth-century illustrated books, most of which were also left to the museum. The books are available in the National Art Library at the V&A, under the title 'The Harrod Collection'.

As a writer of fairy stories and collector of pictures and books, it seems impossible that he might also have collected firearms! However, to my surprise, I discovered an article from the *Times* archives of 1914 which gave the story of his collection. It was so out of character that I thought for some time that it must have been a different Henry Herbert Harrod, who I had been unable to find. The article stated that he had collected firearms for several years, and had a remarkable collection dating from 1700 which, with a total of about 800 pieces, was believed to be the most representative collection in the country.

A chance finding by Sebastian Wormell, Harrods' archivist, revealed further articles. One was from the *Journal of the British Historical Small Arms Association* of December 2006, by Clifford Bryant. This article quotes another article, from the *Daily Express* in 1935 with two photographs (albeit grainy, copied newspaper photographs) of Henry. Henry would have been aged 64 at the time of the article, and these are the only pictures of Henry I have ever found. This piece was headed, 'ONE-MAN ARMS MUSEUM', and subtitled, '£10,000 History of the World's Battles'. It reveals that the collection was housed in a room 14ft by 20ft, on the top floor of Harrods furniture depository. The collection was then valued at £10,000, a sum equivalent to about £350,000 today. I suspect rare collectibles like these guns will have increased in value faster than inflation and so might be worth even more today.

The collection consisted of a huge range of firearms of all ages, some early hand grenades and many bayonets. These guns had killed Frenchmen at Waterloo, Englishmen at Blenheim, Turks at Acre, Russians at Balaclava, English at Cawnpore and Germans at Ypres. The article states he had been collecting since 1906, and spent an average of ten hours per week cleaning and caring for them. The *Express* correspondent interviewed Henry for about two hours. Henry was dressed in overalls and gloves, and touched his treasures with the reverence of a priest with holy relics. He enthused about the items and the history surrounding each:

> 'This belonged to George IV when he was Prince of Wales, silver and gold mounted, and this belonged to Tippoo Sahib, last Sultan of Mysore. But it did not save his life at Seringapatam, where he was killed in 1797.'

Henry himself wrote little about his collection, apart from an article in a *Country Life* magazine of 1921, entitled 'Early Gun Locks'. Henry's knowledge of his subject was such that other firearms historians acknowledged his assistance when producing their works of reference.

It is not entirely clear from the article or further research what happened to the collection. Photographs of pieces that were once in his collection appear in other treatises on the subject, and in 1974 and 1975 parts of the collection were auctioned by Wallace & Wallace. The lack of a mention of any guns in his will suggests it was dispersed before his death. According to the article, he did offer to present his unique collection to the nation but this was, amazingly, rejected. I have searched online for any evidence of remnants of his collection with no success.

Henry Herbert led a pretty relaxed life. The family know that as well as writing fairy stories, he visited several children's hospitals in London, including Great Ormond Street, reading and telling stories to the sick children. He was much loved by his nephews and nieces for the same reason. One of them, Digby Weightman, wrote in 1989 at the age 80:

A character in every sense. An odd character. Never earned a penny having qualified as a solicitor. Income from father of about £400 on which he lived in a hotel in S. Kensington. Wrote several books on fairy tales. Very useful Uncle. Got invited to Sunday lunch and when the rest of the adults fell asleep, he told stories to the children. Spent much of his life going round London Children's Hospitals telling stories to the children.

Very little is known about his personal life. All attempts to discover more through his school, university or the many art clubs in London at the time has proved fruitless.

Henry Herbert Harrod died in 1945, aged 74, at St Mary Abbots Hospital, Kensington, London. His cause of death was given as uraemia (kidney failure) due to senile enlarged prostate. The informant was his sister, my grandmother Beatrice, then residing at the Ashley Court Hotel in Knightsbridge.

Apart from the bequest to the V&A and some personal bequests, his will had a codicil which bequeathed some specific pictures and books to relatives.

There is an interesting postscript to the story of his collection which comes from a further visit by Sebastian Wormell to the V&A archive in 2009 to look again at the Henry Herbert Harrod file. He found an autographed letter from Henry, dated from 1909, which was addressed to the librarian at the V&A. In it he offers to loan the library his 'collection of the illustrated books of the sixties, 1855–1872'. The offer was rejected. What was remarkable about the letter was Henry's bizarre handwriting. Sebastian said it was hard to describe – the letters were made up of narrow strokes and very broad strokes of the pen as the nib is pressed down, rather like an odd form of italic. Curiously, these bulbous broad strokes run horizontal, parallel to the line of script, creating something of the effect of a string of beads – very calligraphic and neat, but difficult to read. I am not sure what a graphologist would make of it.

With some difficulty, the letter has been 'translated'. After a while, it becomes more obvious. It reads:

Dear Sir,

I have in my possession a large and almost complete collection of the illustrated books of the Sixties, 1855–1872; that is books illustrated with wood engravings after Winsham, A. Hughes, Tenniel, Rossetti, Middais, Doyles, Pinwell, Boyds Houghton, etc. The collection numbers some 200 Volumes, and I shall be very pleased to loan the same to the Library under your charge.

Yours truly, H.H. Harrod.

AMY CAROLINE HARROD AND THE WEIGHTMANS

Amy was the fifth child and fourth daughter for Charles Digby, who must have been hoping for more boys. She was born in 1875 at Ditton Marsh, near Esher.

A family photograph of her in her twenties shows her to have been a striking young woman. At the age of 32, in 1907 Amy Caroline married Arthur James Weightman at St Paul's Parish Church in the village of Rusthall, near Tunbridge Wells. Amy had been living with her widowed mother in the Red House, Tunbridge Wells, and was given away by her mother, though she entered the church on the arm of her brother, Henry Herbert. Arthur was aged 44, and his father and mother had both died a few years earlier. He was living in his parents' house in Croydon. He was the second son of James Milward Weightman, a solicitor.

It had been almost twenty years since the last wedding of one of Caroline Harrod's children, and it looks as though they went to town in celebration. Amy had seven bridesmaids; four were her nieces, Margery and Katherine Conder, aged 17 and 9 years respectively, and Dolly and Gladys Martin, aged 13 and 11 years respectively; and three were her husband's nieces. There were 218 guests.

Several newspaper reports of the wedding were shown to me by their grandson, James. One states:

Yesterday afternoon, St Paul's Church, Rusthall, a western suburb of Tunbridge Wells, was the scene of a pretty wedding. Artistic decorations had been carried out, and the ceremony was largely attended, the rain storms which threatened to interfere having ceased soon after mid-day ... she wore a dress of ivory duchesse satin, in semi-Empire style, with Court train, the bodice and train being trimmed with exquisite Brussels lace, the gift of her mother. A fine Brussels net veil covered a spray of orange blossoms ... The bridesmaids wore Empire Gowns of white Breton net, and Valenciennes lace, over underskirts of glace silk, veiled with chiffon. Their picture hats were white net and silk with white ostrich plumes, and their ornaments consisted of pear brooches, the gifts of the bridegroom. The bride's mothers dress was of heliotrope Irish poplin trimmed with white velvet and beautiful old Flemish lace, with bonnet to match ... The breakfast and reception were held at the Spa Hotel [conveniently only a few doors away from the Red House]. Later, Mr and Mrs Weightman left for Bournemouth for the honeymoon. The bride's travelling dress was of fine cloth in Nattier blue, with hat to match, with shaded ostrich feathers, and a set of beautiful white fox furs were worn.

Arthur Weightman worked as a 'chemical agent'. He had an office in the City of London, in St Mary Axe, off Leadenhall Street. The 1911 census is more specific; there he is described as an 'agent for a lead manufacturer'. He spent his working life trading, mostly with Europe.

James and Philippa, Amy's grandchildren, have helped to fill in some details of the Weightman family. James is a retired actuary living in Cirencester. He is the owner by inheritance of several Charles Digby Harrod treasures, including his portrait, his Bible and the presentation items from Morebath.

Philippa has documented the Weightman ancestors back through many centuries, and has produced a beautifully illustrated scroll to show this. Her history of the Weightman family can be traced through fifteen generations to about 1500. A branch of the family goes back to Richard de Rodvile, living in the time of William the Conqueror in the eleventh century – a total of more than twenty-four generations. All the families involved originated in that area of the Midlands situated along the present A5 road, on the Leicestershire/Warwickshire border, near the towns of Nuneaton and Hinckley.

After their marriage, Arthur and his wife lived south of London, and moved to the definitive family home at 'Allerford', Silver Lane, Purley. Presumably the house was named after the same Allerford in Somerset; it obviously held happy memories for them all.

Arthur and Amy Weightman had three children: Digby born in 1908, John in 1911 and Mary in 1913. Arthur Weightman died in Purley, Surrey, in 1925, aged 61, as the result of a road traffic accident. Amy Caroline remained at Allerford House and died seventeen years later in 1942, aged 67.

Digby Milward Weightman, their eldest son, uniquely carried the names of both his paternal and his maternal great-grandmothers. He became a solicitor. He married Lavender Maureen Leck in 1940, at Purley, and from 1950 spent over twenty years in Foxley Lane, Purley, the same road that some of the Conders had lived in thirty years earlier. Digby Weightman was Charter Mayor of Croydon between 1970 and 1971, and was created a Freeman of the Borough in 1977. Apart from my father and my Uncle Michael, Beatrice's son, he was the only other one of his generation, the grandchildren of Charles Digby Harrod, to whom I have managed to talk personally.

BEATRICE MARTHA HARROD

Beatrice Martha Harrod, my grandmother, was Charles Digby and Caroline's fifth daughter. She was known to the family as Bea or Bee.

I did not know her at all. What has been learnt about her has been, of necessity, second or third hand, and has certainly not produced a favourable impression of her. She was pretty well universally disliked by most of her relatives.

On the Harrod side of the family, Natalie Oliver, a great-granddaughter of Charles Digby and grand-niece of Beatrice, was not too fond of Aunt Bea: 'She seemed rather pompous towards my father's family.' She never forgave Beatrice for the aloofness she displayed and her lack of contact during the illnesses and deaths of Natalie's grandparents, Rennie and Fanny Conder. She blamed it on Beatrice's delusions of grandeur. She told me:

> Michael [Uncle Michael, Bea's son] was invited at the beginning of 1939 to Windsor Castle as a young officer to mix with the two princesses and Aunt Bea was invited once to dinner there. But I really couldn't forgive her in totally ignoring Granny in her old age – no letters, or visits.

Apparently the lack of contact was despite Rennie contacting Beatrice Martha about his wife's terminal state. They felt that Bea owed them some attention after the help they had given her earlier in her life.

Jean Pitt, another granddaughter of Rennie and Fanny, thought she was 'snooty'. Natalie Oliver wrote in 1989, 'Great Aunt Bea ran away from home and stayed with my grandparents [Fanny and Eustace Reynolds Conder], who were married and much older. I'm afraid I never enquired why she ran away.' Another letter from Natalie to Jean, also from around 1989 and written soon after the death of their Aunt Katherine, confirms the story about Bea living with her sister Fanny for a spell. She says that she remembers her grandfather Rennie talking, at the time his wife went into a nursing home, when he had had no contact with Bea, 'she had run away from home and stayed with them.'

Anna, the wife of Uncle Michael and daughter-in-law of Beatrice Martha, has no fond memories of her either. Bea was opposed to her marriage to her son and proved difficult throughout their married life, relenting only when she was near death and needed Anna to be with her. Peter Conder, another grandson of Fanny, said, 'Bea and the two daughters were about the most toffee-nosed people I knew and certainly made me feel a poor relation.'

Her husband's family also disliked her and were opposed to her marriage to their son.

In trying to understand why Beatrice may have been as described, reasons can be found in her story that would have been likely to make her feel bitter and twisted about how things turned out for her. She had a privileged upbringing and started life, like all her siblings, in a comfortable, loving and financially secure family. Was her temperament in her nature, or did circumstances cause the problem? We can never know without first-hand accounts of her earlier life, but my bet is that her later life had played the major part. This story, as suggested earlier, is told elsewhere.

Beatrice was born in April 1877, soon after the family had moved to their splendid new home of Armitage Lodge in Sydenham. Charles Digby would have been in his pomp, with things going well for him in business and at home. Indeed, Great Britain was also doing very well at the time. On 1 January that year Queen Victoria was declared Empress of India; in February, there was the first cricket test match between Australia and England in Melbourne – Australia won by 45 runs (I have no doubt Charles Digby, a keen fan, may occasionally have been distracted by the scores in the newspapers of the day); on 12 April, Britain annexed the South African Republic and this same year Edison invented the microphone and the phonograph.

Beatrice lived in Sydenham until she was 12 years old, when the family moved to the West Country. Her daughter-in-law, Anna, remembers that Beatrice was an accomplished pianist, an avid 'smocker', and that she spoke fluent French. These were attributes learnt, presumably, during these early years. The latter ability, the speaking of French, is the subject of some conjecture in her own story. It has previously been mentioned that Beatrice, along with the other three of the four youngest sisters and her mother and father, were missing from the 1901 census. They were all probably abroad then, and Beatrice also spent further time abroad in the following decade, so perhaps she learnt her French at that time.

Further details of her before the age of 30 were very hard to find. More recent research has filled some of those gaps. Beatrice had moved with her parents to Allerford, and later Morebath at the end of the nineteenth century. Her father, Charles Digby, died suddenly in 1905 and afterwards she followed her mother to the Red House in Tunbridge Wells in 1906, and lived there until 1909.

OLIVE MARY HARROD

She was born in 1880 in Lewisham, and was the sixth daughter and seventh child of Charles and Caroline. She caused some confusion during research as she is listed in error as Alice M. Harrod in the 1881 census. In 1901, she is missing from the census, like her other young sisters. There are very few details available about her and no photographs have been found.

She was well liked by her nephews and nieces. Jean Pitt wrote:

> I think mother's [Margery Caroline Conder] favourite Aunt was Olive, there was only eight years between them [in fact ten years], they seemed to go on holiday together before mother married and I have a book of postcards given by Olive to Mother in memory of a holiday all over Exmoor.

Olive travelled in 1934, on her own from Liverpool to Montreal on board the *Duchess of Bedford*, and returned two months later. Her address is given in the ship's manifest as South Park, 11 Lansdowne Road, Wimbledon, SW20, and she was still at this address, according to the telephone directory, in 1937.

She died in 1951, aged 70 in Eastbourne. She left a modest estate with several individual bequests to charities, and the rest to her sisters and brother.

EVA MARGUERITA HARROD AND THE RODGERS

She was the seventh daughter and the last child, and was born in Sydenham in 1881. Charles may have decided to give up hope of another boy after Eva; Caroline was now 41 years old and this may have been the end of the line, both literally and metaphorically.

I have had a lot of contact with her granddaughters so have accumulated information and photographs about Eva and her descendants. Penny Blyth in Canada told me that Eva went to finishing school in Paris, so one presumes she must have been aged about 20 then, so it would have been in about 1901. Perhaps the members of the family who were missing in 1901 were on a trip which included either seeing Eva in France or taking her there. Perhaps the other daughters had done the same.

Eva's future husband, Dr Frederick Millar Rodgers, proposed to her on the steps of St Paul's Cathedral. Though spelt 'Miller' on his birth records, Millar was the correct spelling of the family name. They married in 1912, like her sister Amy at St Paul's Church, Rusthall.

Frederick was born in 1876 in Clayton-Le-Moors, near Blackburn. He was the youngest of three sons of the Reverend Thomas Rodgers and Jane Millar. Thomas was a Wesleyan minister, like his brother Isaac. So Eva was the third daughter to marry a son of a Nonconformist minister.

The Rodgers family have been traced back to Frederick's great-grandfather, Thomas Rodgers, who was born in about 1770 in Ecclesfield, Yorkshire, a village close to Sheffield and Rotherham.

Frederick qualified in Manchester and practised initially in Hull, where his parents were living. Prior to his marriage he had decided on a career in what today would be called mental health, but was in those days much more to do with mental illness, variously dubbed madness, feeble-mindedness, insanity or lunacy. He became one of the physicians at Winwick Hospital, Warrington, which was the County Lunatic Asylum for Lancashire, and by 1919 he was a consultant psychiatrist.

Psychiatry was in its infancy, and patients were admitted to hospital for lengthy periods with not just the full range of mental illnesses recognised today but sadly also for many social reasons, including illegitimate pregnancy. Admission was often at the request of relatives, mostly fathers or husbands, who judged the patient difficult to manage. Some of the hospital inmates were drunkards or vagrants. These hospitals were crowded and hopeless places for people who should never have been there in the first place. Treatment, as we know it today, was primitive and included psychoanalytical therapy (Freud had been in full flow for some years), malaria-induced fever, insulin-induced comas, lobotomy and primitive forms of electroshock therapy. The general opinion of much of the remaining, supposedly sane, population was that they should just be shut up away from society forever.

These institutions were vast establishments like small villages, with large numbers of buildings and their own small farms, catering and laundry facilities. They were almost completely self-sufficient. In 1911, Winwick Hospital held about 2,200 patients, tellingly all identified in the census by initials only. There were about 300 members of staff, including maintenance staff of all sorts, assistants and nurses, with just four doctors and a medical superintendent.

When I was a medical student in the mid 1960s, I was able to see a similar institution myself when I was studying for a short while at Claybury Hospital in Essex. Although it was nearing the end of its days, it had probably changed little in the previous fifty years. By chance, I have visited Winwick myself during the 1990s when, as a general practitioner, I went there to undertake a course on hypnotherapy in the psychiatric department. It was a typical, grim, Victorian asylum building. It finally closed in 1998.

Penny Blyth said that she was told that the three children of Frederick and Eva were born in the house in the grounds of the hospital. She said, 'There was a tunnel connecting the house to the hospital – the only one with a key to the gate in the tunnel was my grandfather. My mother remembers being allowed to ride bikes in it on rainy days.'

Sometime in the late 1930s Frederick retired and, together with Eva, they built and moved to a house in Bexhill, where they lived for the rest of their lives. Jean Pitt remembers, 'my brother John was evacuated to Eva in Bexhill for a short time in WWII.' During the Second World War Eva's daughter Jean had to teach her mother to cook as she had never done so previously!

Frederick and Eva are remembered fondly by their grandchildren. Frederick was known as 'Pop' and Eva as 'Granny' or 'Mop'. Jocelyn Broughton, another granddaughter, recalls Eva as being both 'lovely' and yet 'formidable'. Helen Yarwood recounts that her grandmother was rather strict, 'on one occasion she threatened to serve up my dinner for breakfast if I didn't eat it all. I didn't, she did!'

Frederick died when Penny Blyth was very young but she remembers, 'he had lovely hands – healing hands I think you would call them.' Later Granny used to buy Penny's riding clothes for her in Harrods when Penny stayed with her in the summer. Granny had obviously begun to lose it, as they had Christmas crackers every day with their breakfast!

Frederick died in 1955 in Bexhill, when he was aged 78. Eva lived until 1964.

There are interesting stories about the three children of Frederick and Eva. Not only are some of the family quite exotic, but the history I have uncovered shows that family myths are not always absolutely true. Charles Thomas Rodgers was the eldest child and was born in 1913. He joined the army between the wars becoming a 2nd lieutenant in 1934. He had two marriages.

His first marriage was to the excitingly named Vaudine Louise Agassiz. The marriage as a whole seems to have been odd, and a rather dark period of his life. Vaudine, according to the records, was born in 1912 in Patrington, East Yorkshire. Patrington is just not an exotic place at all; it is a small hamlet on the very flat land between Hull and the North Sea coast named Holderness. There is a small creek connected to the River Humber.

Jeanann, the only daughter of Charles and Vaudine, thought her mother had been born in Whitby, about 65 miles further north, although it may be that the family were based there during her childhood. Though the Agassiz name is relatively rare, they were an active lot and there are an awful lot of them to be found in the records. Usually an uncommon name aids the family history researcher, but although the records show that Vaudine was a name often used in the family none of the Vaudines identified were the one I was trying to find. No Agassiz family were found in the 1911 census in east Yorkshire, they were all in London and environs, or Hampshire.

Jeanann was given to understand that Vaudine's father was a submarine captain, killed during the First World War. He was Thomas Roland Agassiz, born in 1870 at Gosport, Hampshire. His ancestors were a military part of the clan. His father was Lieutenant Roland Lewis Agassiz, a Royal Marines officer born in Cologne, Germany, and his grandfather, Lewis Agassiz, was also a Royal Marine. So the story seemed reasonable.

Thomas Roland Agassiz's career was in the Merchant Navy and then in the RNR. He obtained his Board of Trade Certificate as a mariner in 1897 and rose through the ranks during the following ten years. Late in 1913, just before the First World War started, he was commissioned as a commander and served on a series of mine-sweeping vessels in that role. Most of these were armed, commandeered trawlers or motor yachts. They acted both as mine sweepers and patrol and protection vessels for merchant shipping. He had two spells in command of the armed admiralty motor yacht, *Conqueror II*. She had been built in Hull, east Yorkshire, in 1889, for the Vanderbilt family in New York, so presumably was a smart boat.

During Agassiz's second spell of service in September 1916, the *Conqueror II*, together with HM Trawler *Sarah Alice*, was in the process of trying to investigate an unidentified merchant steamer north of the Fair Isle when they were attacked by the German submarine *U-52*, commanded by Kapitän Hans Walther. Between July 1916 and September 1917, Hans Walther and his boat sank thirty-two and damaged a further four ships of various nationalities. The total tonnage sunk by him was 89,000 tons and he damaged 13,700 tons.

During this engagement, both naval boats were sunk and nineteen minutes later the merchant steamer was sunk. This turned out to be the 2,788 ton *St Gothard*. Seventeen lives were lost on the *Conqueror II*, including the commander, and sixteen on the *Sarah Alice*. The crew of the *St Gothard* were saved. The crew of *Conqueror II*, including Commander Agassiz, are commemorated on the Portsmouth Naval Memorial.

So, Thomas Roland Agassiz was Vaudine's father, but who was her mother? The only marriage listed for Thomas Agassiz was at the end of 1914, when he married Winifred Ann Smith in Portsmouth. This was two years after Vaudine's birth, but of course does not mean Winifred was not her mother, and there are no other candidates.

Nothing much more is known about Vaudine's early life. There is a record in the passenger lists at the National Archives, of a journey from London to Mombasa in Kenya in May 1920, undertaken by Vaudine and her mother. Her mother is recorded as a dressmaker, aged 39, and Vaudine, aged 7. Later events suggest this was a one-way journey, and no return journey has been found.

Charles Thomas Rodgers was said to be the third husband of Vaudine Agassiz, though there is no documentary evidence to confirm this. They married during the Second World War in Kenya, so no details are available, and no records of his war service have been found for him. Her previous marriages were presumably also in Kenya. Their only daughter, Jeanann, was born in 1943. Charles and Vaudine did not last long after this. Charles met his second wife, Noreen Alba Hale, when Jeanann was 6 months old. Vaudine was then about 30, and Charles left her and Jeanann soon afterwards.

Vaudine was not yet finished, though. When Jeanann was 5 years old, Vaudine married Desmond Kenzo Knight (presumably her fourth husband) in Kenya. He became Jeanann's 'Dad'.

Desmond and Vaudine were married for over forty years. Jeanann lived in Kenya until she and her husband went to Australia in 1974. Desmond and Vaudine followed in 1976 and they lived in Western Australia until they died. Vaudine died aged 81 in Bunbury, Western Australia. There were no other children.

Jeanann Rodgers married Richard Andrew Barbour in 1964 and they had three children. After nearly thirty years living in Kenya and then thirty years in Australia, Jeanann and Richard lived and worked at Kisampa Camp in Tanzania. Kisampa is a private community conservation sanctuary that adjoins the unique coastal Saadani National Park in eastern Tanzania. Conserving this area was the passion of the Barbour family.

Charles Thomas Rodgers married Noreen Alba Hale in 1946. Noreen was born in 1912 in Buenos Aires, Argentina. Her mother's father had been in Argentina as manager the Anglo South American Bank, whilst her father, Horace, after an illustrious rowing career at Eton and Balliol, worked there as an importer of agricultural equipment and later arms and munitions. Noreen had obviously been married before as her name was given as Pearson when she married Charles.

Charles continued in the forces after the war. He spent some time as a liaison officer in Washington DC, in America, where their only daughter, Jocelyn, was born in 1947. He served as colonel with the Cheshires in Korea. After that he returned to the USA, still working in the army. Later, after leaving the army, Charles went to work for Lonrho, the London and Rhodesian Mining and Land Company, in Rhodesia. He died at a cricket match in Oxted, Surrey, in 1989 whilst there with his daughter Jocelyn.

Jocelyn Mary Rodgers was the only child of Charles and Noreen Rodgers. She had US citizenship by reason of her birth. She married Martin Broughton in 1974 in Chelsea, London. They had met whilst they were both working with British American Tobacco (BAT) in Hong Kong. Trained as an accountant, Martin later became chairman of BAT; he has also been chairman of the Wiggins Teape Group, chairman of Eagle Star and became chairman of British Airways in July 2004. He was president of the CBI from 2007. He is a keen Chelsea football fan, and was most recently in the news for his part as temporary chairman of Liverpool FC in 2010, negotiating the sale of the club.

The rationale for this long explanation of the origins of Jeanann and Jocelyn can now be revealed. With all the convolutions and intricacies of their father's marital situation, Jocelyn did not know her half-sister, Jeanann, existed until she was 23 years old. Frederick Harrod Rodgers was the second child of Frederick and Eva Rodgers, born in 1916. Although qualified as a solicitor, he spent most of his life in local government.

Jean Mary Rodgers was the third child of Frederick and Eva, and was born in 1920. Her daughter, Penny Blyth, gave details of her story.

She married her first husband, Major Donald John Scott, a Canadian officer, at the end of 1942, when the Canadians were stationed in Sussex. Don was killed in the D-Day landings at the Falaise Gap in France. Their best man, Jimmie Blyth, who was Don's roommate at the University of Saskatchewan, was also serving with the Canadian forces in France, where he was wounded. Jimmie came back to England after the fighting in France – and married Jean himself!

Jimmie had been made a major at the age of 24, and ended the war as an acting lieutenant colonel. He returned to Canada with his troops at the end of the war, sailing on the *Queen Mary*. Jean followed later on a bride ship. He worked in the power industry and later the brewing and soft drinks industry, including Canada Dry, where he became president and chairman of the board.

Penny Jean, who was born in 1948, was their only child.

An interesting addition to the story of Jean Mary Rodgers materialised in 2014. I was contacted by a retired British Army officer after he saw my family tree on Ancestry. Tony was born in June 1942 and had been adopted as a youngster, and he had had a very happy family life. He had been born a Rodgers. He was keen to trace his birth mother, who he knew to be Jean Rodgers. He thought from my tree that he might have been an illegitimate son of Don Scott and Jean Rodgers, conceived before their marriage. He had already done quite a lot of research about Don. He hoped I might know what had happened to Jean Rodgers and be in contact with any relatives.

It had been some years since my last contact with Jean's daughter, so I was by no means certain whether Jean was still alive. She would have been 94 years old. I was able to contact Penny and break the news to her that her mother had a further child, and she had a half-brother. Jean was still alive, though very frail, and Penny had to broach the subject slowly and carefully with her mother. It turned out her mother had had a relationship with another Canadian soldier before marrying Don Scott, and Tony was the result. Jean came round to the idea that her secret was out and Penny was delighted to find a brother.

The happy end to the story is that Tony and his wife flew off to Canada soon afterwards and they were all able to meet Jean and Penny and get to know each other.

EPILOGUE

I am very proud of my illustrious ancestors, despite their occasional indiscretions. However, I do wonder from time to time whether the Harrods of today is such a glorious institution because of or despite my relatives.

Comparing the store to other similar stores suggests that a good start in life is not necessarily a guarantee of success; look at what happened to Whiteley's. But plenty of London stores which were founded in the nineteenth century, or even earlier, have thrived and are still in a healthy state today. John Lewis started as a draper's apprentice. He opened his own store in 1864 in Oxford Street. He became a great benefactor with a reputation for looking after his staff; a feature of the company that still continues today. No one could argue that the store has not been successful.

William Debenham invested in William Clark's small London draper's shop in Wigmore Street in 1813. Starting as Clark & Debenhams, it was later renamed Cavendish House. Of particular interest to me is that they opened several provincial stores, including one in my own town, Cheltenham, in 1823. It prospered, and the management split with Debenham returning to London. The Cheltenham store that remained is called Cavendish House. As what goes around comes around, John Lewis has this year, 2016, taken over an arcade site from Debenhams in Cheltenham and will have a department store here once again.

There has always been a flux of stores which get swallowed up in a group and then change hands. Harrods were involved for a while in the House of Fraser group, and Debenhams in its time took over

Marshall & Snelgrove and Harvey Nichols, but they have all changed ownership since.

The Army & Navy Co-operative Society was formed in London in 1871 by a group of army and navy officers. It became a limited company in the 1930s, and expanded into other stores in the 1950s. They were acquired by House of Fraser in 1976 but the name was lost when the stores were rebranded after 2005.

Arthur Lasenby Liberty opened his business in 1875 selling exotic fabric, with a lease on half a shop in Regent Street. He had already worked in Regent Street for twelve years. Over the following years the store continued its growth by buying neighbouring properties and pursued its interest in fabrics and design. Although Liberty died in 1917, in 1924 the distinctive mock-Tudor store was constructed from the timbers of two Royal Naval ships: HMS *Impregnable* and HMS *Hindustan*. The shop has changed hands several times and in 2010 it was taken over by a private equity firm.

William Fortnum used his position as footman to Queen Anne to kick-start his career. His landlord, Hugh Mason, joined him and their Piccadilly grocery store opened in 1707. It has always concentrated on provisions, and although other departments have been added it has never tried to have universal coverage. The shop has changed hands in the last few decades and is now privately owned by an investment company.

Benjamin Harvey opened a linen shop in 1831. He died in 1850 and his wife ran the shop in partnership with James Nichols, who married Harvey's niece. Following demolition, a new building was completed in 1894. It was owned for a while by Debenhams, and subsequently Burtons who bought Debenhams, but it has changed hands since then only once, and is now listed on the stock exchange. In the recent years the group has opened branches both here and abroad.

In 1849, Hugh Fraser and James Arthur started a small drapery shop on Argyle Street, Glasgow. The partnership was dissolved in 1865, but Fraser continued. Between 1936 and 1985 over seventy companies, not including their subsidiaries, were acquired and the group became a national chain and it was rebranded as the House of

EPILOGUE

Fraser. In 2006 it was sold to a consortium of investors and, latterly, in 2014 was acquired by a chain of Chinese department stores.

Michael Marks began selling wares from a bag. In 1884, Thomas Spencer joined him and they opened a shop in Leeds. It is now publicly owned and listed on the stock exchange. Today, it operates 700 stores.

What I do not know is how many potential stores started up in the nineteenth century and never made it into the twentieth century.

Whiteley's makes an interesting comparison; it is really very similar to Harrods. They were both started by a driven individual who did well after humble beginnings. Whereas Whiteley had the vision to see where he wanted to go on his own, Harrods needed the ambition of the founder's son to put the growth into overdrive. Whiteley was fired up by his visit to the Great Exhibition in 1851 when he was aged 20. Both Mr Harrod and Mr Whiteley's shops suffered the setback of a major fire – Harrods in 1883 and Whiteley's in 1897 – but both recovered and continued to progress.

Charles Digby Harrod had seven daughters and a son who was not interested in business. William Whitely had two daughters and two sons, and his sons took over after William's death in 1907. They opened a splendid new store in what is now called Queensway, in 1911.

At this point, I would guess Harrods and Whiteley's were neck and neck in the store stakes, with Selfridges a late starter. Whiteley's thrived for a while, but the sons lost interest and drive, and in 1927 the store was sold to Harry and Gordon Selfridge. It did not thrive and gradually declined in the following decades. Gordon Selfridge did not do very well in the next decade and had many financial problems. In the end, he returned to the retail trade in the USA in 1940.

So why did Harrods continue and succeed, whilst Whiteley's never really recovered from the founder's death? I think the answer lies in what today would be called succession planning. Whiteley's ran out of somebody to pick up the ball, whereas Harrods, more by chance than planning, always found somebody competent to pick up the ball and run. Charles Henry Harrod made an inspired decision when he moved from Cable Street to Brompton Road, but he had run out of steam by 1860 and Charles Digby, despite his youth, was raring to go. Thirty years later, when he was in his turn ready to retire, he had no family to take over.

However, he was well advised to sell up and form a limited company. It was luck that determined that the appointed manager, Mr Smart, failed so early in his career, and that the board moved rapidly to replace him. Richard Burbidge, who proved to be more than capable, happened to be available and the rest is history. There could have been no better individual to take over, and fortunately the correct genes passed to his son and grandson who kept up the momentum in their turns.

So, the critical factor was the ability to react to changes in circumstances. Perhaps for the future of Harrods it was a blessing that there was no one in the family to take over. So often a successful father is followed by a reluctant and less successful son. Throughout the convoluted changes to ownership in the last few decades, someone with drive and ambition has always been able to maintain the reputation of the store. Which leaves us thankfully with the 'best store in the world'.

The Harrods played their part, and I am proud of them. What a shame, though, that I was not the fifth generation of the family in charge!

ACKNOWLEDGEMENTS

The information contained in this story has been sourced from many places, some from official websites, some unofficial, some from individuals who have done their own research and an awful lot from living relatives.

There are a few names amongst those that helped me research and create the book that stand out for me. Mary Rance helped me to understand the importance of accuracy. I have found that accuracy cannot be guaranteed, but it has been strived for. Peter Shilham did a lot of background work in Southwark. Successive archivists at Harrods have given me help and encouragement, notable Nadene Hansen and more recently Sebastian Wormell. Several cousins have given me information, photographs and help, particularly Jean Pitt, Natalie Oliver, Vanessa Ascough, and James and Phillipa Weightman; and there are several more in the Conder, Martin and Rodgers families who have also contributed. There are some no longer alive, like Maughan Innes and Lionel Harrod. My brothers and my own family worked with me in the early stages of my research. Most important of all, my wife Christine has put up with thirty years of my research, both on foot and latterly in front of the computer god.

There are many more in a list that has become too long, they know who they are already.

The author is happy to be contacted with additional information about the Harrods shop or the Harrod family. The address for contact is- HarrodHistory@aol.com. The author will attempt to answer all constructive e mails.

INDEX

Al-Fayed, Mohamed 11
Army & Navy Store 177, 246

Benett's of Derby 10
Birch, Essex 19, 36–7, 44–6, 49, 95, 115
Bunhill Fields Burial Ground 38–40
Burbidge, Richard and family 8, 10, 118, 159, 172–5, 177, 178, 181, 182, 186, 248
Burden, Philip Henry 88–91, 93
Burns, Robert 29–30

Cholera and the Great Stink 83
Clacton 36–7
Cohen, Edgar 143–4, 168, 173–5, 179
Conder, Fanny Elizabeth and family 120, 133, 162, 164, 184, 186, 191, 196, 202, 216–22, 234
Corn Laws 45–6
Countess of Huntington's Chapel, Spa Fields 39–40

Dale, Tim 11, 14, 37, 94, 114, 118, 119, 143, 160, 168
Debenhams 11, 245, 246
Dickens & Jones 11, 15
Dickens, Charles 15, 35, 56, 95

Digby, Elizabeth 19, 36, 75, 81
Digby family 19, 33, 36, 37, 43–9, 82, 84, 95, 97, 98, 100, 115
Doré, Gustav 56, 227

Edwardstone, Suffolk 84–5, 93
Exciseman 27–30, 33–5

Fortnum & Mason 10, 246
Frankau, Gilbert 37, 108, 118–19, 133, 173–5

Godsmark, Caroline Harrod and family 106 113–15, 122, 184, 212–14, 222, 231

Harrod, Beatrice Martha 110, 132 184, 186, 196, 206, 212, 230, 233–6
Harrod, Caroline, sister of Charles Henry 38
Harrod, Charles Digby 14, 37, 75, 82, 84, 94–6, 103, 106, 109, 112–33, 136–65, 216, 222, 225, 231, 232–6, 247, 248
  Armitage Lodge, Sydenham 131–2, 162, 216, 235
  Culverwood and Waldron, Sussex 198–208, 210, 212–13

INDEX

Death 202–14
Devon & Somerset, Morebath Manor 163–5, 173, 175, 186–99, 210, 214, 232, 236
Esher 127, 131, 159, 162, 231
Evelyn Terrace 162, 222
Hill Street/Trevor Place 129–30, 162, 222, 224, 225
Sale of Harrods 168–84
Harrod, Charles Henry 8, 11, 12, 27
  Bethnal Green 82–4, 88
  Brompton Road 88–94, 114, 119–20, 182, 247
  Cable Street 52, 55, 62, 68, 70, 73, 76–9, 82, 85, 88, 116, 207, 247
  Death 153
  Eastcheap 82, 88, 93–4, 109
  Essex 34, 36, 41
  Rosemary Lane 55, 60, 62, 67, 70
  Southwark 14–17, 19–21, 23, 26, 57–8, 68, 70, 75, 82
  Thurloe Place 115–16
  Trial and conviction 57–68, 69–80
Harrod, Emily Maud 130, 186, 196, 212–13, 224
Harrod, Henry Digby 82, 88, 93, 95, 99, 102, 103–12, 115, 116, 122, 153, 184, 186,
  Frank Henry 111, 184
  Lionel 111–12
Harrod, Henry Herbert 130, 161, 182, 186, 196, 199, 212–14, 225–31
  The Harrod Collection 226–31
Harrod, Joseph Digby 82, 88
Harrod, Olive Mary 132, 186, 236

Harrod, William 27–8, 30, 33–4, 38–40, 84, 104, 190
Harrod, William Digby 82, 94, 97–102, 116
Harrod, William Frederick 40–1, 52, 67–70, 78, 81–2
Harrods, The Shop 7–12, 14, 16, 21, 23, 27, 28, 33, 35–8, 40, 43, 44, 57, 58, 67, 68, 89, 90, 92, 94, 100, 107, 108, 110, 113, 114, 118–20, 121–5, 127, 129–31, 136, 138, 140, 142–4, 153, 155, 156, 159–63, 168, 170–2, 174–83, 186, 189–91, 200, 207, 209, 214, 216, 225, 227, 228, 239, 245, 247, 248
  1909 Diamond Jubilee 182
  1948 Centenary Celebration 90, 113, 144, 184
  Fire 136–46, 208
  Employees
    Mr Clancy 128, 141, 145–6, 155, 170
    Mr Cole 158
    Mr Mercer 155–6, 171
    Mr Smart 151, 154–5, 170–3, 248
  Haymarket Stores 143–5, 207
  Humphrey's Hall 142, 145, 148
  Kent's Way 160
  Sale of 165, 168–70, 189
Harvey Nichols 180, 246,
House of Fraser 11, 245, 246

Kelvedon 31–2, 34, 42, 44
Kibble, William and family 108–10, 114–15, 122–4, 136, 142–4, 154–5, 158–9, 222

Ledward, Gilbert 226,
Lewis, John 245
Liberty 246

Marks & Spencer 247
Martin, Grace Miriam Harrod and family 120, 133, 162, 186, 196, 205, 216, 222–4
Mason, Clara Selina 47–9
Mason, Tamah 26–7, 30–6, 38, 41, 43, 84, 104,
Marshalsea Prison 15, 17, 56
Morebath 187–95, 197–200, 210–12, 232, 236

New Zealand 44, 97–102, 161

Panic of 1825 18, 74
Press, Mary Ann Harrrod and family 41–2

Rodgers, Eva Marguerita Harrod and family 132, 184, 237–44

Selfridge, Harry, family and the shop 7, 8, 10, 177, 182, 247
Swan & Edgar 11

Tallis's London Street Views 19–20
Tattersall's 92, 124
Transportation to Van Dieman's Land 69–72

Vernall, Jane Harrod and family 42–3

Weightman, Amy Caroline Harrod and family 131, 162, 184, 186, 198, 214, 229, 231–3
West Kensington Stores 174, 177
Whiteley's 172, 174–9, 245, 247

Wicking family 15–18, 20
Wilton's Music Hall 54

Also from The History Press

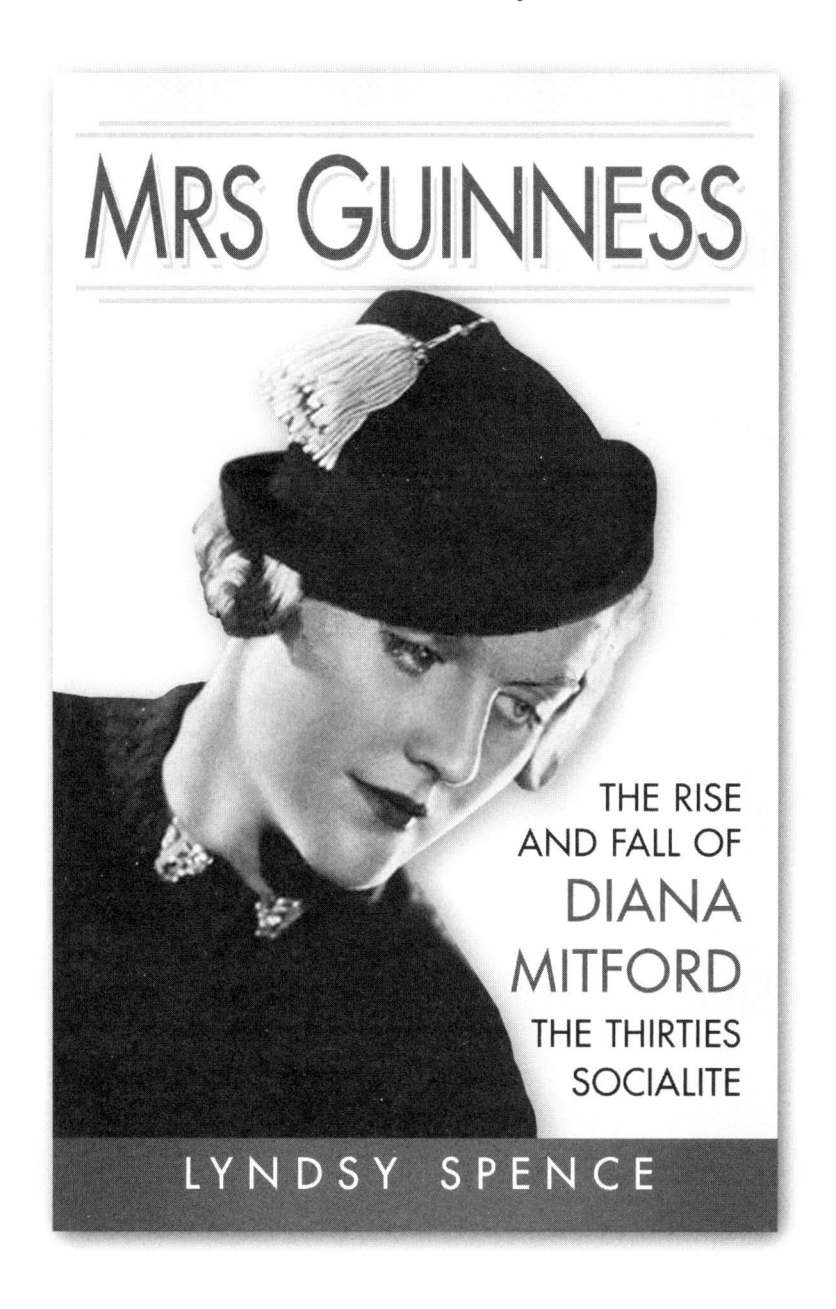

MRS GUINNESS

THE RISE AND FALL OF DIANA MITFORD THE THIRTIES SOCIALITE

LYNDSY SPENCE

The History Press

The destination for history
www.thehistorypress.co.uk

Also from The History Press

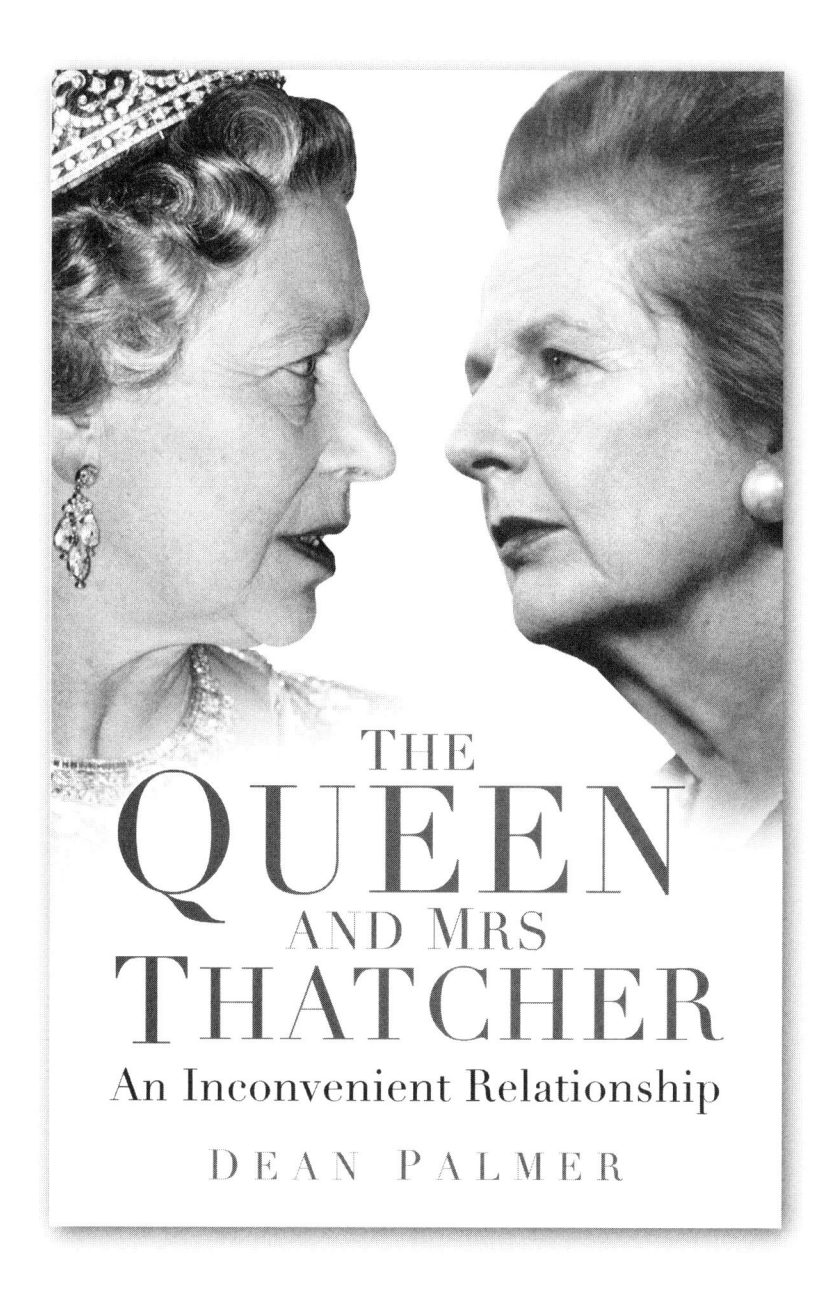

THE QUEEN AND MRS THATCHER

An Inconvenient Relationship

DEAN PALMER

The History Press

The destination for history
www.thehistorypress.co.uk